Rethinking Europe

Rethinking Europe broadens the terms of the debate on Europeanization, conventionally limited to the supersession of the nation-state by a supra-national authority and the changes within member states consequent upon EU membership.

Dominant approaches to the transformation of Europe ignore contemporary social theory interpretations of the nature and dynamics of social change. Delanty and Rumford argue that we need a theory of society in order to understand Europeanization. In doing so the book advances the case that Europeanization should be theorized in terms of globalization, major social transformations that are not exclusively spear-headed by the EU and the wider context of the transformation of modernity.

Gerard Delanty is Professor of Sociology at the University of Liverpool. His publications include *Inventing Europe: Idea, Identity, Reality* (Macmillan, 1995), *Social Theory in a Changing World* (Polity Press, 1998), *Social Science* (Open University Press, 1997), *Modernity and Postmodernity* (Sage, 2000) and *Community* (Routledge, 2003).
Chris Rumford is Senior Lecturer in Political Sociology at Royal Holloway, University of London. He is the author of *The European Union: A Political Sociology* (Blackwell, 2002) and *European Cohesion? Contradictions in EU Integration* (Palgrave, 2000).

Rethinking Europe

Social theory and the implications
of Europeanization

**Gerard Delanty and
Chris Rumford**

Routledge
Taylor & Francis Group

LONDON AND NEW YORK

First published 2005
by Routledge
2 Park Square, Milton Park, Abingdon, Oxon OX14 4RN

Simultaneously published in the USA and Canada
by Routledge
270 Madison Ave, New York, NY 10016

Routledge is an imprint of the Taylor & Francis Group

© 2005 Gerard Delanty and Chris Rumford

Typeset in Goudy by
HWA Text and Data Management, Tunbridge Wells
Printed and bound in Great Britain by
TJ International Ltd, Padstow, Cornwall

British Library Cataloguing in Publication Data
A catalogue record for this book is available from the British Library

Library of Congress Cataloging in Publication Data
A catalog record for this book has been requested

ISBN 0–415–34713–0 (hbk)
ISBN 0–415–34714–9 (pbk)

Contents

1 Theorizing Europeanization

Towards a constructivist theory of society

In recent years Europe has become an object of research and consciousness, but it has not been adequately theorized. Given the number of studies that now refer to Europe this may appear to be an extreme claim. Current theorizing on Europeanization is primarily concerned with conceptualizing the emerging shape of the European polity (see Chryssochoou, 2001b; Wiener and Diez, 2004). Missing from the existing literature is a concern with European society, that is with the cultural presuppositions and societal structures and processes by which social relations are constituted. Although social and cultural issues are coming to play an increasingly prominent role in studies on Europeanization, there is not yet anything like a theory of society in sight comparable to the theory of the state. Institutional processes and policy-making overshadow anything like a theory of society. Certainly there is a strong sociological interest in comparative studies of European societies, that is in comparisons of different national societies. But a theory of society in terms of a theory of the *social* is on the whole absent.

In this chapter an attempt is made to outline a conception of Europeanization in terms of a theory of society beyond national societies. To achieve this it will be necessary to move beyond the limits of institutional and empirical-comparative approaches which presuppose national societies. To an extent philosophical and historical studies on the idea of Europe offer some new perspectives, but on the whole the insights from such studies have not been incorporated into social scientific theorizing (Nelson *et al.*, 1992; Mikkeli, 1998; Morin, 1987; Pagden, 2002; Viehoff and Segers, 1999). Major social theory conceptions of Europe such as those of Castells and Habermas have not led to middle range theories. Habermas's work on Europeanization is predominantly a normative political philosophy which, unlike his earlier work, is not concerned with social scientific analysis. As a result, the normative dimension is not linked with a theory of society.

According to Julia Kristeva (2000), in a view that is now widely shared, Europe must become not just useful, but also meaningful. The normative conception of society that this entails has rarely been considered and yet is implicit in notions of cultural identity, and the European model of society. According to Jeremy Rifkin, there is now a 'European dream' in the making and which will rival the 'American dream' in its capacity to articulate a new vision of society (Rifkin,

2004). What is being implied in these views is that the European project cannot be separated from normative considerations.

The central thrust of the position advocated in this book is broadly a social constructivist conception of Europeanization. This theory of society gives particular weight to the diverse ways in which the social is constructed under conditions that are not fixed or reducible to institutional structures. Unlike neo-functionalist approaches, it does not explain Europeanization simply by reference to national governments operating within an international functional order. A social constructivist approach highlights the multiple ways social reality is continuously created in processes that cannot be reduced to either agency or structures. It is an approach that places particular emphasis on globalization and the historical process of modernity as the context in which Europeanization operates and also draws attention to the cultural foundations of politics and norm building processes.

Why a theory of society?

The difficulties with such a task cannot be underestimated. In the last two decades or so there has been a move away from the traditional concerns of social theory around a normative theory of society. Indeed, many theorists – Urry, Latour, Moscovici, Touraine, Baudrillard, Luhmann – have denied the very coherence of the idea of society. In these approaches, society as a fixed and objective reality has been replaced by global flows and mobilities, networks between diverse things, by forms of collective action, communities of interest, cultural discourses, self-constructing systems – these seem to be the messages from a variety of approaches on the fate of the social. The position taken in this book is that such developments, which are centrally concerned with globalization, do not mark the obsolescence of the social, but bring about new configurations of it (Gane, 2004: 8). The social cannot be equated with national societies for the reasons that have been most accurately spelt out in John Urry's book on mobilities; it is not a territorially bounded entity, but shaped through dynamics and processes that can take variable forms (Urry, 2000a). Although Urry declares the redundancy of the term 'society' in favour of an exclusive focus on mobilities, this is not the only conclusion (Mellor, 2004). Accepting the basic argument that we have entered an age in which many of the assumptions of classical sociology – the notion of the objectivity of society or the idea that sociology is concerned with objects that are to be understood only in relation to the intentions of social actors, for instance – have to be questioned in light of the contingency, transience and uncertainty that has been a feature of recent theorizing. To drop the term 'society' in favour of another term is not the most helpful solution. The social is changing its form rather than disappearing and is therefore open to new definitions.

In arguing for the need for a theory of society, we are not demanding a return to 'grand social theory', but rather looking to what Robert Merton called middle range theories to explain the current situation. Nevertheless, one important aspect of what might be called grand social theory is still of relevance: the concern with a normative foundation of society. Moreover, a normative conception of society cannot be conceived in isolation from a consideration of the cultural foundations of politics and of the historical process of modernity. The debate about post-national society in the context of Europeanization offers a particularly interesting opportunity to rethink the concept of society in a way that critically engages with the classical tradition and contemporary developments in social theory.

There are at least three reasons why we need to have a theory of society in order to understand Europeanization. First, if Europe is to be meaningful, as opposed to merely useful, there is a basic normative problem that cannot be solved without a theory of society. Classical social theory from Marx and Hegel through Spencer, Durkheim and Weber to Parsons and Habermas has always presupposed a normative conception of the social order, that is in some sense a notion of the 'good society'. Although these conceptions of the social order have greatly varied – from critical to affirmative to speculative utopian stances – they tended on the whole to be based on what might be called national imaginaries that express the institutional and normative structures of society. Since the rise of globalization theory and postmodernism in the 1980s there has been a questioning of the assumptions of such imaginaries, along with a growing scepticism of autonomy. It was therefore inevitable that theories of Europeanization would not give a central place to the traditional normative concerns of classical social theory. While there is some evidence to suggest that there is a new interest in normative political theory applied to the European polity (Friese and Wagner, 2002; Habermas, 2001a; Bohman, 2005), there is a noticeable absence of any concern with an underlying theory of society. But these approaches in any case are exceptions. The discourse of Europeanization is dominated by superficial metaphors suggesting a teleological project legitimated by grand EU narratives, such as 'widening' and 'deepening' or 'ever closer union'; vague, if not inaccurate, sociological terms, such as 'integration' and 'inclusion', and morphological metaphors such as 'multi-levelled' governance.

Second, in order to explain the cultural and epochal significance of major social transformations we need a theory of society. This was one of the basic insights of the sociology of Max Weber and, under the changed circumstances of the present time, is still of relevance. It is simply not possible to explain major European transformations alone by reference to changes in the nature of statehood, such as sovereignty, citizenship and constitutions. Obviously this is to make the assumption that major social transformations are occurring in the very nature of modernity. This seems a valid assumption to make, for there can be little doubt that the project of European integration has brought about large-scale social, economic and political change. Along with the worldwide impact of Americanization, wider processes of globalization, generational changes and major shifts in values and identities and socio-cognitive structures, Europe is undergoing significant change. The basic point made here is that a theory of changes in the nature of the state will not explain the epochal significance of the social changes that are occurring (see Balibar, 1991). For this reason a theory of society is required. A great deal of recent literature has tended to focus on citizenship as a partial attempt to deal with some of these normative and sociological issues. However, e concern with citizenship, while producing many valuable insights especially in the direction of post-national membership (see Eder and Giesen, 2001; Soysal, 1994), has tended to reduce the salience of society to late-liberal theorizing on rights and duties. The concept of citizenship has been over-worked as a sociologically useful term to fully capture the most significant aspects of the current situation, which go beyond the question of the participation of the citizen in the polity (see Chapter 5).

Third, in the context of Europeanization there is much evidence to suggest that there are new processes and dynamics occurring beyond the limits of national societies. While a European society as such is not necessarily occurring, it is evident that the European social space is becoming increasingly more salient (see Chapters 6 and 7). This emerging social order cannot be fully understood by reference to traditional comparative methods of analysis which all presuppose national societies and their convergence. It is possible to speak of an emerging European public sphere, overlapping and shared social and cultural worlds, a growing consciousness of Europeaness, transnational complexes, and interconnected economies. Such developments suggest the salience of a theory of society. The problem of, in Norman Davies's terms, 'what is European history' is now also a sociological problem, namely 'what is European society' (Davies, 1996). In an invaluable study, Cris Shore has attempted to refute the possibility of the European Union ever creating anything comparable to national society (Shore, 2000). Shore is undoubtedly correct for the greater part; however, this anthropologically based argument is premised on the assumption that Europeanization is akin to nationalization and should be judged by reference to the normative assumptions of the nation-state. So long as Europeanization is seen as another version of nation-building, that is, as an exercise in supra-nation building, the current state of theorizing on Europeanization will not move beyond a discussion on whether the European Union can compete with the nation-state. A new theory of society will need to address a wider range of issues that take account of transformative dynamics and processes, including new social models, socio-cognitive structures and normative ideals (Balibar, 2004; Eder and Giesen, 2001; Haller, 2000; Therborn, 1995b).

Following on from this, we can identify three distinctive features of the theory of society advanced here as it relates to Europeanization. First, it does not assume a necessary link between European integration/EU and European society. Approaches to the question of European society tend to assume that society exists at the national level but is absent at the European level. Recent thinking on European integration has tended to see the absence of European society as a problem (Armstrong, 2001; Closa, 2001) and that the public legitimacy of the EU and the 'democratic deficit' can only be improved through the institution of European society. Framing the question of European society in this way encourages the view that European society, to the extent that it exists or may exist in the future, will be a product of EU integration. In contrast, we assert that society is an area that lies beyond the scope of the EU project and we must move beyond functionalist and civil society models of society, which suggest that society exists as a corollary of the state and needs to be domesticated by it. The relationship between state and society (inasmuch as they can be conceived as separate realms) is much more complex and contradictory than suggested by the notion of civil society. Societies, even those located within nation-states, are not fixed and bounded entities but are in a constant state of transformation and becoming. Europeanization is properly identified with the dynamics of society while at the same time society is being constituted by Europeanization. In this sense there is a fundamental tension at the heart of Europeanization, which can be seen as a reflection of the fundamental tension within modernity: the tension between open and closed systems of integration and differentiation; or, between the logic of institutions and resistances from the social field, for example, EU treaties on the one side and on the other the revolutions of 1989/90 which together have shaped the face of Europe.

Second, our theory of society places Europe and the EU within the global frame. In short, the only meaningful way of studying the transformation of society is by understanding the global dimensions of society. There are several components to this. As mentioned above, societies can no longer be easily regulated or bounded by national states. There are many global influences which work to make societies less nationally cohesive, including telecommunications, flows of capital, population migrations, and transnational solidarities of ethnicity and belief. Moreover, the idea of global society has gained fresh impetus in a world in which awareness of a world risk society (Beck, 1999) is stronger than ever, and in which cosmopolitan identifications can rest on foundations more solid than an invocation of an idealized world citizenship (Held, 2002; Linklater, 2002; Chandler, 2003). In this context, it should be mentioned that the rise to popularity of the idea of global civil society (Keane, 2003) has given momentum to the notion that society has a transnational or global dimension, and the relationship between state and society is undergoing massive transformation. As such, there are many good reasons to suppose that European society cannot be conceived apart from global society. If Europeanization is located in societal transformation, the dynamics of this transformation are global rather than European. Notwithstanding the regulatory power of the EU, Europeanization is occurring within world society.

Third, we advance the position that the idea of society provides an important resource for both social theory and for thinking about contemporary Europe (see also Mellor, 2004). Society as a normative construct is the necessary social context for any debate on rights, justice, citizenship, belonging, and identity. Understandings of what constitutes society, how it can be transformed, and to what ends, will always be the subject of contested reasoning. In contemporary thinking, contestation over society has become dominated by the notion of civil society, and it is noticeable that at the core of much recent thinking on European society (or its absence) has been a presumed nexus between supra-national institutions, citizenship, and civil society (Soysal, 2001). Similarly civil society has come to dominate discussion of the 'good society' (Edwards, 2004). We argue, that the notion of civil society is too limiting to be of use in elucidating the nature and dynamics of European society, recent work on transnational and global civil society notwithstanding (see Chapter 10).

In sum, in order to understand the nature of European material, cultural and political realities today a theory of society is needed. In the course of this chapter the basics of such a theory will be outlined. It will suffice to mention at this point that our approach can be roughly described in meta-theoretic terms as a social constructivist one; that is an approach that sees society as constructed by social actors and public discourses under the manifold conditions of globalization. What emerges out of these processes is often unclear and highly contingent and needs to be understood more fully from the perspective of a wider theory of modernity. But we can say that Europe is being socially constructed out of disparate projects, discourses, models of societies, imaginaries and in conditions of contestation, resistances and diffused through processes of globalization. What is being claimed in this is that Europeanization is a process of social construction rather than one of state building and one in which globalization, in all its facets, plays a key role in creating its conditions. A social constructivist approach draws attention to contestation and also to reflexivity since social actors and discourses are often reflexively constituted. The argument to be developed goes beyond this in also clarifying normative issues. The thesis is that there are cosmopolitan currents evident in globalization and that these are particularly articulated in certain processes of Europeanization (see Beck, 2003).

At this point it can be stated that the term 'Europeanization' will be used instead of the more conventional term 'European integration'. The latter has too strong connotations of cohesion to be useful and does not make clear the different dimensions of integration, for example functional integration in terms of market integration or democratic integration (Calhoun, 2003). Europeanization itself is a term which has been employed in many different ways in recent literature, and no consensus on its meaning exists. Although it remains a 'fuzzy concept' (Jachtenfuchs and Kohler-Koch, 2004) in the most common usage it denotes the processes by which national politics and/or policy processes are increasingly dominated by EU agendas and/or the ways in which EU norms are domesticated in member (and non-member) states: in short, 'domestic changes caused by European integration' (Vink, 2003). It is common to encounter references to the Europeanization of domestic politics and in this sense Europeanization implies the intrusion of EU issues and priorities into national political decision making (Imig and Tarrow, 2001). Europeanization is not simply a one-way process however and the extent to which national actors mobilize at a European level is also seen to be a marker of Europeanization (Ladrech, 2002; Statham and Gray, 2005).

Other usages of Europeanization point in the direction of social transformation (Tarrow, 1995). In this sense, it can denote a reorganization of territoriality and peoplehood (not limited to the EU) leading to a new social and political order (Borneman and Fowler, 1997). Alternatively, it can refer to a multi-dimensional process of transformation which goes beyond the EU's institutions to embrace a concern with networks and boundaries, the export of the EU model, and the inter-penetration of national systems (Bach, 2000; Olsen, 2002). Featherstone (2003: 20–1) sees Europeanization as a series of processes which includes, but goes beyond, national adaptation to the dynamics of EU integration. On this view, Europeanization includes the emergence of cross-national policy networks and communities and shifts in 'cognition, discourse, and identity'. These features of Europeanization are conceived as responses to European developments within a multi-levelled polity. This highlights a general tendency to see Europeanization in solipsistic terms: a global dimension or context is absent. Whilst recognizing that the term Europeanization is becoming overused and under-theorized in much the same way as European integration has been, there are still good reasons to use the term, not least of which is the (minority) tradition of equating Europeanization with social transformation. Europeanization, as employed in this book, signals the following: a concern to go beyond institutional frameworks to examine the dynamics of society; an awareness of the importance of cultural dynamics; the centrality of contestations generated by multiple perspectives on issues central to European transformation; the importance of a global context for understanding European developments; and a dissatisfaction with the ways in which questions of European transformation have been framed within political science discourses on the EU.

Finally, it must be noted that global perspective will also entail what Dipesh Chakarbarty has called 'deprovencializing Europe' in the sense of not generalizing developments specific to Europeanization to the rest of the world (Chakarbarty, 2000).

Europeanization, globalization and social theory

A brief survey of Europeanization and social research will provide a useful point of departure for an outline of Europeanization in terms of a theory of society. The first point to be mentioned is that the current uncertainty in the meaning of 'Europe' is reflected in European social research. There are simply many conceptions of Europeanization as a research agenda. Many of these could be divided into two general groups, institutional approaches that are mostly directed at the European Union and comparative studies that are generally studies of national societies in the context of EU-led processes. This leads to some problems and questions, for instance are European societies becoming more similar as measured by EU integrationist ideology? Is Europeanization to be understood merely as process of change or is there an emergent social reality?

Much European social research is merely comparative national and regional case studies. In such studies the objective is simply comparing similarities and differences between various European countries and their regions (for example, Crouch, 1999). Moreover, comparative research, rather than being seen as having too many limitations in a world where transnational and supra-national forces are at work, has been sustained over recent years by a number of important developments, and cannot be seen as antithetical to approaches which embrace Europeanization. Indeed, a need to understand Europeanization now forms a pretext for further comparative studies: the extent to which different nation-states are Europeanized (Borzel and Risse, 2003). The rise to prominence of 'contentious politics' as a field of study has further encouraged comparative national research at the same time as emphasizing the necessity of a European context for carrying out this research. It should be noted that much of the recent work on 'contentious Europeans' concludes that European citizens are Europeanized to differing degrees depending upon national contexts (Imig and Tarrow, 2001; Kriesi *et al.*, 1995; Koopmans and Statham, 2000). This work can also be seen as a reaction to the limits of comparative cross-national research and is dominated by notions of convergences and divergences whereby the nation-states are relatively stable entities that change accordingly as the EU impacts upon them. Europeanization in this sense is a variable process underpinned by a logic of increasing societal convergence. EU studies has also witnessed a rise in the influence of comparative politics, a move which draws attention to the polity-like qualities of the EU. If the EU is conceived as a political system (Hix, 1999) then its institutional structure and policy-making mechanisms can be compared to those of nation-states. This approach takes EU integration as given and focuses on questions of institution and capacity building and the ways these converge throughout the member states.

European integration studies can be contrasted with what can be called transnational approaches to Europeanization. Arising largely from the growing involvement of sociology and anthropology, the emphasis has shifted away from an analysis that is specifically focused on the EU as the main actor and unlike cross-national research, transnational approaches are not essentially comparative (Boje, van Steenbergen and Walby, 1999; Bellier and Wilson, 2000; Le Gales 2002). The main thrust of transnational approaches is to identify processes and dynamics that occur in several societies and are therefore transnational or 'European'. Such processes of Europeanization will in general refer to new state–society relations, especially the interconnected nature of societies. But transnational approaches are evident in studies on European borders, migration, public spheres and civil society movements and the formation of post-national identities and loyalties. The move beyond an exclusive concern with the EU and institution-building has not led to a move away from the basic concern with looking at Europeanization as entailing processes comparable to large-scale nation-building. Not too surprisingly, many of these studies draw critical conclusions as to the viability of a European society. It might be suggested that the prevailing approaches lack a theory of society adequate to explaining the current situation. Europeanization is generally understood to be a process emanating from national societies as a result of the impact of the EU and in particular the transnation-alization of the state.

The alternative theory proposed in this book is to view Europeanization in terms of a particular response to globalization and as such is neither the result of the transnationalization of state nor the integration of societies (Nederveen Pieterse, 1999; Rumford, 2002). However, this is not to suggest that this book echoes the popular view that Europeanization, in the form of EU integration, has accelerated due to the threats posed to Europe by (economic) globalization. In other words, that the single market and monetary union were defensive reactions to globalization (following the success of which the EU has developed the capacities with which to shape globalization, both in Europe and the wider world). Perhaps the most celebrated attempt to portray the relation between globalization and the EU in this way is that of Manuel Castells, who writes that, 'European integration is, at the same time, a reaction to the process of globalization and its most advanced expression' (Castells, 2000c: 348; see also Castells, 1998).

In contrast to the economistic and integrative interpretation offered by Castells we suggest that three important dimensions of the relationship between the European Union and globalization can be identified. The first highlights the tension between processes authored by the European Union and the wider globalization-inspired transformations occurring in Europe. For example, the content of citizenship rights in Europe are more the product of global regimes of personhood rights than EU membership (Soysal, 1994; Cesarani and Fulbrook, 1996). The second draws attention to the ways in which globalization works to fragment as well as to integrate, for which the term 'fragmegration' is sometimes employed. From this perspective, globalization renders impossible the project of constituting Europe as an economic, political and social unity. The third recognizes that near pan-continental territorial expansion and the construction of the world's largest trading bloc have given the EU aspirations to be a shaper of globalization. In this regard, it seeks to establish itself as an alternative to the US and has developed evangelical models of governance to promote the European social model as a successful blend of economic growth and social justice (Lamy and Laidi, 2001).

The aim, then, is not to look for a specifically European kind of society (see Crouch, 1999). The perspective that is suggested here is one that does not see the EU as the principal actor and does not operate on the assumption of integration as the fundamental principle at work. In contrast to transnational approaches, the emphasis shifts to the impact of global forces in Europe and the emergence and development of global dynamics. Whereas transnational approaches would see the EU as being constructed from within, globalization approaches would view the EU and Europe more generally as shaped by global processes. Whereas transnational approaches would emphasize the increasing interconnectedness of European nation-states, globalization approaches focus on the lack of boundaries between Europe and the world (Meyer, 2001a). From this perspective, Europeanization includes an awareness of the Europe/non-Europe relationship, the recasting of the idea of European borders, and the impossibility of fixing inside/outside relations.

Europeanization recasts debates on Europe in terms of societal forms emerging from new relations enjoyed by individuals *vis-à-vis* the globe. As such, Europeanization eschews institutional and integrative explanations for the transformation of Europe in favour of explanations which focus on society rather than institutions and the state. At root, the dynamics of Europeanization are bound up with the processes of globalization and novel forms of social transformation to which they give rise. Whereas EU studies interpret Europeanization as a response to largely economic globalization, Europeanization can be more usefully seen as a cosmopolitan response to globalization. This will now be elaborated more thoroughly, since theories of globalization alone will not provide an adequate foundation for a theory of society. Drawing from central concepts in social theory, a conception of Europeanization will be proposed that grounds it in a theory of society conceived in terms of an open field of social possibilities.

Europeanization between integration and differentiation

Two key concepts in social theory are integration and differentiation. These notions are highly relevant to an understanding of both globalization and Europeanization. The following discussion will attempt to outline a conception of Europeanization in terms of a wider theory of globalization using these terms.

To follow a distinction made originally by David Lockwood and later by Jürgen Habermas, two kinds of integration can be distinguished: social integration and system integration (Lockwood, 1964; Habermas, 1987). This is particularly helpful when it comes to Europeanization as an unpacking of the notion of integration as in the term 'European integration'. European integration – assuming that the term integration is appropriate at all – is not something that is self-explanatory or clearly defined. There is something to be gained by examining it in the terms of social and system integration. Undoubtedly most accounts of European integration presuppose a particular understanding of integration as system integration and assume that this translates into cultural cohesion (see Pahl, 1991). By system integration is meant forms of integration achieved primarily through states and markets, but also through law and technologies, and which have a functional role. The media of power and money underlie it. Social integration, in contrast, refers to integration through the media of cultural and social structures. In Habermas's terms, social integration is anchored in the 'life-world', that is in essentially communicative and symbolic forms. Normative questions play a greater role in social integration than in system integration, which is driven by the more objective imperatives of instrumental rationalities whose primary form is not symbolic.

Without entering into the controversies on the distinction between social and system integration, there is some value in applying these terms to Europeanization in order to distinguish the socio-cultural logic of integration from systemic processes. It might be suggested that increasingly social integration is playing a greater role in Europeanization, but the nature of this particular form of integration is not simply a mapping out of systemic forms of integration. Indeed, there is much to indicate that there may be tensions if not resistances between these forms of integration. For example, in Habermas's theory, integration is not inherently something desirable, since one pervasive form it takes is the 'colonization of the life-world', which occurs when system integration erodes social integration (Habermas, 1987: 332–73).

No account of integration, whether social or systemic, can neglect the dimension of differentiation. Integration is articulated through processes of differentiation. Differentiation can be functional, as in the Parsonian sense of functional differentiation, and can also be autopoetic, that is self-constructing.

In the latter sense, system differentiation is the term Luhmann used to refer to forms of differentiation that are driven primarily by the need of a given system to distinguish inside from outside (Luhmann, 1982, 1995; see Rasch, 2000). System differentiation and functional differentiation entail different logics. The latter refers to the specialization of functions within a system, whereas the former concerns the construction of the system in relation to another system.

Processes of integration and differentiation relate to each other in complex ways, as the social theory of Luhmann testifies (Rasch, 2000). It is not simply the case that there is a prior differentiation that is overcome by integration, for instance by a process of societal convergence. Differences – distinctions, exclusions – do not precede integration but are produced by the very logic of differentiation, according to Luhmann who draws attention to numerous and often incommensurable orders of interpretation emerging and producing different logics of exclusion. Nor is it the case that there is a prior homogeneity of functions that becomes more and more differentiated leading to new and more fragile kinds of cohesion, as Émile Durkheim argued in 1893 in the *Division of Labour in Society* (Durkheim, 1960). In complex societal systems, such as the European Union, integration and differentiation are articulated alongside each other. We can see how system differentiation is becoming more important today with the concern with borders, the identity of Europe, immigration and security. Functional differentiation, on the other hand, is one of the main logics of system integration, while social integration continues to be resistant to many expressions of systemic integration.

The principles of integration and differentiation are particularly pertinent to globalization, which as argued earlier is a more general context in which to consider Europeanization. Globalization is a process that entails forms of social and systemic integration but unfolds through differentiation. New kinds of differentiation – as opposed to the older ones based on specialization – are organized into the decentralized and often horizontally connected units of the global network society. Globalization produces new sets of distinctions between inside and outside as, for example, between rich and poor, those who have access to information and those who do not, as well as fragmenting previously existing social structures and creating new kinds of borders. Neither states nor transnational agents, such as the EU or UN, control the field of globalization, which is characterized by contingency and indeterminacy; it is not a modernist, state-led process comparable to nation building. With globalization there is no master plan. Globalization takes many forms: economic globalization, political and legal globalization, and cultural globalization are the major ones. Globalization is a dynamic that acts upon the local. The consequences can vary from hybridization and indigenization to transnationalism. Globalization can be reproductive – that is, affirmative of the status quo – or transformative; it can work through processes of social and system integration and unleash different logics of differentiation.

Examples of such complexes of integration and differentiation produced by globalization are societal cross-fertilization, such as various kinds of hybridities, nested identities; interdependencies, mutually overlapping and interpenetrating links and networks; expanded interdependence as well as assertions of autonomy and arising from this symbolic conflict; and the diffusion of common models and universalistic norms. These complexes are particularly evident in Europeanization. European societies are becoming more and more interlinked, without an overall European society as such emerging. This interpenetration of societal systems is occurring within the wider context of globalization, since it is not only European societies that are becoming more and more embroiled in each other but as a result of migration and global culture other social and cultural worlds are becoming diffused within the European societies. Emerging out of these, too, are new conflicts over boundaries and identity, that is conflicts arising from system differentiation on the one side and on the other conflicts arising as a result of tensions between social and systemic modes of integration. There are forms of integration that extend beyond the immediate horizons of societal systems – be they those of national societies or the EU itself – and which may be designated cosmopolitan. This is especially relevant in the case of making sense of the enlargement of the EU. It has been widely recognized that the existing neo-functionalist framework of integration is inadequate when it comes to explaining the enlargement of the EU for the simple reason that this process cannot be understood without taking into account the interaction of the EU with those countries seeking membership (Nugent, 2004; Wallace, 1999). In other words, it requires a model of integration that will be able to take account of a wider context of complexity.

The upshot of this suggests a social contructivist theory of Europeanization, that is a theory of society that stresses the open-ended process by which the social field is shaped. Viewing Europeanization as a dimension of globalization – in which roughly the same logics occur – rather than as a transnationalization of the state, the role and function of social factors can be more adequately accounted for. As a constructivist process, Europeanization can be seen as a form of reflexive creation in which the entire process produces its very own terms. This suggests a conception of society as an emergent reality. This will now be clarified.

Europeanization from a social constructivist perspective

Social constructivism is a reflection of the general trend towards context that has been a feature of post-empiricist social science in the last few decades. Sometimes called social constructionism, it was implicit in the theory-led post-empiricist epistemologies of science since Popper and can also be traced back to the Hegelian-Marxist notion of society as a human artefact rather than being naturally given. However, constructivism proper makes sense only with the awareness of the reflexive nature of social science as part of society while at the same time being distant from it. The most well known statement of social constructivism is Peter Berger and Thomas Luckmann's *The Social Construction of Reality*, which outlined a view of social institutions as constructed by social actors. Central to this approach was a view of everyday knowledge as opposed to scientific knowledge playing a major role in the construction of social reality (Berger and Luckmann, 1966). However, this approach did not go beyond a weak notion of institutionalization in terms of a largely phenomenological social theory which aimed to be an alternative to structural functionalism. Moreover, it did not entail a reflexive self-understanding of social science in that it accepted uncritically existing forms of social institutionalization. The term social constructivism will be used in this book as an alternative to the weak sense of social constructionism in Berger and Luckmann and as an alternative to the strong sense associated with 'scientific constructivism'.

Constructivism has been particularly associated with the sociology of science and technology. It was implicit in Max Weber and Robert Merton's studies on how the social factors into the world of science and, as already mentioned, a weak notion of constructivism was integral to the sociology of knowledge, which was based on the insight that social reality is created by everyday forms of knowledge. Increasingly stronger conceptions of constructivism entered the social sciences, beginning with the 'scientific constructivism', sometimes referred to as the 'Strong Programme', which argued all of science was itself constructed. In the major works in the field, a view of constructivism was developed that stressed the creative process by which reality is manufactured or assembled. In these theories, the constructive process cannot be reduced to agency or to structures, but occurs in a mediated context in which agency is embedded in structures that are at the same time the outcome of the action of social agents. Based on the work of Luhmann and others, so-called 'radical constructivism' emerged around notions of self-constructing systems, where agency and structure are replaced by informational systems.

Today social constructivism has abated as a specific theory of science, although it is now central to many epistemologies (Gergen, 2001; Velody and Williams, 1998). Some of the extreme positions have been severely criticized (Hacking, 1999). Within science and technology, actor-network theory has replaced many of the earlier positions. The tension between constructivism and realism has been overcome, with the recognition that both are compatible (Delanty, 1997b). This is evident in the writings of philosophers such as Rom Harré, Jürgen Habermas and Hillary Putnam, who represent a pragmatic realism that leaves considerable room for constructionism (see Delanty and Strydom, 2003: 372–7). In Habermas's terms, constructivism is the outcome of a pragmatic view of social reality as democratically organized in discursive contexts (Habermas, 2003b).

Constructivism is now entering political science and international relations (Wendt, 1999). This belated development can be compared to the early reception of constructivism in sociology where it offered an alternative to positivistic accounts of social reality as given. Constructivism in political science provides an alternative to the dominant theories of neo-functionalism and realism. In European studies, it suggests an alternative to inter-governmentalism and actor-centred approaches (Checkel, 1999; Christiansen *et al.*, 2001; Risse, 2004a, 2004b). It is certainly very pertinent in the context of the enlargment of the EU, a process that cannot be so easily explained in neofunctionalist terms (Miles, 2004). However, it is still a marginal approach and lacks the influence of neo-functionalism and its various schools. Undoubtedly the reason for this is because it is ill-suited to explain problems in the transnationalization of the state, questions of security and foreign policy. For this reason, it is at most a corrective to neo-functionalism rather than an alternative. However, as Thomas Risse has argued, constructivism has much to offer (Risse, 2004a, 2004b). This is a position that we support but take a different view on the aims of a constructivist approach. Conctructivism in political science and international relations generally amounts to a critique of neofunctionalist attempts to explain processes of internalization by reference to the functional needs of national governments for cooperation. Constructivism in contrast draws attention to the role of values, norms and identities in which national governments are also embedded.

As indicated earlier, the conception of Europeanization that is advocated here is one that recognizes the wider context of globalization and of social factors rather than being primarily concerned with the transnationalization of the state. For this reason the merits of a social constructivist approach are not limited by the analysis of the formation of systems of governance but extend far beyond it. One of the major claims made in this book is that globalization is the context for Europeanization and that a social constructivist approach is particularly pertinent to this. A social constructivist approach is based on the following points.

The first characteristic is a concern with the reflexive nature of social science as a self-questioning endeavour that recognizes that science is part of society. Reflexivity has generally been held to entail the incorporation of the perspective or standpoint of the social actor in the research process, which does not objectify social reality and nor does it take anything for granted. In this respect, the reflexivity of science suggests a critical perspective that sees science as contextualized while at the same time capable of standing back from social reality. More generally, reflexivity concerns the application of something to itself; it therefore indicates self-implication. The 'reflexive turn' in the social sciences has been catalysed by the recognition that no one theory or combination of theories is capable of apprehending the world. In this sense, social science is reflexive in as much as it recognizes its own limitations. This recognition has been further stimulated by the fashion for contextualizing the social science of modernity within developmental or historical perspectives, thereby generating a self-awareness which works to both limit the range and scope of the social sciences and promote the idea that they need to be superseded. Postmodernity is one product of this 'reflexive turn'. In short, the social science of modernity has not been able to answer all the questions which it has posed itself and has become more reflexive as a consequence. On this reading, reflexivity signals 'a heightened awareness that mastery is impossible' (Latour, quoted in Beck *et al.*, 2003: 3). Such developments can be viewed in very negative terms, opening up new avenues of relativism and/or pessimism: 'The social researcher is left to reflect upon the futility of their enterprise in terms of the scientific inadequacy of their discipline. They can thus conclude that there are no conclusions to be reached concerning their social world!' (May, 1999: 3.1).

More positively, sociological debates on reflexivity have taken shape around the idea that modernity is undergoing a transformation. This is the sense in which we can understand Beck's idea of 'reflexive modernization': an attempt to re-capture the dynamic of modernity from the grasp of postmodern theory (Beck *et al.*, 2003: 3). In addition, and perhaps more importantly, interest in reflexivity has also been stimulated by the recognition that modernity has been relativized by globalization. There has been a marked shift away from the idea that globalization should be understood in terms of the global diffusion of modernity (Giddens, 1990), towards the idea that the relation between globalization and modernity is more complex and contradictory and that we need to recognize multiple or entangled modernities (Therborn, 2003). As such, reflexivity should be considered in conjunction with globalization, thereby offering sociologists an important way of re-contextualizing modernity. Modernity can now be seen as being driven by globalization, not the other way round (Robertson, 1992). In this case, reflexivity points to alternative developmental schemas and a reassessment of frameworks of theory and concepts central to the sociology of modernity; society, state, and citizen, for example. Reflexivity is concerned centrally with the search for concepts and frameworks with which to apprehend a dynamic and changing world (Beck, 2000b).

Second, one of the chief features of social constructivism is the argument that agency and structure are mediated in cultural contexts. Structures are created by social actors who are embedded in particular contexts. Constructivism is a reaction to the view that social actors act on the basis of motives that can be rationally explained without reference to the specific context in which actors find themselves; it is also a response to the reduction of agency to structure. Neither structure nor agency alone explain anything. The turn to a mediated view of structure and agency must be seen in the context of the so-called 'cultural turn' in the social and human science since the 1980s (Chaney, 1994; Hall, 1999; Bonnell and Hunt, 1999). This was characterized by a strong tendency to explain interest by reference to identities and more generally to stress the salience of culture in the constitution of social realities. The famous notion of the 'invention of tradition', although not explicitly constructivist, is also close to the emphasis in constructivism on the creative process by which reality is fabricated out of various elements in highly contextualized conditions (Hobsbawm and Ranger, 1983). This trend can be seen in terms of the wider turn to context in the social sciences and has led to an anti-reductionist epistemology. By this is meant the recognition of the manifold nature of social reality and the multiplicity of numerous possible interpretations. But constructivism is more than a mere emphasis on context; it also implies a stronger relational conception of social actors and structures. In this respect, it suggests a dynamic process of movement, networks and mobilities rather than a static view of the social world (Strydom, 2002: 153–4; Emirbayer, 1997). Furthermore, constructivism also encourages the development of relational politics in place of both the reification of networks on the one hand, and territorialist assumptions about political space on the other. Relational politics emphasizes the social practices which comprise networks and movements and understands these practices to exist in global spaces (Amin, 2004; Massey, 2004).

A third consequence of the constructivist view of social reality is that nothing is forever fixed or immutable. Social reality is the product of a process of becoming and is open to new designs. In this sense, constructivism has generally been held to be tied to a radical democratic ethos that the world can be shaped by human design (Unger, 1987). This suggests a discursive dimension to the constructivist process, that is the view that social realities are shaped in conditions of contestation and negotiation. Social reality is negotiated in discursive contexts rather than being simply given. Habermas's theory of discourse is particularly useful in conceptualizing how social worlds are normatively created through deliberative reasoning (Habermas, 1996). Although criticized for its formalism and inappropriateness to many situations, it does draw attention to the discursive context in which a good deal of institution building and social action occurs. In particular, it draws attention to the discursive articulation of normative structures. Discourses are also articulated in the context of socio-cognitive structures.

Finally, an important aspect of social constructivism is the socio-cognitive dimension (DiMaggio, 1997; Eyerman and Jamison, 1991; Strydom, 2002: 116–17; 153–7; Zerubavel, 1997). This concerns the creation of frames, imaginaries, worldviews and cultural models, which go beyond the immediate discursive context and express emergent forms of social reality. A socio-cognitive approach entails an analysis of the frames, symbolic structures and codes of social discourses with a view to uncovering their contested claims and possibilities of resistance. It involves looking at discursive modes of expression and experience in a relational field in which issues are defined, or framed, and articulated within highly competing and contested conceptions of the world. Of particular salience are the cultural resources, that is frames and codes, and repertoires of justification that social actors use in defining their situation and view of the world and the learning that evolves from the emergent cultural models.

The constructivist process also entails the creation of such socio-cultural frameworks as, what Cornelius Castoriadis and Charles Taylor have called, 'social imaginaries', that is the evaluative frameworks that people use to 'imagine' their social surroundings (Taylor, 2004: 23; Castoriadis, 1987). These socio-cognitive frameworks play a role in shaping social reality while at the same time are continuously constructed. Europe is itself one such socio-cognitive form and is immersed within a wider one, which can be called a cosmopolitan frame. The cognitive dimension of social constructivism concerns less the immediate context and discursive situation in which social reality is constructed than cultural frameworks that are both produced and which at the same time influence the creative process. It can be mentioned in this context that one of the major socio-cognitive forms is modernity itself, namely the belief in the self-transformative capacity of modern societies to shape themselves in the projection of their imaginary.

This conception of social imaginaries goes beyond Taylor's use of the term – as a moral order – and also beyond Benedict Anderson's well known notion of 'imagined community', which is predominantly affirmative (Anderson, 1983). In his major work, originally written in 1964, *The Imaginary Institution of Society*, Castoriadis argued that the radical imaginary, which derives from the creative forces of the human psyche, drives the social imaginary, which tries to domesticate it by reducing it to institutional forms (Castoriadis, 1987). The creative imagination is a powerful impulse at work in all cultural systems of meaning and derives from the basic capacity of people to create symbolic representation. All societies have a central imaginary in order to answer basic questions relating to their identity and orientation to the world. For Castoriadis this extends beyond the institutional forms of society with a vision of an alternative society. This is what he calls the radical imaginary, which is expressed in a belief in the project of autonomy which constantly challenges the institutional social imaginary:

> History is impossible and inconceivable outside the *productive* or *creative imagination*, outside of what we have called the *radical imaginary* as this is manifest indissolubly in both historical *doing* and in the constitution, before any explicit rationality, of a universe of *signification*.
>
> (Castoriadis, 1987: 146)

For Castoriadis, the main struggle in modernity is between the radical imaginary based on the project of autonomy and the institutional imaginary based on rational control. The existence of the imaginary institution of society enables a society creatively to self-constitute itself and give it an orientation in the world. Without the radical imaginary of autonomy this project would be largely affirmative and reduced to functional aspects. The radical imagery refers to a society's capacity for transcendence. In this sense it refers to a conception of society as an emergent reality (see Mellor, 2004).

Castoriadis's theory has a strong constructivist tendency, which is evident in his argument that

> the social imaginary must assemble-adjust-fabricate-construct itself as society, and as this society it must make itself be as society and as this society, starting with itself and with what 'is there', in a manner appropriate to and in view of being and this particular society.
>
> (Castoriadis, 1987: 260)

In a later work, he reiterated this vision of the social order: 'Each society is a construction, a constitution, a creation of the world, of its own world. Its own identity is nothing but this "system of interpretation", this world that it creates' (Castoriadis, 1993: 9).

In sum, then, a constructivist approach highlights the transformative capacity of societies; it asserts the creative self-constitution of social realities; and recognizes that imaginary significations enter into the ongoing process of social construction. In this book we strongly emphasize the cognitive constructivist position for the reason that this best describes what we take to be the current and critical phase of Europeanization, namely under the conditions of globalization a conflict of competing conceptions of political community and cultural models of society. Emerging from the various competing frames and codes of a manifold of social actors is a discursive transformation that is generating a new conception of social reality, normative models and imaginaries which are not yet fully embodied in a political order or institutional framework.

As discussed earlier, Europeanization entails complex logics of integration and differentiation, which in interacting with each other under the wider conditions of globalization, produce various fields of tension leading to different levels of societal emergence. The first point to be made is that it is not enough to say that Europeanization is just a multi-levelled polity. The morphological metaphor, while being in many ways apt in describing the different levels of governance in the EU, does not capture the interpenetrating and transformative links between the different levels of what we can now more adequately call social and system integration. In social constructivist terms there are diverse logics by which social reality is produced and no master plan or dominant social actor that controls the reality creating process. Europeanization is a multi-directional process. This is also true of territory (Ruggie, 1993).

This account of Europeanization strongly emphasizes the discursive dimension, which is highlighted by the growing salience of public spheres, social movements and democratic currents. The aim of the analysis is to show that globalization is a condition or context that opens up possibilities for different forms of action and modes for what Alain Touraine has called 'historicity' – the capacity of a society to act upon itself and determine its future – to emerge and define the social field (Touraine, 1977). In all of this language plays a very important role. Social constructivist approaches strongly emphasize the role of language in constructing social and political realities (Wodak *et al.*, 1999; Fairclough, 2000). This emphasis on the discursive also avoids simplistic appeals to 'culture' to explain everything (Orchard, 2002). A social constructivist approach to Europeanization identifies the following as the key dynamics or logics of development in the social construction of Europe: (a) societal interpenetration, (b) the transformation of the state, (c) discursive and socio-cognitive processes, and (d) the transformation of modernity.

(a) Europeanization as societal interpenetration. European societies are becoming more and more mixed. As a result of the common currency, migration, multiculturalism in consumption and life styles, educational exchanges, tourism, transnational transport systems as well as cheaper travel, European societies are becoming increasingly hybrid. This is not the same as saying they are becoming more and more integrated or that there is a convergence in social patterns, but that these societies are less separated, more embroiled and entangled in each other. This can come about just as much from the negative aspects of modern society, such as crime, pollution, terror, and social pathologies of various kinds.

(b) A transformation of the state is central to Europeanization. The relationship between the changing nature of the state with new forms of governance in the EU will be examined at length in Chapter 8. It is argued that debate on the state-like properties of the EU must take account of both the influence of globalization on the EU and the ways in which the EU has consciously acted upon its mechanisms of government by, for example, creating European policy spaces in order to advance European (rather than national) solutions to social problems. In doing so it constitutes European space as a governable entity (Barry, 1993; Lawn 2003).

In social constructivist terms, this entails an emphasis less on supra-national governance and institution-building than on the social shaping of national and transnational interests through collective identities and context bound considerations. Although most neo-institutionalist approaches recognize the role of culture and collective identity in the expression of interests, they strongly stress agency. A social constructivist account of the Europeanization of the state – EU institutions, the *Aquis*, the European Constitution, etc. – would give a greater role to identity. More importantly, it points to a much stronger tension between systemic integration and social integration as the axis on which the Europeanization of the nation-state is played out. In terms of system differentiation, foreign policy on both national and EU levels is now increasingly having to confront a situation in which the nature of security no longer deals with a clearly defined 'outside': the nature of security has changed considerably, with shifting inside/outside relations and the impossibility of any clear demarcation. Finally, a social constructionist approach will stress the impossibility of any single outcome. In this respect, the debate and framing of the European Constitution is a good example of the social construction of the European polity in a process of contestation, negotiation, persuasion, and power in which multiple actors are involved. As mentioned above, language is important in framing the terms of debate and thus in creating the discursive context in which the political reality emerges.

(c) Europeanization as discursive and socio-cognitive transformation. This is partly the context in which the Europeanization of the nation-state occurs, but it is also more. One of the most important, and neglected, dimensions of Europeanization is the discursive field which, in the language of social constructivism, has reality creating properties. Europeanization entails different levels of societal emergence. The interaction of different identities, interests and social projects generates new realities. For example, different conceptions of political community – ranging from left and right to national and Eurosceptical – produce fields of discourse in which competing claims are worked out in the public sphere. What is significant about these discourses is that they are not directly controlled by the social actors involved; instead, they have constantly to re-situate themselves in these discourses, which, in Foucault's terms, are productive; that is they are generative of the very terms of debate, limiting what can be said and done, creating conditions of the possibility of action and of Self and Other relations. Thus the postulation of an Other can very easily become reversed in the othering of the Self, as the example of the discourse of the Extreme Right illustrates. In other words, given the absence of fixed reference points, the discursive logic of Europeanization is highly contingent. There are no authoritative definitions of what constitutes the 'we', the 'other', 'inside' or 'outside', as is also evidenced by the cultural politics of borders and memories (see Chapter 5). Discursive transformation leads to socio-cognitive transformation whereby social imaginaries are articulated that go beyond the immediate context and have learning possibilities. For example, it is now possible to think of Europe in terms of a concept of Europe, as opposed to a notion of national interests.

This is a particularly important aspect of Europeanization and to which considerable attention is given in this book. The basic argument to be developed is that the state does not define a people's imaginary. New conceptions of peoplehood can be found in the cosmopolitan currents that are a feature of Europeanization. The cosmopolitan imaginary is one such imaginary that is currently emerging. But there are also others which can be called, following Boltanski and Thévenot, 'orders of justification', that is different cultural repertoires or regimes of evaluation (see Boltanski and Thévenot, 1991, 1999; Thévenot and Lamont, 2000; Silber, 2003). This is the most under-theorized research dimension of Europeanization and where the most fruitful application of constructivism can be applied in a way that reconciles micro and macro analysis. Europeanization can thus be conceived of in terms of multiple and competing orders of justification articulated through different cultural repertoires (national, transnational, cosmopolitan, etc.) and forms of sociality.

(d) Europeanization as the transformation of modernity. Finally, a social constructivist perspective draws attention to the transformation in modernity in Europe. The foundations of the European Union were, like the foundations of the nation-state, in a particular model of modernity, which is now reaching a critical juncture. In the context of postcommunism and the enlargement of the European Union, as well as wider dynamics of globalization, a new model of modernity is taking shape in Europe which is no longer exclusively based on a narrow western conception of modernity that culminates in the state and national elites. There is also a geopolitical reconfiguration of Europe with the eastern enlargement of the European Union. It may be suggested that it is now modernity itself that is being constructed out of the current developments in Europeanization (see Chapter 2). Modernity emerged in the context of societies embarked on state-building and industralization, the contemporary situation is characterized by consumption and communication under the conditions of globalization. This does not mean that modernity is being overcome, but that the current process of Europeanization must be located in the transformation of some of the central questions constitutive of political modernity (Wagner, 2005).

The chapters that follow will elaborate on these processes of Europeanization beginning with the question of modernity and moving through the other major issues, such as the cultural and discursive construction of Europe to a consideration of the social and political dimensions of Europeanization. The main argument that has been made in this chapter is that the process we are calling Europeanization cannot be reduced to state-centric approaches or to governance theories. In emphasizing globalization as the wider context in which Europeanization is occurring, diverse logics of the social construction of Europe can be identified, ranging from collective identities and imaginaries to new state–society relations and social models.

Recognition, cosmopolitanism and Europe

In closing this theoretical and preliminary chapter some remarks on the normative underpinnings of the theory of society espoused here will be made and these will serve as a preliminary outline for arguments to be developed in the subsequent chapters. Chapter 5 will take up some of these themes around a more sustained discussion of normative structures with respect to issues of citizenship and cosmopolitanism and in Chapter 6 with respect to the debate about the European Model of Society. It would be beyond the scope of this book to establish a fully developed normative philosophy. In the present context we can only refer to some of the most important considerations that are suggested by some of the major normative theories and to establish some connections with respect to Europeanization.

As argued earlier, normative claims must be grounded in a theory of society. On the basis of this claim the thesis can be advanced that neither liberal conceptions of political community nor communitarian and republican positions are adequate to account for developments associated with Europeanization. The liberal concern with individual liberties and rights, while being an important aspect of Europeanization, is not the defining characteristic of political community in Europe today.

Notwithstanding the important concern with human rights and the rights of citizenship, there is much to indicate that contemporary European society has moved beyond a liberal conception of political community. Communitarian oriented positions make too much out of a belief in the existence of a people, whether national or European, that has a basic cultural foundation. Republican variants, including some deliberative approaches, while departing from the assumptions of communitarian in the view that political community is underpinned by a cultural community, are also limited in their belief in the existence of a people albeit one defined in terms of a 'demos', that is a civil society that transcends the divisions of party, class, ethnicity, gender and other lines of cultural and political division in late-liberal society.

It will suffice to mention here that there is a dimension of analysis missing from all of these approaches to normative concerns. This is the idea of an order of recognition. As put forward variously by Pierre Bourdieu, Charles Taylor and Axel Honneth, all societies are based on what might be called an order of recognition. According to Bourdieu, all societies are based on a fundamental principle of recognition, meaning that people desire to be recognized by others in terms of worth, status, and reciprocity. However, Bourdieu's main concern is 'misrecognition', which is the cultural logic of symbolic capital, that is the way in which power and principles of social organization transform the basic orientation towards recognition into a cultural system of symbolic meanings using different forms of capital (cultural, economic, social, etc.) (Bourdieu, 1984). For Taylor, in contrast, recognition is at the heart of a liberal political community which must acknowledge minorities and their cultures (Taylor, 1994). The need to respect others is a vital human need which arises from the dialogic condition of social relations. But in the public sphere demands for recognition are more complicated than in the private realm. Taylor's essay highlights the problem of conflicting demands for recognition and where there is no obvious solution if there is to be equal recognition. While Taylor implied the need for some degree of cultural protection and thus initiated the communitarian debate, Honneth's conception of recognition addresses a different set of issues (Honneth, 1987).

Although close to Taylor in his theory of recognition, Honneth develops a version of recognition that avoids the affirmative communitarian pitfall and one that is more compatible with a cosmopolitan position. His argument is that all societies require a social order of recognition in which individuals have the means to create identities based on self-confidence, self-respect and self-esteem. For this to be possible a legally institutionalized order is required in which the autonomy and respect of individuals is guaranteed along with networks of solidarity. Honneth's thesis is that such an order of recognition is not given, but is created through social struggles, 'the moral grammar of social conflicts'. In this way normative principles emerge out of social contexts and historical processes.

Drawing from this notion of recognition, the case is made here for a normative conception of Europeanization as a cosmopolitan condition (see also Beck and Grande, 2004). Some of the major issues in debates and controversies today concern precisely the problem of recognition: the recognition of different cultures, the integration of minorities, the legal status of refugees, problems of racism and discrimination, the nature of sovereignty and citizenship, etc. Given the wider context of globalization in which to view such developments, a cosmopolitan perspective suggests the most viable way in which to view the struggle for recognition. The problems that are raised by the politics of recognition cannot be contained within national parameters and require a broadening of horizons. The upshot of Honneth's approach is that the normative integration of society depends on building structures of social recognition and resisting tendencies towards social fragmentation.

The normative approach to Europeanization in this book owes a lot to Honneth's theory of a social order of recognition. In this respect, the idea of cosmopolitanism associated with Europeanization can be linked to a social theory grounded in a normative conception of society. One of the major weaknesses of current theorizing on Europe is the absence of a social philosophy. Political philosophies – of which Habermas's is the most advanced – are often abstracted from an analysis of the social constitution of political goals. The recent concern with citizenship is an example of a retreat into a discourse of rights that is rather strangely based on late-liberal views of the polity rather than on a conception of social justice or a politics of social well being. The articulation of a social conception of society is one of the major challenges for all European societies, especially for the European Union, and one which cannot be eschewed by appeals to slogans such as cultural notions of Europe or to superficial political ideas.

In the most general sense the notion of cosmopolitanism, as used here, refers to the transformation of cultural and political subjectivities in the context of the encounter of the local or national with the global. Cosmopolitanism captures the existence of a level of reality that is being constituted by Europeanization whereby cultural models are emerging and articulating new visions of social order and which crystallize in different forms, discourses, speeds, and agencies. The empirical manifestations of cosmopolitanism require a critical and anti-reductionist approach that sees the social world constituted as an emergent reality and with transformative capacities. The cultural significance of Europeanization can be associated with cosmopolitanism rather than with something specific as a European People, a European society, a European supra-state, or a European heritage. This view of cosmopolitanism draws attention to dynamics of becoming that arise when the national and global interconnect.

It is possible to conceive of European identity as a cosmopolitan identity embodied in the pluralized cultural models of a societal identity rather than as a supra-national identity or an official EU identity that is in a relation of tension with national identities. As a cosmopolitan identity, European identity is a form of post-national self-understanding that expresses itself within, as much as beyond, national identities. Post-national and cosmopolitan currents are evident within national identities, which should not be seen, as in Castells's terms, merely resistant to global forces. The local global nexus is often the site of major social transformation. This is the significance of Europeanization, which can be understood as a reflexive relation of the national and global levels.

In this respect Europeanization is more than a matter of different levels of governance as is suggested by the notions of subsidiarity and multi-leveled governance; it is also not merely a matter of cross-cutting links between different societies, as is indicated by the network society. What these perspectives miss is, firstly, the extent of such processes, which link into the wider global context and, secondly, the dynamic and transformative movement that occurs. As a networked framework, horizontal links exist between European societies, vertical links between European societies and the EU, and transversal links between European societies and the global, as well as between the EU and the global.

The kind of cosmopolitanism that this suggests is more than the simple co-existence of difference, in the sense of multiculturalism. The relation is not one of co-existence because the various levels co-evolve and as they do so an emergent reality is produced. For this reason the cosmopolitan perspective advocated here entails a recognition of the transformative dimension of societal encounters. The cross-fertilization that occurs when societies come into contact leads to more fixed societal forms on the one side and on the other a certain logic of convergence. Europeanization is leading to greater convergence but this is also consistent with plurality. This is more than the superficial motif of 'unity in diversity', since the term generally refers to the supposed co-existence of nation-states and regions within the broader arena of the European Union and its continued expansion. The point is rather that the integration of societies entails differentiation, which is not a contrary logic. This corresponds closely to Beck and Grande's notion of 'cosmopolitan integration' (Beck and Grande, 2004). The obvious convergence of European societies does not mean some overall cohesion or uniformity. It is undoubtedly for this reason that Europeanization is ultimately difficult to democratize, since the cosmopolitan currents that accompany it tend to produce difference and with this comes more and more points of view and contentious demands (see Trenz and Eder, 2004). The democratic deficit thus becomes a structure feature of the European polity.

Main themes of the book

Based on a social constructivist approach, our book argues for the need to theorize European society, and we view Europeanization as both social transformation and a cosmopolitan condition within the context of the more general changes represented by globalization. We argue, in short, for a theory of society as a corrective to the tendency within conventional European and EU studies to develop theories of the state, integration and governance while largely ignoring the question of society. As we show in Chapter 1, the widespread and ongoing social transformation of Europe, occasioned by fundamental changes to the dynamics of modernity, requires a theory of society within which to contextualize Europe, and because European developments are rooted in social transformation and not in institutionalization, social theory is well placed to make a significant contribution. What emerges is a Europe in a process of becoming and in which peoples are seeking to orientate themselves in a post-western, post-national, and post-welfare state configuration of societies dominated to a large degree by, but ultimately not answerable to, the European Union. This process of becoming – Europeanization – is also connecting Europeans to issues, processes and identifications which have a cosmopolitan complexion: becoming European is also about being a part of the world.

With this in mind the book deals with a broad range of themes central to the question of European society. In particular we address the historical transformation of Europe and the interplay of civilizations that have constituted its cultural dynamic. We also deal with a cluster of issues concerning identity, belonging, loyalty and citizenship in the context of the emerging cosmopolitan dimension to Europe. In addition, we address themes occasioned by the dominant position of the European Union in considerations of contemporary Europe: supra-national governance; the organization of European space; polity-building; the possibility of a European civil society; and the development of a European Social Model. The project of Europe-building embarked upon by the EU is generally seen in terms of supra-state institutions, polity building or new forms of governance. The argument here is that a focus on European society not only serves as a corrective to this rather one dimensional agenda but it also broadens the terms of the debate. A focus on society means that Europeanization cannot be reduced to EU state-building: European society does not 'fit' inside an institutional model of Europe.

The cultural diversity of Europe, so often seen as a barrier to political integration, is not limited to its nation-states. Chapter 2 focuses on the historical transformations which continue to shape Europe, and which have resulted in contemporary Europe taking on a post-western orientation in which a new east has emerged to shape Europe. From such a perspective enlargement is not just about the EU becoming larger and more diverse. It is also about the transformation of Europe, the relativization of western Europe, and an awareness of many Europes shaped by multiple modernities. Europe is best thought of as a 'civilizational constellation'.

The question of European identity has long accompanied the transformation of Europe, and has taken on a new salience with the debates leading up to the development of the EU's draft Constitutional Treaty for Europe, recent enlargements to the east, and the prospect of Turkey's accession. The question of European identity has frequently been posed in such a way as to assume its incompatibility with national identities. Chapter 3 looks at how this idea is increasingly challenged, not only from positions within social theory, but also within EU discourse, where the identity of Europe (if not Europeans) has come to be represented by the idea of 'unity in diversity'. Despite its obvious attractiveness it is argued that this conceptualization of collective European identity does not account for other European identities, individual and societal, which point to a more cosmopolitan orientation for Europe.

Associated with this is the question of what it means to be European, given that the EU is unable to generate anything comparable to a national identity or the hyphenated identities which are characteristic of being American, for example. Although collective European identity is weak and a European demos has not been created by the EU's project of integration, it is possible to say that Europeans exist. Chapter 4 examines the shifts in attachment and loyalty away from the nation-state: increasingly loyalty is conditional and depends less on patriotism and residence and more on the consummation of democratic legitimacy. The nation-state no longer has a monopoly over collective action, conceptions of the 'good life', and the meaning of belonging. Cosmopolitan identifications, including but not limited to an association with Europe, offer an alternative way for individuals to imagine their history, personhood and attachments in the world.

The cultural logic of Europeanization points to the importance of the public sphere and the changing nature of citizenship as a crucible for forging European identity. In Europe, and also elsewhere, citizenship has been transformed from its modernist association with the rights and duties associated with membership in a national community. Citizenship is now a marker of difference and has been recast through its encounter with post-national membership, human rights regimes, and pluralized notions of national belonging. Chapter 5 looks at questions of citizenship and the public sphere in a Europe in which national culture and belonging can no longer fulfil the function of social integration. The chapter also looks at the Europeanization of commemoration and the way in which European publics are (to differing extents) engaged in a new politics of memory. The emergence of a European culture of apology and collective mourning is examined in the context of the institutionalization of public memory and attempts to negotiate a way between the alternatives of a memoryless history or remembrance as guilt.

The European Social Model, so central to the European Union's sense of self, particularly in dealings with the rest of the world, is the topic under consideration in Chapter 6. In one sense, the attempt to formulate a social model can be understood as EU recognition that the project of integration requires a social dimension and a vision of the collective good in a post-welfare state Europe. The social model developed in recent EU discourse is revealed to be future-orientated and closely associated with the drive for greater economic growth and competitiveness. This is the idea of Europe as a learning society, which while remaining a top-down project, offers a basis for reorienting citizenship and governance around a coherent vision of a European future, albeit one which is highly individualistic: a vision of the 'good life' rather than the 'good society'. It is argued that although the idea of the learning society is constructed as functional for both integration and economic growth it projects the concerns of European citizens beyond the confines of Europe towards a more cosmopolitan orientation.

The organization of European space beyond an assemblage of nation-states is of considerable importance in contemporary thinking about Europe. Nonetheless, much thinking on Europe is predicated upon a territorialist logic and the assumption that European space must be the outcome of integrative developments. Chapter 7 examines the nature of European spaces and borders, the dynamics of which are becoming increasingly interrelated: borders are more and more assuming the characteristics of spaces. It is argued that there are two spatial dynamics at work. The tension between networks and places tends to be interpreted in EU discourse as leading towards integration. The dynamic of fragmentation versus autonomy suggests that Europe is not necessary becoming more unitary or cohesive. The chapter focuses on how these dynamics are played out within the EU's policies towards its 'near abroad', and the creation of new 'borderlands' which comprise zones of interaction without 'hard' borders.

The question of what kind of state the EU presents has generated much debate in contemporary social science, and remains largely unresolved. In recent years there has been a marked 'governance turn' in EU studies to account for 'levels' of decision making above and below the nation-state; the ideas of network governance and multi-level governance being especially popular. Chapter 8 takes up these themes and identifies the main characteristic of EU governance as being the creation of European solutions to European problems deployed in European spaces. What is novel about EU governance, it is argued, is not so much the mechanisms of governance employed by the EU but the new spaces through which Europe is governed. This is reflected in a new lexicon of spatial governance: polycentricity and territorial cohesion pertain to European, not nation-state governance. It is further argued that conventional theories of EU governance have failed to develop anything like a theory of society, and understandings of the new spatialities of state spaces have not been extended to consideration of new social spaces.

Questions of EU governance have become connected to the idea that the EU is engaged in polity-building and preferred to the outmoded notion that a supranational state is emerging. Chapter 9 looks at the ways in which current debates on the Euro-polity are disconnected from wider social scientific debates on the idea of a world polity which hold the potential for useful work on the EU-as-polity, particularly a new comparative politics which does not take the nation-state as its baseline. It follows that the issue of whether the EU is becoming a polity cannot be answered outside the context of the relation between the EU and the rest of the world, and the relation between the EU and globalization. While the debate on polity-building provides a useful opportunity to place Europe in a global framework of interpretation it is argued that a theory of polity is no substitute for a theory of European society.

European society, to the extent that it been theorized at all within EU studies, has been viewed through the lens of civil society, and this tendency has been reinforced by both the governance turn and the preference for seeing the EU as a polity. The idea of civil society also reinforces an interpretation of the EU as an aggregate of its nation-states. Chapter 10 looks at the possibility of a European civil society in the context of the ideas on global civil society developed in social theory and elsewhere in recent years. What is revealed is an anomaly: there appears to be more evidence of global than European civil society. The reason for this, it is proposed, is that EU studies takes a restricted view of civil society, seeing it as something to be organized by the EU and built after the model of national civil society. It also tends to employ the understanding of civil society found in political science accounts of the development of the European nation-state. Theories of global civil society, on the other hand, do not assume that it has nation-state foundations and draw upon natural law assumptions about the rights and capabilities of humans, translated into the language of human rights in the contemporary context. It is argued that work on global civil society constitutes a valuable resource for studying the nascent European civil society, and also forms a bridge to a more cosmopolitan orientation to European civility.

2   History, modernity, and the multiple conceptions of Europe

European transformation in historical perspective

For over 100 years the question has been asked again and again as to the cultural form of Europe.[1] What is Europe? Is there an underlying European idea from which politics might be grounded? The answer to such questions partly depends on who asks the question and how they view history. Every age has constructed Europe in response to the concerns of the present situation. But this invented nature of Europe does not mean it is only a construction of discourse and ideology; it is also a site of cultural contestation and political possibility.

Originally the question of Europe arose in the sixteenth century in the context of threats to Christendom and continued, as its secular successor, to be loosely associated with the ideas and ideals of a civilization that could claim to be European (since the only contending civilizations were conquered by Europeans). But this was to change. Since the beginning of the twentieth century the stage of world history had slowly moved beyond Europe and its civilizational heritage had now to define itself with respect to the west, now principally represented by the United States of America, and the communist 'Asiatic' east. Europa migrated westwards once again (as the myth of the Rape of Europa recalls of an earlier migration when Europa migrated from Asia Minor to the lands we now call Europe). But in this later migration Europe lost its identity, which was claimed by the wider, and predominantly American, west. With the leadership of the west in the hands of America, Europe could no longer claim to represent European civilization, which in the aftermath of fascism had betrayed itself. In fact civilization had become a residual category, that is that which is left when culture has been extracted. As the German distinction between culture (*Kultur*) and civilization indicates, civilization has been exhausted but culture can be preserved so long as it maintains a distinction between its high and low variants.

Thus, for much of the twentieth century, it was the high culture of civilization, not the low culture of nationalism or the materialism of the nascent mass society, that was the crucible in which Europe was defined. But this was, to use Hegel's term, an unhappy consciousness, an alienated mind that had lost its connection with itself. The discord between mind and reality in European thought influenced conceptions of European identity. The most influential writings on Europe all defined Europe as an idea, a cultural discourse of the mind, an essence, based on myth. The assumption was that Europe is based on a cultural idea and that this idea can be embodied in a political form, albeit one that had yet to be realized. We need only think of works such as Husserl's *Crisis of the European Sciences*, Paul Valéry's *The Greatness and Decadence of Europe*, Karl Jaspers *The European Spirit* or T. S. Eliot's *The Unity of European Culture* to witness this discord in the European idea between its culture and political forms (Delanty, 1995a, 1995b).

There have been two attempts to 'recapture' Europa, one institutional and the other revolutionary. The first was in the historical treaties of Paris (1951) and Rome (1957) which gave birth to the EEC/later EC, and renamed European Union in 1992 with the Maastricht Treaty. The second was in 1989 and 1990 with the fall of the Berlin Wall and the demise of the state socialism arising from the revolutions in central and eastern Europe. With the European Union and the creation of new European institutions such as the Council of Europe culture became associated with the emerging reality of a European polity and became, for a time, diluted in a project that has been dominated by economic and social concerns and increasingly with politics. Politics in the 'new Europe' has caught up with culture. With the collapse of state socialism in central and eastern Europe, 'the return to Europe' as it was called put questions of civil society at the forefront of new debates on the meaning of Europe. With these developments, the abstract question of culture had been eclipsed in the way the discourse on culture had earlier eclipsed civilization. Whether in the vision of a 'Europe of regions', a 'post-national European civil society', a 'European federation', it began to look like a European identity was consolidating and in a largely political form.

However, ten years later, with the enlargement of the EU, the 'return to Europe' – or the making of a 'new Europe' – has lost its utopian promise. In the post-communist constellation, the rise of nationalism, incomplete democratization and the unsettling effects of capitalism, which have led to major social and geographical disparities, have retarded, not advanced, the promised European ideal. The economic and political consolidation of the European Union, on the other side, has also led to a growing scepticism of a common European identity emerging. With the widespread recognition among western populations that Europeanization is leading to a growing democratic deficit and a deeper crisis in loyalties, the question of the possibility of a European identity is once again on the agenda. But the mood is different: xenophobia has replaced euphoria. The 'new Europe' has been troubled by rising xenophobia and cultural backlashes, fuelled by fears of immigration (Holmes, 2000b). Many of the potential new member states were, and continue to be, divided on the question of membership. Until now Europeans aspired to the unity of 'Europe' secure in the knowledge it was not possible. A project that was once led by the conservative right has become the refuge of a besieged democratic left.

The question of culture and identity has thus returned with many people asking the question as to the cultural form of Europe. Until now Europe has been largely defined by reference to geographical, cultural, political and historical factors, which allegedly have been the basis of a unique civilization out of which emerged a distinctively western model of modernity. The European liberal democratic nation-states and the European Union are thus supposed to be the political manifestation of a *European* modernity and a *European* civilization. The assumption of a unitary civilization which leads to a single trajectory in political modernity will be critically discussed in this chapter. In this chapter the argument will be proposed that Europe is best defined in terms of a multiple, as opposed to a unitary, conception of modernity. The multiple forms of modernity in Europe are an expression of the civilizational diversity that has been a feature of European history. For this reason the idea of a European civilizational constellation rather than a single and narrowly defined civilizational model is a more appropriate notion. Looking at European history today in light of the current transformations that have been taking place for some time, it is possible to venture the claim that what is occurring is not just a change in the nature of the state, but a major shift in modernity. In Chapter 8 changes in the nature of statehood and governance are discussed. The present concern is rather with the wider geopolitical configuration of Europe in terms of a reassessment of European history and modernity. Modernity is therefore the central issue. A consideration of modernity will provide the context for a discussion of issues of political community and identity, which will be a topic of the subsequent chapters.

From our current perspective we can see not just one but many projects taking shape and as they do Europe can be seen to take a new form, whose contours are as yet unclear. The following are some of the main points which will be elaborated on in the course of this chapter. First, Europe can no longer be conceived of in terms of the West, which is itself undergoing major change. Second, in geopolitical terms, Europe is not just one thing but many: there are several 'Europes'. Third, the postcommunist era has not led to the erasure of the East but its reconfiguration. In this context what is particularly significant is that a new 'East' has arisen and which will be more important in shaping Europe. This is largely represented by Turkey but also includes Russia.

In view of these considerations, the eastern enlargement of the European Union is especially important in redefining the meaning of Europe and opens many new perspectives on European modernity. It is argued in this chapter that a new approach to the very meaning of European civilization is also timely. Europe has always had two faces, a western and an eastern one. We are now witnessing a new expression of the latter, and with this comes too a new identity for Europe. It is possible to suggest that in fact Europe is becoming more and more post-western.

The chapter proceeds as follows. Different conceptions of Europe and its borders are first discussed, focusing on the western, central and eastern faces of Europe; the second section develops this plural conception of Europe in terms of a civilizational approach to Europe as a constellation of civilizations; the third section looks at the question of multiple modernities in light of current transformations and theoretically in terms of processes of self-construction; the eastern enlargement of the EU is the subject of the next section. The chapter concludes with some remarks on the cultural and historical significance of the new 'eastern' face of Europe.

Borders and definitions of Europe

Since the invention of cartography, borders have played a major role in defining Europe. Empires, states and transnational trade and political organizations have had territorial borders. Mountains, rivers and seas have been amongst the oldest markers of territories in Europe, but have generally been more like metaphors to define politically and culturally shaped entities. Europe has been mapped by numerous borders, both internal and external, but it is not essentially a geographical entity. The Carpathians are not any more of a border than the Pyrenees and the Urals are far less of a geographical obstacle than the Alps. The absence of absolute geographical boundaries has been reflected in the variable and highly symbolic nature of human-made borders that have been a feature of European history. This has been particularly the case with the border between Europe and the non-European world. The Greeks variously believed the Sea of Asov, the Nile or the Don marked the boundary of Europe and Asia and, in the view of Herodotus, the Adriatic was the western border.

For the Greeks, to the extent to which they had a notion of Europe, it was a political system based on freedom rather than a geographical entity. Indeed, the Greeks did not always see Hellas as part of Europe. The Mediterranean Sea is often considered today to be a natural border defining the southern limits of Europe, but for the seafaring civilizations of antiquity it constituted a natural unity, in contrast to the largely unknown territories of the European landmass. The Straits of Gibraltar and the Bosporus, now seen as civilizational borders, in fact once were the meeting place of cultures. For the British, on the other hand, the Atlantic Ocean is supposed to be less a border than a common transatlantic Anglo-Saxon culture. Borders have changed, along with their functions, which have ranged from symbolic functions, administrative devices to control the movement of populations and economic growth, and military functions. Borders are not final frontiers, but zones of interpenetration and are often permeable on one or more of the many levels that they mark.

The frontier can mark the point where the metropolitan centre begins to lose control over the periphery; but it can also represent the power of the state to define its territory. This ambivalence of the border as is reflected in the literature on borders in EU law tends to distinguish borders from frontiers, with the former referring to the external limits of the EU and the latter internal distinctions, such as the border between regions and states (Müller-Graff, 1998: 15). Although this distinction does not exist in every language, as in German which has only the word *Grenze*, frontiers are precise and defined by customs and police controls. Literally they are a front line, while borders on the other hand are fuzzy and have the character of boundaries, lines of demarcation that are often defined in cultural terms or by reference to geographical factors (Anderson, 1996; Anderson and Bort, 1998; Coakley, 1982). Boundary construction is a feature of all human collectivities and one of the key markers of ethnic groups and of community more generally, as has been commented on by many anthropologists who have noted the symbolic function of boundaries (Barth, 1969; Cohen, 1985).

We cannot insist on strict definitions, but using these terms with due regard to their contested nature, it can be argued that the outer limit of the EU is becoming more like a border at precisely the same time that national frontiers within the EU are becoming diffuse. Schengen has abolished frontiers between several western EU countries, but includes within it Norway, which is a non-EU country. The result of this double dynamic is that the outer borders of Europe – the demarcation of Europe and the non-Europe – will not succeed in becoming what Webb in a classic work on frontiers has called 'a great frontier', a new imperial *limes*, for all borders and frontiers will remain contested boundary constructions (Webb, 1952). In short, we may be witnessing the dissolution of fixed frontiers, but borders with all their uncertainty and symbolic contestation remain.

One of the most important borders in modern history has of course been what Winston Churchill named the Iron Curtain. This has been more of a hard or closed border and has served to define the edge of Europe; an absolute line of demarcation, rather than a point of intersection between two territories. The western border of Europe has been closer to what the American historian, Frederick Turner, called in a different context an expanding frontier rather than a closed one and which has lacked one of the functions of the border, namely to separate insiders from outsiders (Turner, 1921). In this respect the western border has been the basis of the idea of Europe as the West, a limitless frontier, and allowed the expansion of European civilization westwards into the Americas and beyond. As such, there is no western border, just the open horizon of the Western world with its universalistic culture. The eastern and southern borders of Europe, while being more complicated, have not always been hard borders. Throughout European history these borders have taken a great diversity of forms, zones of exchange, buffer zones or marches, liminal zones, administrative units, trading blocks, nations. Hard and soft borders have been mutually reinforcing.

The disappearance of the Iron Curtain has not led to the end of borders, but to new kinds of borders, the 'soft' borders epitomized in the slogan the 'clash of civilizations' and which in the view of some are reflected in the outer borders of 'Fortress Europe.'

Such borders, which have global significance, have played an important role in European history, but a closer look reveals a more complicated story. While the eastern border has often been a hard border, looking further back into European history, this frontier was the basis of the expanding borders of the Roman Empire, whose *limes* established the foundation of the geopolitics of Europe. The fact that the Roman Empire was not only transnational but also an inter-civilizational entity without fixed borders made it inevitable that modern Europe would not be able to rest on secure territorial foundations (Whittaker, 2000). There is no clearly defined eastern border and it can be argued that in fact it is the constantly changing eastern border that has been the defining feature of Europe's geopolitics. This border has suffered the fate of the grand narratives of the past, dissolving into a plethora of mini-borders. With the end of communism and the incorporation of Poland into the EU in 2004, Oder–Neisse has lost its symbolic role as a border; the inclusion of Cyprus in the EU has pushed the eastern border closer to Syria and Lebanon.

Borders of different kinds have been a feature of the continent, especially between East and West. The eastern border has taken many different forms and has shaped the geopolitical configuration and identity of Europe to a very considerable extent (Delanty, 1996a). The border, often described as a fault line, that runs from the Baltic to the Adriatic Sea has divided Europe for much of its history. The most striking feature of this border is that it has changed many times in the course of the twentieth century, from the interwar period to the post-1945 era, and in the present post-Cold-War period it has changed once again (Dingsdale, 2002). This border has separated the western democracies from the authoritarian communist ruled societies, but it has also separated the various Soviet bloc countries – GDR, Poland and what was then Czechoslovakia – from each other. But these were borders that have constantly changed, especially between Hungary and Austria and between Austria and Slovenia (Meinhof, 2002). In the case of Poland, the borders have changed numerous times since the eighteenth century. The actual axis itself has also shifted, for the pre-1945 Polish–German border was much further east than today's Oder and Neisse border. Russia's western frontier has shifted westwards. As a result of the enlargement of the European Union to include these former communist countries, a new border has arisen which divides the former central European countries from the further eastern countries, Bulgaria and Romania.

Where some of these borders were once permeable, as the border between Romania and Hungary was due to its overlapping ethnic population in Transylvania, they have now become more rigid, a consequence of the enlargement of the EU to include the latter. A new border has arisen between what is now Slovakia and the Czech Republic. It was the very permeability of the Austro–Hungarian border in 1989 that led to the dissolution of communism and the end of the Cold War. Here the border marked an opening in Europe to a new era. Since then, the eastern border is being pushed in different directions, opening up new borders as a consequence of Schengen, as well as liminal zones, as the example of Kaliningrad illustrates, international protectorates such as Kosovo, and unsettled border areas, such as Transylvania, with its Hungarian population, and Cyprus where the Greek–Turkish border has brought to the heart of the enlarged EU a major and unsettled dispute. It is indeed paradoxical that as borders have been diminishing within the existing EU, they are becoming more visible in central and eastern Europe as well as the EU's outer frontier with the rest of the world. Major symbolic conflicts are being fought around these borders by societies in which national autonomy has been relatively recent and in which it is often associated with the need to deny large minorities of rights. This suggests that in fact Europe is not old at all, for most of the frontiers in Europe were created in the twentieth century as a result of state building and the dissolution of the older empires (Foucher, 1998: 233).

The renegotiation of borders has been one of the characteristic features of European history. While the driving force in general has been the necessity to define political boundaries – whether those of particular states or of political organizations ranging from NATO to the EU – a wider and no less important force has played a key role in this, namely the 'soft' borders of civilization, such as

those of Christianity and the symbolic borders that have been part of the received
wisdom of the past, such as the notion of a European continent.

As a continent, Europe is indefinable. Paul Valéry described Europe as 'a little
promontory on the Asian Continent' (Valéry, 1962: 31). Yet, the myth has
remained that Europe is a continent apart from Asia. Where does Asia end and
Europe begin? Can a continent that is little more than promontory have borders?
The answer largely depends on from where the question is asked, for Europe is
perspectival. Until the end of the Cold War, in the view of many western
Europeans, Europe ended at the Iron Curtain. From the perspective of Poland,
the Czech Republic and Hungary, Europe has a central core rooted in traditions
of civil society, democracy and Roman Catholicism (Delanty, 1996b). The result
for Central Europe has been the migration eastwards of the border with Asia,
which increasingly is being brought as far as Turkey and Russia. But this is a
decidedly political and cultural definition of the continent. The British have
generally excluded themselves from the 'continent', a metaphor for western Europe
(Kumar, 2003). It is an undeniable fact of European history that a continental or
geographical identity has never been found. Europe's geopolitical space has been
defined by a mix of civilizational, continental, and political factors (see Jönsson
et al., 2000). Europe is a term that cannot be reduced to a geographical, a
civilizational or a political form, for it is all three together. As a civilization it
emerged out of the Roman pan-EuroAsian Mediterranean civilization; as a
continent it occupies an uncertain space on the Eurasian landmass somewhere
between Madera and Cyprus or between Iceland and Malta to take the outer
reference points; and as a political entity it has been shaped by the internal struggles
between empires and states that followed from the Carolingian Empire, whose
geopolitics effectively defined what has come to be known as western Europe.

The divisions in European history go beyond rivalries between states (Fontana,
1995). The Carolingian Empire gave to Europe an enduring geopolitical mould.
The division of Christendom into two parts from 1054, following the earlier
separation of the Roman Empire in the sixth century, was decisive in bifurcating
Christian Europe into a Greek east and a Latin west. The excommunication of
the Byzantine church in that year laid the foundation for subsequent divisions,
culminating in the fourth crusade in 1204 which was a crusade led by one Christian
church against another. Although this division was not initially one of a separation
of Europe and Asia, it effectively became one in the aftermath of the fall of Constantinople to Islam in 1454. The migration northwards of Byzantine Christianity
to Moscow, the 'Third Rome', gave some legitimacy to the claim that Russia was
European. By the time of the Reformation in which Latin Christianity divided
between a Catholic south and a Protestant north, the myth had been created
that Europe was interchangable with Christendom. This was when Spain was
unified and the reconquest of the Iberian Peninsula began at the same time as the
European 'discovery' of Americas. With the expulsion of Islam from the Iberian
Peninsula, and unification of Castile and Aragon, Spain ceased to be a borderland
between Islam and Christianity and invented the myth of global leadership. With
this a new idea of Europe consolidated: an Oceanic, or Atlantic, Europe, that was

eventually led by Britain and a continental Europe divided between France, the Russian and Austro-Habsburg Empires.

It was the Habsburg dominated Christendom – from the Iberian Peninsula to central Europe – that promulgated the myth that Europe and Christendom are one and the same. From the sixteenth century onwards, Europe became defined in opposition to the Ottoman Islamic Orient. The actual word 'Europe' itself began to be used with increased currency from the sixteenth century when the Ottoman Empire made its first onslaught on the Habsburg Empire (Hay, 1957). The Protestant heritage – itself deeply divided between numerous sects – on the other hand did not to the same extent define itself against Islam. Indeed, the beginnings of Britain's alienation from Europe began with the Reformation, which in dominating Scandinavia acquired a strongly Nordic character. Despite the fissure between north and south, it was the west versus east divide that was the abiding axis in defining the shape of Europe. Nevertheless, given the extent of the divisions in western Christendom since the Reformation, the absolute nature of the east versus west divide should not be overestimated. Recent evidence in fact suggests that the cultural and political lines of communication between the east and west were far from adversarial, especially between the Protestant west and the Islamic east (Jardine and Brotton, 2000). However, this is also true of the German eighteenth-century enlightenment as well as later German thought (Harrington, 2004; Osterhammel, 1998).

Since the east–west axis has shifted so many times in European history, it is not possible to specify where 'Europe' ends – or where it begins. In any case the borders are contested and are continuing to be negotiated. As Norman Davies has shown, there is not just one east–west axis that has remained constant since the days of the Carolingian Empire: there is a wide range of other borders and divisions in European history, including the fault lines of the Reformation (Davies, 1996). Taking Scüzs's threefold model of Europe, it is possible to define Europe in terms of western Europe, with its origins in Rome and the Carolingian Empire, a central Europe consisting of Hungary, the Czech Republic, Slovakia, Poland, Hungary, and a truncated eastern and south-eastern Europe, including the Balkans, Romania and Bulgaria (Scüzs, 1988). Northern Europe, which until the Reformation was more or less outside Europe, and the European Mediterranean from Spain to Greece, can be considered part of a wider Western Europe. In short, there are many 'Europes'. If Europe was once shaped by the pull of Rome, on the one side, and on the other by Byzantium, it became defined by the tension between the United States and Russia in the twentieth century, with the result that the inner divisions in Europe became reflected on a global level. Given the role of the eastern border in the making of Europe and the obvious fact that Europe contains large parts that do not fall under the general category of 'western', it must be concluded that the plurality of Europe is more than a diversity of cultures and nations, but extends into its very civilizational nature. In other words, as a geopolitical entity Europe is as much eastern as it is western.

Since the end of communism and the enlargement of the EU to include many of the former eastern European countries, the very terms central and eastern have been reinvented. Most notably, there has been a rebirth of central Europe, which is not an enlarged and central part of the EU, and as a result the designation eastern Europe has been pushed further east (Delanty, 1996b). Given that the countries to which the designation refers are themselves seeking EU membership and some of which, such as Ukraine and Belarus, exist in a close relation with Russia, which for them is the east, the very terms east and west are losing their traditional referents and are best abandoned in making sense of Europe. Within the Balkans, a new east–west distinction arose following the break-up of Yugoslavia, with countries such as Slovenia and Croatia positioning themselves in an ideologically charged Roman Catholic and liberal west to distinguish themselves from an allegedly more Asiatic Serbia. In this west–east contest, it is interesting to note that the Islamic populations of Bosnia and Kosovo were allied to the liberal West, suggesting that the identification of the East with Islam is not as fixed as has often been thought. Widespread public opposition to the Iraq War in 2003 and 2004 in European countries expressed more hostility to the United States than to Islam.

In view of these considerations and in light of the renegotiation of borders today, there is some sense in defining Europe itself as a borderland, as Étienne Balibar has argued (Balibar, 2004: 220). This is to draw attention to the impossibility of defining Europe geographically, given the lack of stability in its borders (Berezin and Schain, 2003b). Robert Barlett has shown how Europe was created out of a continuous process of colonization and expansion into borderlands (Barlett, 1993). Europeanization is now more than ever located in what were once borderlands. The relation between inside/outside is therefore changing rapidly. As Balibar has commented, 'the notions of interiority and exteriority, which form the basis of the representation of the border, are undergoing a veritable earthquake' (Balibar, 2004: 5). If this is correct, then, both the conventional view of Europe as the west as well as the new discourse of 'Fortress Europe' need some revision. Undoubtedly the western, Christian Carolingian centre of Europe played a major, if not decisive, role in defining Europe, but it did not set down immutable frontiers. The frontiers and borders of Europe have been possible only in relation to the appropriation of other centres in a history that has been one of changing relations between cores and peripheries. Both Europe and its borders are discursive constructions. Where Europe ends is one question but where the EU should end is a quite different and more political question, as William Wallace has argued (Wallace, 2003).

The European civilizational constellation

If there are several 'Europes' – western, Nordic, central and eastern – does this mean there is no such thing as Europe? Is it possible to speak of a Europe as a civilization or is this a myth that is best abandoned along with any attempt to define Europe geographically? There is a sense in which Europe can be defined: Europe as a civilizational constellation. Conceived of as a civilizational constellation, Europe can be defined in civilizational terms without the usual western-centric notions and assumptions associated with the term and obscuring the diversity of Europe. The major geopolitical components of the European civilizational constellation are: the western Judaeo-Christian, Russian-Slavic and Islamic-Turkish civilizations. European modernity has been shaped by not one, but by all three civilizations, which opened up different routes to modernity.

By civilization is meant a family of societies, or a constellation of societies, formations of the *longue durée* which are open to significant internal changes and adaptable to new circumstances (Arnason, 2003a: 304). A civilization has a foundation in material life and while not reducible to a specific spatial location, it can be related to a geopolitical field. The term 'constellation', as used by Walter Benjamin and T. W. Adorno, refers to a juxtaposed rather than a fixed or integrated cluster of changing elements, which do not have a common foundation or underlying meaning. In giving form to a configuration of elements, the constellation constitutes a unity in difference. A civilization is a constellation of societies and a civilizational constellation therefore is a configuration of civilizations. Civilization analysis as pioneered by Shmuel Eisenstadt and Johann Arnason is an alternative to nation-state centric approaches in comparative historical and sociological analysis (see Arnason, 2003a; Eisenstadt, 2000a, 2003). In this view, civilizations are multi-dimensional formations in which basic cultural orientations interact with dynamics of political and economic institutions shaping families of societies. Civilization analysis aims to provide a foundation for a conception of modernity as multiple and is also relevant to an understanding of the historical roots of globalization in inter-civilizational encounters. In short, questions of globalization, modernity, and the encounter of civilizations, are highly pertinent to a civilizational perspective. In the present context, what is important is the civilizational dimension to European modernity. While nations and states have been critical in shaping modern Europe, a civilizational perspective provides a wider picture of the roots of modernity and the constellations of societies that it produced. Moreover, the impact of globalization cannot be seen as a radical rupture from history, but must be located with respect to the dynamics and societal structures that have emerged in the historical process of civilizational development (Morin, 2002; Mozaffari, 2002).

This emphasis on Europe as a civilizational constellation shifts the focus away from states and, moreover, stresses less the internal regions within Europe to a consideration of the wider civilizational basis of European history. Although states have been the major actors in shaping history, a perspective on civilizations highlights the cultural, geographical and political factors that together have been constitutive of modernity. Modernity cannot be explained exclusively by reference to state formation but requires reference to other matters such as consciousness of globality. Furthermore, in light of recent scholarship and changing perceptions of western civilization, any account of Europe will have to include the active relation with the east. This is partly because the origins of European civilization lie in the appropriation of eastern civilizations, but in the present context of more importance is that a large part of the European civilization has itself been formed in relation to two Eurasian civilizations, the Russian and Islamic civilizations. In stressing the role of these components of what is being called the

European civilization constellation, we are drawing attention as much to the nature of the interaction as to the diverse traditions. Indeed, it could be argued that Europe has been formed by precisely the interaction, cross-fertilization, cultural borrowing and diffusions of its civilizations. Europe must be seen as a constellation consisting of links rather than stable entities or enduring traditions or an overarching idea that can be basis of a political design. The following is a necessarily brief outline of the European civilization constellation.

The occidental Judaeo-Christian civilization is itself a constellation of societies shaped by empires and states along with the Roman and Christian heritage. This is the civilization that has shaped European and indeed western world history and is the civilizational model of modernity to which the current EU owes its identity (Geremek, 1996). As a civilization, its defining features are the universalistic culture of science, art and music, as reflected in the Renaissance and Enlightenment. The tradition of revolutions and the creation of democratic liberties, civil society, secularism and republican government has of course been an undeniable feature of European civilization. Historians and philosophers have emphasized different aspects of Europe in an effort to characterize the distinctive nature of its civilization. Weber stressed the rationalizing tendencies of 'universal significance' in western Europe and which gave a particular impetus to capitalism, science and formal law, while Marx stressed the social movements of the nineteenth century, and Husserl and Patocka drew attention to the European philosophical mind (Husserl, 1965; Patocka, 2001). Western Europe has reinvented itself throughout history; indeed, it has done so to a point that makes it difficult to say what Europe actually is and what is European and what is borrowed from non-European sources (Hobson, 2004). In terms of culture and geopolitics, western Europe has been a constellation of forces that have been characterized by a high degree of renewal. Rather than look to just one aspect of western European civilization, a more plausible solution is to define it in terms of a continuous capacity to reinvent itself. As a civilization based on rebirths or renaissances, reformations, revolutions, and enlightenments, western European civilization does not rest on an indubitable origin as such or even a geographical territory; rather it is characterized by a mode of cultural transmission, which includes the transmission of the culture of other civilizations and societies. In the context of what is now an enlarged EU, the assumptions upon which identity are based may need to be reconsidered. The historical roots of this western civilization – Athens, Rome and Jerusalem – were not European in the western sense of the term 'European'. Classical antiquity and origins of Christianity were Mediterranean in the sense Fernand Braudel used the term (Braudel, 1972/3). Western civilization is based on a history that was never entirely European, but became Europe in a process of borrowing, translation and diffusion (Brague, 2002). The major examples of this are Hellinization, Romanization and the subsequent adoption of the Roman heritage by Christianity, the Renaissance and scientific revolution and age of discovery, and exploration and imperialism which led to the diffusion in Europe of non-western inventions and marked the 'rise of the west'.

From the beginning European civilization was divided between western and eastern faces, which are represented by Russian civilization and Islamic civilization.

Because of their major importance Russia, Islam and the Christian west must be defined as civilizations in that they are characterized by distinctive geopolitical or spatial configurations, which are generally related to major empires, distinctive cultural models, which are linked to a universalistic religion, and a dominant social imaginary, such as a historical narrative. The Russian and Ottoman empires were major imperial powers in which distinctive civilizations crystallized. Other important empires, such as the central European Habsburg Empire or earlier the Polish Lithuanian state, did not have the same civilizational significance and were mostly regional variants of one of the main civilizations. Judaism is a more complicated case; but – as a way of life, a religion, and culture which are diasporic – cannot be considered a civilization in the strict sense of the term, since it cannot be related to a geopolitical field encompassing a family of societies and a political order. Instead, it can be seen as part of the cultural diversity of European civilizational constellation rather than being a civilization in its own right. From the point of view of a civilizational analysis, it must be more specifically considered part of the occidental Judaeo-Christian civilization.

Russia, with its roots in the Byzantine tradition, represents another major part of the European civilizational constellation. Southern Russia has been part of Europe far longer than many regions which we consider to be core European countries (Hobsbawm, 1997: 289). As a Eurasian civilization and deeply rooted in the Orthodox tradition, Russia warrants being called a civilization distinct from western civilization (Arnason, 2000; Buss, 2004). In taking over the mantle of Byzantium and Orthodoxy in the wake of the fall of Byzantine civilization to the Ottomans, a distinctive civilization consolidated in which the Christian heritage was tied to a Slavic Eurasian culture. This mix of western and eastern, European and Asian components was the defining feature of Russian civilization and the basis of its route to modernity. In Russia modernity unfolded though an active and close engagement with the west and earlier with the Byzantine tradition. As a European civilization, Russia was the main focus for eastern Slavs and those western Slavs in Central Europe who identified with the nascent Slavic cultural project as it consolidated from the eighteenth century onwards. The cultural and political programmes inaugurated by Peter the Great were an attempt to assert the western European face of Russia. The nineteenth-century invention of the Ural Mountains marking the border between Europe and Asia was one such attempt to show that that Russia had a European and an Asiatic side (Bassim, 1991). Whether the Russian Revolution was the assertion of the Asiatic or the Western component of Russian civilization has been endlessly debated, but certainly it was possible only as a result of the impact of the western revolutionary tradition. In any case, it was in Russia that one of the most important experiments in modernity occurred (Arnason, 1993). The communist programme, 1918 to 1991, was the major expression of a counter-modernity that was a product of a European civilization based on western (the national state tradition), Eurasian (Slavic) and classical (Byzantine) traditions. In Russia today these traditions are being renegotiated (Billington, 2004; Neuman, 1996).

Since the fall of Constantinople in 1453 and the subsequent expansion westwards of the Ottoman empire, it is possible to venture the claim that a third major component of the European civilizational constellation is constituted by the Islamic Mediterranean, and principally represented by modern Turkey as the inheritor of the Ottoman legacy. This is not to neglect the importance of the earlier history of Islam in Spain. However, whether this constitutes a separate civilization is questionable, since after the defeat of the Moors there was little historical continuity in civilizational terms, despite the important cultural influence of Spanish and Sicilian Islam. This is also the case with the Mongols, who converted to Islam in the thirteenth century, but did not leave a discernable Islamic culture in Russia, which they occupied from the thirteenth century until the formation of the Muscovite State in 1480. In terms of a civilizational model, the Islamic component of European civilization is principally, but not exclusively, represented by the Ottoman and Turkish civilization. The Ottoman Empire brought Islamic civilization into the heart of Byzantine Europe and while a later arrival to Europe it is an important – but an all too neglected – part of the European civilizational constellation. Throughout the Middle Ages, both Spain and Russia were under Islamic rule. According to Jardine and Brotton, the Renaissance was formed out of encounters between the Orient and the Occident and that in the fifteenth and sixteenth centuries east and west met on more equal terms that was later the case. Some of the most potent symbols in European culture derived from the East and that the borders between east and west were more permeable than was later thought (Jardine and Brotton, 2002; Brotton, 2002).

The conventional approach is to see Russian civilization as the inheritor of the Byzantine tradition in the aftermath of the fall of Constantinople, which ceases to be European, except in the narrow geographical sense. The civilizational approach adopted here on the contrary would suggest that the Ottoman tradition represents a third European civilization and one based on Islam. This is also the position taken by Jack Goody, who has argued for a transcontinental European civilization that includes Islam, which has the same roots as the Judaeo-Christian civilization. Europe has never been purely isolated and purely Christian (Goody, 2004: 14). Today Islam is represented principally by Turkey, which is relatively small but a reminder – especially in the context of the enlargement of the European Union – of a third route to modernity (Bozdogan and Kasaba, 1997; Göle, 1996; Kaya, 2004). The Mediterranean geopolitical face of Europe is becoming more and more important in the wider Eurasian and Mediterranean definition of Europe. Malta, for instance, is another example of this, albeit of a Christian country that has played a role in mediating the civilizations and cultures of the Mediterranean.

Multiple modernities and European transformation

The civilizational perspective discussed in the foregoing has emphasized the deeper formations of material and symbolic culture and societal models that underlie the much discussed cultural diversity of Europe. In other words, the cultural diversity of Europe is more than the diversity of its nations but is an expression of the constellation of civilizations that make up Europe. In drawing attention to the civilizational context, the transcontinental nature of Europe was noted as an important feature of its history. On the basis of these points it can now be argued that modernity can itself be conceived as a multiple condition which is continuously constructed. This is in line with recent theories of multiple modernity (Eisenstadt, 2000a, 2003). In the most developed version of this thesis, the argument has been proposed that the divergent patterns of modernity are to some extent grounded in civilizational frameworks (Arnason, 2003a).

What is modernity? The term signals a condition of self-confrontation, incompleteness and renewal in which the localized past is reshaped by a globalized present; it expresses a self-confidence in the transformative project of the present time as a liberation from the past; modernity is the belief in the possibility of a new beginning based on human autonomy, the belief that the world can be shaped by human agency; and above all it is the consciousness of global or world cultural concepts. In Agnes Heller's words: 'Everything is open to query and to testing; everything is subject to rational scrutiny and refuted by argument' (Heller, 1999: 41; see Delanty, 2000a). This was a consciousness – which was radical and therefore both liberating and destructive – that first emerged in Europe and, while not being specifically European, it was carried to the rest of the world since the sixteenth century and the subsequent history of modernity bore the impact of its European origins. These origins were reconstructed by America in the twentieth century but today modernity is global; it is no longer exclusively western. Global modernity is not uniform and has had many routes into it and has diverse expressions (Therborn, 1995a). Today the defining features of modernity are no longer those that can be seen in European terms, but global and that there are parts of the world where the consciousness of modernity is more intense than in the west. The critical point is that modernity is neither entirely singular nor plural, universal nor particular, but an ongoing process of transformation that arises in the encounter of the local and present time with the global. This is why modernity cannot be equated with globality as such; it arises when the particular – the local – encounters globality.

This encounter can be seen in terms of cultural translations, that is as a translation that transforms, or dislocates, both subject and object. For this reason modernity as such has no location, but is a continuous process of construction. Modernity entails a high degree of conflict, leading some to define it in terms of liberty versus discipline, autonomy versus fragmentation, democracy versus capitalism (Delanty, 1999; Wagner, 1994). As a 'field of tensions', to use Johann Arnason's term, modernity is a process of ongoing contestation arising as a result of dynamics of tensions and conflicts, between the pursuit of power and the aspiration towards autonomy (Arnason, 2003a).

There is general agreement that modernity does not take one form but many. The most interesting approach in this respect is the idea of 'multiple modernities' or – to use a term some authors favour – 'alternative modernities' (Gaonkar, 2001). In this view, which is associated with the work of a very broad spectrum of scholars, modernity is pluralized into numerous societal and cultural forms (see also Kamali, 2005; Kaya, 2004; Taylor, 1999). When generalized to the wider world, modernity needs to be radically de-historicized, it is argued; it cannot be conceptualized in terms of some of the western processes of modernization. When viewed in this light, it would even appear that the notion of a singular modernity has in fact inherited too many of the assumptions of modernization theory, for instance certain assumptions about nation-state formation, capitalism and secularization. The idea of multiple modernities points to an epistemic break from a conception of modernity as a historical condition that with some delays and modifications has been generalized to the rest of the world. Eisenstadt (2000b) and Wittrock (2000) argue that modernity itself refers to the features that are common to the diverse forms of modernity. Mouzelis (1999) has argued that modernity is not westernization and its key processes and dynamics can be found in all societies.

The notion of multiple modernities is not entirely without problems. One problem for instance is that the current debate does not appear to have advanced beyond a general recognition that modernity takes more than one form. The result is that the concept is in danger of being over-pluralized. A problem, too, is that the idea of multiple modernities might reinforce a view of different modernities isolated from each other and being static, rather than processual, transformative and interpenetrating. Some authors have proposed the notion of 'entangled modernities' to explain the immeshed, interconnected nature of modernities and that there is not just multiple but overlapping ones (Arnason, 2003b; Therborn, 2003). Modernity is something that can exist in different forms within particular nations and cultures. The suggestion that modernity exists not just in multiple but overlapping, entangled forms points to something previously neglected in the social theory of modernity and which was always central to the older modernization theory, namely an emphasis on transformative processes and, as Johann Arnason argues, interconnections (Arnason, 2003b). No account of modernity in global perspective can neglect the interactive and, driven by this, transformative mechanisms and processes. The point is that 'modernities' do not simply exist as coherent or stable units, but are in a constant process of change due to the nature of the particular forms of interaction, selection, combination, adaptation and processing of cultural codes, resources, imaginaries etc. A variant on this theme is the notion of hybrid modernities, which is best associated with postcolonial theory and with globalization theory (Gilroy, 1993; Nederveen Pieterse, 2004; Venn, 2000). Nederveen Pieterse stresses the mixed character of 'new Asian modernities', which he sees as shaped by globalization and constituting alternatives to the nineteenth-century legacy of colonialism and its conceptual dichotomies of tradition and modernity, community and society, etc. In this view of modernity, hybridity, syncretism, creolization, bricolage becomes the defining feature of modernity, leading to what has been also been called 'cosmopolitan modernity' (Nava, 2002).

For the purpose of this book, the idea of modernity in the European context must be regarded as both multiple and hybrid. There is not one single societal model of modernity, but several and which can also be seen in civilizational terms. Relating the diverse forms of modernity to civilizational frameworks, a more deeply rooted historical sense of modernity as a transformative project becomes more plausible. One important aspect of this is the role of civilizational encounters, since as previously argued the European civilizations have not been separated from each other, but are part of what has been called a civilization. For this reason, too, the modernities that developed in Europe have borne the imprint of their civilizational context and encounters. With new inter-civilizational encounters, major shifts in modernity occur. This is precisely what is happening today: major social transformations in modernity are leading to a reconfiguration of the European civilizational constellation. In this book we make some limited claims that one expression of this is a new modernity based on cosmopolitanism. But we need to clarify first the nature of the current social transformations in modernity.

Some of the major social transformations that have occurred in recent times are the following: the end of communism and emergence of a multipolar world; the changing nature of Americanization and the rise of militant Islam; the power of global civil society; economic and technological globalization; and new dynamics of Europeanization. The demise of communism and the subsequent unification of Germany, the triple transition to market economies, democracy, and national autonomy for central and eastern Europe and the eventual membership of the EU of many of these countries has been the major transformation in Europe in recent times. It has led to a shift in political influence from France to Germany. The course of German history has been one of the major forces that shaped the course of modern European history. Post-unification Germany has achieved a stability, or 'normality' to use the German expression, that is likely to remain; but the great changes that have occurred in Germany have implications for Europe as a whole in economic and political terms. The trend towards a stronger constitutional and more federal EU is a direct consequence of German power. The consolidation and Europeanization of central Europe and to a lesser extent of the further eastern countries is to a considerable extent the result of German influence. More generally, the demise of communism has changed the relation of Europe to the United States and Russia. The post-Cold War world is a multi-polar one in which Europe is only one of the players, but nevertheless a player distinct from the United States. What has in effect come to an end is the unitary notion of 'the West' and the emergence in its place of a multiplicity of geopolitics and with these new models of modernity (see Bonnett, 2004).

If Europe has changed, so too has the United States. Since 11 September 2001, but probably going back to the election of the Bush administration, there has been a turn to what many critics have called 'empire' (Hardt and Negri, 2000). In direct opposition to the prevailing assumptions about globalization and international governance, there has been an unequivocal assertion of unilateralism, political authoritarianism and military objectives. The current nature of Americanization has implications for Europe. Americanization and Europeanization are two quite different logics and while both are products of a more globalized world for the first time tensions and differences are evident. Where Americanization is allegedly responding to the rise of militant Islam and is primarily driven by security, Europeanization is a multi-directional development that is not primarily politically driven. This change in the nature of Americanization can be regarded as a major shift in modernity since it calls into question for the first time some of the fundamental promises of an earlier modernity, namely the belief in the law governed state.

The global assertion of American power is occurring at the same time as the power of global civil society is becoming ever more apparent (Keane, 2003). Global civil society is evident in the growing volume of transnational debates, movements, and politics and has led to the expression in various forms of a global ethics (Singer, 2003). This is now a real force in the world and is a response to the need for global ethical solutions to problems associated with climate change, the role of the World Trade Organization, human rights and humanitarianism, and foreign aid. A global ethics is evident in ways of thinking, feelings, social movements and struggles, in soft laws as well as in international laws, tribunals and treaties. This has not just arisen as a result of abstract ideas, but as a result of the visible existence of new social actors who effectively constitute the new social spaces of global civil society.

Europeanization cannot ignore such developments, which are influencing the context and content of politics in Europe. As a major shift in modernity, it marks a fundamental move beyond the nation-state as the exclusive principle of sovereignty.

Finally, economic and technological globalization, which Castells has called a second industrial revolution, has led to a major restructuring of the economies and social structures of European societies bringing about new relations between centres and peripheries across countries as well as within them (Castells, 1996). This can be counted as a significant shift in modernity to the extent that it has led to new dynamics in the relation between cultural frameworks and institutions, offering new opportunities for autonomy but also bringing with it new kinds of power and problems. Touraine has characterized this shift in modernity as one that has moved from a modernity based on production to one based on consumption and communication and which he sees as the context in which to interpret Europeanization (Touraine, 1994: 17).

What is emerging out of these social transformations is a shift in modernity, but one that is leading not to a single new modernity but several. It is unlikely that the EU or any state will be able to control or impose its societal model or political programme on the kind of modernity that is now taking shape. The most significant aspect of the current situation is the global context and, related to this, external factors. No longer is Europanization a narrative of the Europeanization of the nation-state and the resolution of conflicts within European societies or something that can be explained in normative terms, such as the desire to achieve lasting unity or peace. As Europeanization moves out of the older models of postwar period – the European rescue of the nation-state – other challenges face it and as they do so, new justifications have to be found. The current hiatus is one in which new cognitive models are being shaped.

Implications of the enlargement of European Union

The enlargement of the EU to include most of central and eastern Europe and beyond can be considered in the context of the developments discussed in this chapter. Viewed as a simple enlargement of the EU, it can be seen as merely the latest in its several enlargements, such as incorporation of the British Isles and Denmark in 1973, Greece and the Iberian peninsula in the 1980s and in 1995 the Nordic enlargement with Finland and Sweden, along with Austria. However this would be too simple. The eastern enlargement is qualitatively different, quite aside from being also an enlargement on a far greater scale; it can be seen as significant step in the reshaping of modernity in Europe and its civilizational framework. In this respect it is an interesting example of a major transformation in Europe. The actual facts of the enlargement are relatively undramatic (Fuchs and Klingeman, 2002; Gowan, 2002; Nugent, 2004). However, when viewed in a wider context, the implications for Europeanization are considerable.

Enlargement entered the agenda of the EU in 1993 with the Copenhagen European Council, which made the historic promise that

> the countries in Central and Eastern Europe that so desire shall become members of the Union. Accession will take place as soon as a country is able to assume the obligations of membership by satisfying the economic and political conditions.[2]

This was also stated in the Maastricht Treaty, but it was not until the Nice Treaty in December 2000 that steps were put in place to prepare the EU for wholesale enlargement by 2004. Estonia, Latvia, Lithuania, Poland, the Czech Republic, Slovakia, Malta, Cyprus, Hungary and Slovenia finally joined the EU on 1 May 2004, increasing membership of the EU to twenty-five countries. A decision on accession for Bulgaria and Romania has been delayed until 2007, the likely entry date for their inevitable membership. Turkey, which had been on the candidacy list since 1999, was finally given approval in December 2004 to begin negotiations to join the EU.

This will not be the end of the enlargement process. At its meeting in Santa Maria da Feira in June 2000 the European Council agreed that all of the countries in the western Balkans – Bosnia and Herzegovina, Serbia, Albania, Macedonia – are 'potential candidates' of the European Union. The stabilization and association process, which is the EU's policy in this region, allows these countries to move towards integration and with financial support from the EU. It is unlikely that the Caucasian republics – Armenia, Georgia and Azerbaijan – will join the EU, despite being recognized by the Council of Europe as part of Europe. However, in a not too distant future this cannot be excluded.

Russia has expressed an interest in opening discussion with the EU on the consequences of enlargement, but membership is unlikely ever to happen. Gorbachev's idea of a 'common European house' has lost its appeal in Russia today and there are no indications of anything more than increased cooperative links with the EU. The framework for the integration of Russia into a common European economic and social space is represented by the partnership and Cooperation Agreement. Since the accession of Finland, Russia is now a direct neighbour of the EU, which consequently will be drawn more and more into cross-regional controversies. However, it is a different matter for Ukraine, Belarus and Moldova, where there is interest in eventual membership.

The post-2004 European Union now has a population of 450 million and twenty official languages in its twenty-five countries. Many of the new members – with the exception of Poland with a population of almost 39 million – are small countries, and some such as Malta and Cyprus are barely larger than many European cities. This institutional reshaping may have adverse effects for the pre-2004 smaller member states, such as Ireland, Greece, Denmark and Portugal. There can be little doubt that the major western countries will continue to dominate an enlarged EU and will economically benefit from it. However, what is likely to change in a significant way as a result of the geopolitical reshaping is a change in the cultural composition of the European Union. Politically and economically the EU will remain dominated by the western core countries, but in terms of geopolitics and cultural frameworks it is a different matter. In this sense, it is possible to speak of a civilizational change away from an exclusive orientation built on the presuppositions of western modernity and its civilizational trajectory.

What is going on in central and eastern Europe cannot be so-easily called 'westernization' in the sense of the imposition of a coherent structure and culture underpinned by the *Acquis Communautaire*. Although many people in central and eastern Europe, as well as people further into the Eurasian belt, see themselves as western and European and want to have more not less of the 'west', they all mean different things by this. The debate about joining the EU in the ten newly joined member states was in almost all cases a deeply divided one, with different collective identities coming to the fore. This reinforces a point made in the previous chapter that Europeanization entails resistances, reconstructions, negotiations; it is not a unilinear and uni-directional process driven by a logic of societal convergence or integration. The EU has of course had a homogenizing effect, especially in terms of legal compliance, but as argued in the previous chapter the logics of both social and system integration produce very diverse results. The encounter of western, central and eastern European countries is not just an encounter of different countries, but of different logics of social and systemic integration and related routes to modernity.

The eastern enlargement has brought the EU into societies which have experienced quite different routes to modernity from the western societies, for the new member states – with the exception of Malta and Cyprus – have been former communist countries. In this sense, different modernities have come together in an encounter that was not the collision that many expected it to be. Most of the new states have been engaged in the triple transition to capitalism, democracy and national autonomy, and many of these countries have disputed territories and major ethnic divisions. The incorporation of the central and eastern

European countries will be quite different from the earlier assimilation of the British Isles, the Scandinavian countries and the Iberian Peninsula and Greece because of the scale of the operation and fact that the enlarged EU will be more politically and culturally diverse than was previously the case. Enlargement means too that the European north–south axis will be overshadowed by the expanding west–east axis, where closure will be more difficult to achieve, for there are no natural frontiers.

This is not to suggest that the Mediterranean is a natural frontier. In the 1980s the Moroccan government raised the question of possible membership of the EU (Featherstone and Kazamias, 2001). It is interesting to observe that the existing EU already contains two enclaves in North Africa in the form of the Spanish territorial enclaves of Ceuta and Melilla. The original EEC contained Algeria, which prior to its independence was a region of the French republic (Hansen, 2002). It is not impossible to imagine that in a few decades from now some North African countries will join the EU. In any case the European Union is now embarked on an enlargement process which is potentially open to societies that lie far from the original 'Carolingian' core states and the legacy of the Second World War which gave to it the original justification for its creation, namely the attempt to bind France and Germany into a common economic and administrative framework to ensure lasting peace.

Moreover, the earlier enlargement processes were largely responses to economic and political aspirations which on the whole made the deepening of the EU towards 'ever greater unity' possible to a degree. This will certainly not be the case with further expansion. The goals of balancing efficiency with social justice and democratic legitimacy may be overshadowed by issues of security, immigration and crime. Aside from the piecemeal pacing of the earlier enlargement processes, the incorporated societies had long histories of relative political and economic stability and their inclusion did not greatly challenge the fundamental assumptions of the EU. The exception to this was of course Greece, which had experienced political instability as a result of the coup of the colonels in 1967, but was otherwise considered to be the cradle of European culture. Moreover, there were certain cultural similarities between these countries. The wider Cold War context also played a major role in consolidating the membership of the EU in capitalism and democracy.

As the borders of the EU move closer to Russia and with the eventual entry of Turkey, extending into Asia, the identity of Europe will become more and more 'post-western.' This is not an anti- or a non-westernism, but a condition defined increasingly by the legacy of an earlier modernity which will have to be negotiated with other modernities. Turkey's close relationships with the countries of central Asia will also have implications for the present countries of the EU, which will have borders with Iran, Syria and Iraq. In short, the borders of the EU will no longer be within Europe, but will be with Asia. In this respect it could be suggested that the eastern enlargement is different from all earlier enlargement processes since it will raise new questions concerning the very identity of Europe. Enlargement in this case is not just about getting bigger. It is also about a very decisive kind of cultural transformation in terms of both the identity of Europe and in terms of the rise of new kinds of symbolic conflicts over identity and belonging. If it is true that the European Union had been at the decisive point of supra- or transnational transformation, this will be arrested with enlargement where national autonomy will be a top priority for many of the incoming countries, many of which have only recently experienced national autonomy.

There is also the question of religion which is likely to become more and more a site of cultural contestation. Despite its apparent secular nature, the EU in fact rests on very Christian cultural assumptions, as Joseph Weiler has argued (Weiler, 2003). Most countries have Christian political parties and several (Denmark, Britain, Greece) have state churches and quite a few are monarchies based on Christian culture (Spain, Britain, Belgium, Netherlands, Denmark, Sweden and, although not a EU member state, Norway). Catholic social teaching has played a major role in the vision of the EU as based on solidarity, integration and subsidiarity. While Christianity does not have a formal role to play in the European polity, it is frequently used as a legitimation of the existing institutional arrangement. In the context of Turkish membership and the drafting of the European Constitution there has been considerable debate on the foundations of the EU in Christianity. In the more fervently secular countries, such as France, secularization has generally served the dominant culture leading to accusations of intolerance and an incapacity to cope with diversity. With the entry of Poland the Catholic underpinning of the EU is likely to be strengthened. Perhaps more importantly, the countries of the EU will have to accommodate Islamic and Orthodox populations. To be sure there has already been within the fifteen member EU a major Orthodox tradition as represented by Greece. However, with the inclusion of other Orthodox populations, such as Bulgaria and Romania, religion is likely to become more visible in the public sphere, especially where it is more closely tied to national identity. Even though the Turkish state is highly secular, the inclusion of a large Islamic population will certainly have implications for the definition of European identity as one framed in the Christian tradition. Within Turkey main support for Turkish membership has come from the Islamic based Justice and Development Party, a moderate Islamist Party, which in the historic election of 2002 won two-thirds of parliamentary seats and formed the present government (Önis and Keyman, 2003). While the rise of a modern Islamic movement within Turkey demonstrates that Islam and European democratic traditions are compatible, the terrorist attack on British interests by Islamic suicide bombers in Istanbul in 2003 is a reminder of the potency of religion on the margins of Europe. Despite the secularization of western Europe, the view persists that Europe is Christian and that Turkey cannot therefore be European (Robins, 1996). This view does not fit comfortably with the view that by virtue of its NATO membership Turkey is part of the west.

This is not to suggest that there will be a clash of civilizations. The available research seems to indicate that there will not be cultural clashes or social and political incompatibilities (Cederman, 2001; Zielonka, 2002). The differences between the ten new member countries and the older fifteen member states fall within the extremes that already exist within the latter group (Laitin, 2002). It is less a clash of civilizations than a reconfiguration and reconstruction of modernities. Nevertheless, a new 'east' has arisen which is playing a major role in shaping Europe. While for the moment this is largely represented by central Europe, the significance of Turkey, on the one side, and on the other Russia in shaping Europe cannot be underestimated.

Conclusion: towards a post-western Europe?

This chapter has attempted to show that a broader and more historically grounded view of Europeanization draws attention to the coming into being of, what might be cautiously called, a 'post-western' Europe, that is a Europe that is no longer based on a singular, western modernity, but multiple modernities. Viewed in the longer perspective of history we get a more differentiated picture of a civilizational transformation in modernity. In civilizational terms, Europe extends well into Eurasia and much of the wider Mediterranean cannot be excluded from it. The interaction with Russia and Turkey and those countries shaped by them is critical in this respect. While there is no doubt that western Europe and the EU is playing a leading role in shaping central and eastern Europe and the wider Eurasian belt, its capacity to impose a unitary societal model on Europe is limited. As other factors, not least of which is the wider global context, enter into the picture, the civilizational composition of Europe shifts and with it new and different models of modernity take shape.

The enlargement process, and those soon to follow, means that Europe is becoming more poly-centric, with more than one centre and also more than one historical origin. Europeanization is multi-directional and articulated through different velocities. The speed of the enlargement process, for instance, suggests that there is not one logic but several; it is a graduated and highly indeterminate process of social construction.

In this sense too it can be said that enlargement is not just about getting bigger but is about transformation, since the EU is changing as it expands and as it does so it forces other parts of Europe to change. In constructivist terms, we can speak of this process as one of self-creation. Europeanization defines and redefines itself in a constant process of construction in which different models of interpretation emerge defining and being defined by the process of construction itself. While it is true that the construction of Europe as a self-creative process cannot be seen as the narrative of a subject or the expression of a historical logic, it can be interpreted in Habermasian terms as opening up post-national possibilities in which communicative forms of social integration may be possible. In a large and multifaceted entity such as the European Union, or indeed any modern polity, social integration cannot rest on tightly defined cultural values. Exactly what kind of values and cultural presuppositions will be discussed in the next three chapters.

3   Is there a European identity?

European self-understanding beyond unity and diversity

Given the preoccupation with identity in recent times, it was inevitable that the question of Europe would be posed in terms of that concept (Cerutti, 1992, 2003; Cederman, 2001; Delanty, 1995a; Garcia, 1993; Herrmann *et al.*, 2004; Stråth, 2000, 2002; Wintle, 1996, 2000).[1] The resulting notion of a European identity has led to a confused debate, not because Europe cannot have an identity or because the bearers of such an identity, Europeans, do not exist, but because the very idea of identity in this debate has rarely been clarified. Do we mean a collective identity, a variety of interlinking collective identities, an aggregation of personal identities, a broadly defined cultural category or civilizational idea, or an official EU cultural or political identity? Whether Europe is unable to compete with national societies because national identities are more real or powerful than collective ones depends on what kind of collective identity we mean when we refer to large-scale social groups or societal complexes having an identity.

European identity is a question of collective identity and as such, theoretically, is no different from the question of national identity. Thus, rather than begin with the vexed question of whether a European identity is replacing national identities, a more fruitful approach is to address the problem of collective identity in the context of major social and political transformation. As many studies have documented, Europe has been part of many national identities (see Herrmann *et al*, 2004; Malmborg and Stråth, 2002). From a constructivist perspective, the notion of a European identity can only be understood with reference to a discourse in which competing claims are worked out rather than a straightforward notion of culture (see Orchard, 2002). Rather than relate the identity of Europe to a set of cultural values, goals, territory or people – what in general may constitute the cultural *content* of the idea of Europe – it is more fruitful to see it in terms of a socio-cognitive *form* consisting of repertoires of evaluation, discursive practices, and identity projects which could be characterized in terms of dialogic rationality. In this respect there are clear parallels with notions of discursive democracy and what may be called a cosmopolitan European identity, as will be argued in later chapters.

Moving from the question of the history, civilization and modernity discussed in the previous chapter, the concern of the present chapter, then, is with problems in defining Europe in terms of identity and culture without a Durkheimean conception of culture as a moral totality. Beginning with a discussion of the question of collective identity, the chapter moves onto a critical analysis of the idea of European identity as one of unity in diversity.

Some conceptual issues

Identity is a contested and much abused term. Various theorists have argued against it, claiming, variously, that it is incoherent and as a collective phenomenon it conceals a latent authoritarianism or includes in it too much to be conceptually useful (Bauman, 2004; Niethammer, 2000; Brubaker and Cooper, 2000; Gleason, 1983). We will not enter into a defence of the use of the term, but will use it as a default term for group consciousness, collective 'we' feelings (Eisenstadt and Giesen, 1995; Giesen, 1998). Drawing from a variety of theories, ranging from social identity theory to sociological and anthropological theories, in brief summary four salient aspects of identity can be highlighted and need to be considered in any discussion of the concept.

First, identity arises only in relation to social action and is processual or constructed. Neither individual persons nor social movements nor whole societies begin with a fully formed or articulated identity. Identities are created in action and express not an underlying consciousness or essence, but the self-understanding and self-recognition of the social actor. Since this changes in the course of time, the identity of the actor will also change (see Jenkins, 1996; Laclau, 1994; Melucci, 1995, 1996).

Second, identities have a narrative dimension: they can be seen as the stories people tell about themselves in order to give continuity to their existence. Such narratives are the basis of memory (and forgetting) and express the performative and public aspect of identity (see Somers, 1994). For this reason identities do not simply refer to characteristics, such as a national character, but to a discursive mode of self-understanding (Potter, 1996). The role of language is thus very important in the shaping of identities.

Third, identity concerns a relation of self and other by which the identity of the self is constituted in symbolic markers. In this sense, identity is based on difference and thus exists in a relational context, which under the conditions of modernity entails reflexivity. In this context it should also be noted that identity presupposes a subject, that is, a social actor who can be an individual or a group. In modern societies collective identities are constructed by social actors out of the available cultural resources; they are not simply given but take the form of a project and can be mobile or transferable to others (see Castells, 1996; Eder *et al.*, 2002; Friese, 2002; Giddens, 1991; Wagner, 2001).

Fourth, a point that needs to be made in any discussion of collective identity concerns what are generally referred to as multiple identities. Collective identities often are distinct but they only rarely exist in a zero-sum relation; they can be overlapping (as in hyphenated identities), nested, cross-cutting, mixed (or hybrid), or co-existing. Ethnic, regional, political and national identities relate to each other in different ways. On the level of personal identities this is particularly the case as individuals rarely have only one identity, but many, and these exist in varying degrees of tension with each other (Calhoun, 1994; Christiansen and Hedetoft, 2004; Friedmann, 1994; Hall and Du Gay, 1996; Herb and Kaplin, 1999).

These four aspects stress the constructed nature of identity, which must not be seen as an entity that either transcends or is prior to social reality. Identity is not an idea or a cultural given, but a mode of self-understanding that is expressed by people in ongoing narratives and situations; moreover, the boundaries between identities are fluid, negotiable and contested. All identities are constructions, regardless of whatever kind they are. Certainly, they may not appear to the people who possess them that they are constructed; but from the perspective of the social scientist nothing is simply natural or given. For this reason the distinction frequently made between the essentialistic and constructed nature of identities is a false one.

A second set of distinctions must also be made. Identities can be either collective or personal. It is important not to conflate these – the identities of individuals and the identities of social groups – as they entail quite different structures and developmental logics. Social identity theory, strongly influenced by psychology, generally collapses personal and group identities (Breakwell and Lyons, 1996; Capozza and Brown, 2000; Tajifel, 1982). A collective identity, it needs to be noted, is not simply the aggregation of individual identities, but the self-understanding of a particular group (for instance, a religious or ethnic group or a social movement or political party). A collective identity will not necessarily result from personal identities and can exist without a direct relation to them. For a collective identity to exist, a social group – which can evince either cultural or political identities or indeed both – with a collective project must exist. Collective identities articulate a group identity (Bloom, 1990; Eder, 2000b; Eder et al., 2002; Melucci, 1996; Giesen, 1998). Without these distinctions, the concept of a collective identity is a meaningless construct. Many introspective national debates on identity, for example in Germany and Ireland, remain on the superficial level of 'Who are we, what is our identity?', and fail to take into account the wider social and historical context in which these claims are made. It appears that this is also all too often the case with the question of European identity.

However, what is important is to distinguish between collective identities as such and wider societal or civilizational identities. These are frequently confused, so that what in fact are cultural categories are attributed the status of fully articulated collective identities. The notions of an Irish identity, a Chinese identity, Jewish identity, black identity, etc. are cultural categories which can be the basis of different collective identities, but are not themselves identities in the same sense as more concrete collective identities. In the case of these diasporic identities, the term covers a broad cultural spectrum of diverse groups or possibly a whole society. Irish identity, for instance, includes Irish Americans, those of Irish descent, citizens of the Republic of Ireland, the Northern Irish, and the Anglo-Irish. Similarly, British identity is a societal or civilizational identity or a broader cultural category which includes the Scottish, the Welsh, the Northern

Irish, the Anglo-Irish, the English, and a wider variety of ethnic groups. The term may even be understood as including the national identity of the Republic of Ireland. Most national identities are broad cultural categories or societal identities which include within them more concrete collective identities.

In modern societies, collective identities that encompass the entire society generally have to take the form of categorical identities in order to be able to include the diverse membership of the society; they are what Émile Durkheim called 'collective representations', that is, the ideas that symbolize the identity of a society (Durkheim, 1995; see also Moscovici, 2000). These collective representations refer to very broadly defined cultural models and could also be called 'imaginaries.' As collective identities, it is necessary to go beyond Durkheim in that collective identities are more than self-images or representations but articulated modes of self-understanding. For present purposes we can distinguish between personal identities, collective identities and societal identities.

On the basis of these conceptual considerations, several points concerning national and European identity can be made. Virtually every kind identity – personal, collective and societal – exists today in a state of flux and contingency. The cultural logic of modernity has led to a situation in which all identities are forced to define self-understanding in non-essentialistic terms. This is true of most religious and ethnic identities, as it is of national and other political and cultural identities, for none of these can assume the existence of secure foundations.

As a result of globalization, multiculturalism, global civil society and cosmopolitan political and cultural currents, societies are becoming more and more pluralized and interpenetrating, and less and less discrete wholes anchored in unique cultures and territorial nation-states. The result of these major shifts in culture and politics is that national identities are changing; they are becoming more decentred, liquid and reflexive in their awareness of their limits, and through societal cross-fertilization more and more mixed. The European space has grown to the extent that it is no longer possible to say what is national and what is European. In Europe today, there is no national identity that exists on the level of a simple collective identity, i.e. a coherent self-contained identity that is underpinned by a particular social group. All national identities are becoming more like societal identities, that is, broadly defined cultural categories. In post-liberal European societies, the nation has become a contested category of belonging for diverse social groups. The self-understanding of culturally mixed European societies is inescapably elucidated in post-national forms of consciousness.

National identity has ceased to fulfil the function of social integration; the nation no longer fits into the sphere of the state, providing the latter with an identity and cultural legitimation (Delanty and O' Mahony, 2002). Globalization has unleashed numerous processes of differentiation, as well as of de-differentiation, and these cannot easily be resisted by recourse to nation-building or to nationalism. The loss of capacity to create enduring forms of social integration is due not just to the changing role of the nation-state, but also to the fact that culture in general has lost its integrative function. Collective identities cannot simply anchor themselves in secure cultural reference points; they also have a socio-cognitive function in constructing new fields of discourse and meaning for society (Eyerman and Jamison, 1991; Zerubavel, 1997).

Viewed in this perspective, there is no tension between national identity and European identity. National identities are not closed to cosmopolitan influences or based entirely on non-negotiable cultural assumptions. The relativizing of cultural values in late modernity has led to a greater self-scrutiny in national identity, which is no longer codified exclusively by political elites or reflective of the cultural form of the nation-state. There are few national identities that do not contain critical, reflexive and cosmopolitan forms of self-understanding. The idea of a morally superior European identity that somehow transcends national identity must be rejected as an implausible construction. To varying degrees, all national identities in Europe contain elements of a European identity, which is not an identity that exists beyond or outside national identities. For example, the major expressions of German national identity today contain a strong sense of a European Germany; national identity and European identity do not exist in a relation of tension, but of complementarity. This is also the case with regard to Finnish, French, Irish, Greek and Italian identity, as well as others. In these cases, the nation already contains within it a post-national moment.

In sum, the question of national identity and European identity is largely a matter of how we define identity in the first instance. The suggestion made here is to see identity as a process or a developmental logic with learning possibilities rather than as a fixed and unchangeable state. Both European identity and national identity are embroiled in each other and reflect some of the major shifts in culture and identity that have occurred in recent times. The most significant of these shifts is the move from substantive to what Zygmunt Bauman has termed liquid identities (Bauman, 2001, 2003).

Defining European identity

The notion of a European identity can mean several things. As the previous discussion suggests, we can speak of European identity on the level of personal identities. In this case, it is a matter of individuals identifying with European culture or politics. People increasingly describe themselves as European. However sociologically interesting this may be, the proliferation of Europeanized personal identities does not produce a European collective identity as such. To be sure, consciousness of being European characterizes the identities of many individuals, and the growing Europeanization of social relations has increased the extent of personal European identities. But this does not necessarily amount to the existence of a European collective identity (although it could result simply in more cosmopolitan identities among Europeans). As argued earlier, a collective identity derives not from numerous personal identities, but from a distinctive social group or institutional framework that articulates a collective identity. For such an identity to exist there must be a means of expressing an explicit collective self-understanding.

There are not many examples of a collective European identity in this sense of the term, despite the efforts of numerous Europeanists to create one (Shore, 2000,

2004). Attempts to create an official collective identity for the European Union, identity generally serve a legitimating function. The Maastricht Treaty (1992) makes a vague reference to the goal of 'reinforcing European identity and its independence in order to promote, security and progress in Europe and the world.' European collective identity in this sense has clearly become more pronounced in recent times with the proliferation of symbols of Europeanness, an emerging EU cultural policy, the euro currency, a passport, and scientific and educational policies aimed at enhancing a consciousness of Europe. Despite the absence of a shared language, these developments are not fundamentally unlike the earlier attempts by national elites to create national identities, although they are more fluid. Whether an enlarged EU will be able to articulate a collective identity comparable to a national identity is questionable. However, what is more certain is that the EU is having an impact on personal identities, with more and more people expressing an identity with Europe. Citrin and Sides (2004) find that complementary attachments to nation and to Europe are increasing, while identifications with Europe are not as intense as national identititification. For example the EU may influence personal identities, but will not necessarily influence collective identities (Breakwell, 2004).

Taking the third sense of identity previously discussed – societal – European identity can be viewed in a different light. In addition to the empirical fact of an increase in the number of personal European identities and the obvious attempt of Brussels to construct a European collective identity, we can also speak of a wider European cultural identity but which is distinct from EU policy and politics. In this case, European identity refers not to a capitalized *Identity*, but *identities* in the plural, such as national, regional, political, etc., that are defined by an orientation to a broad cultural conception of Europe. Here, European identity is a generalized mode of self-understanding through which groups, whole societies, movements, as well as individual citizens, define themselves and their relation to others. In so far as it has an identity, the EU is an example of such a categorical identity and thus includes other identities within it. In so far as these identities change, the identity of the EU will change. An example of this is the incorporation of new countries into the EU.

As argued earlier, collective identities also take the form of broad cultural categories that are not group-specific but more akin to cultural imaginaries. Such categories are reference points for specific identities to take shape. In this sense, European identity refers to specific modes of self-understanding that have arisen from the increased interpenetration of European societies and from a certain 'liquidification' of national identities. In this broader sense, a European subject as such does not exist in the way distinct groups of people exist. But this does not mean that it cannot exist. As a cultural imaginary, European identity is a process of self-recognition and exists as a constellation of diverse elements which are articulated through emerging repertoires of evaluation.

This European identity corresponds to a dialogic view of culture. According to Jürgen Habermas, the identity of a 'post-national' society can be based only on cultural forms of commonality that accept certain basic principles – e.g. procedural rules for conflict resolution, communicative solutions, and the limited patriotism of an identification with the constitution (a 'constitutional patriotism') – rather than on territory, cultural heritage or the state (Habermas, 1994, 1998, 2001b). He argues that no society can simply opt out of the critical and reflexive forces at work in modern culture. In this view, unity is merely the limited universalism of modern values such as criticism and reflexivity. The characteristic feature of Habermas's argument is that these values go beyond the typical liberal values of respect for others, tolerance of difference, and so on, by giving a greater role to critical scrutiny and self-confrontation. Thus, rather than simply looking for a common or underlying cultural identity, the emphasis is on a transformative type of self-understanding. The kind of European identity that this suggests is one that expresses cosmopolitan currents in contemporary society, such as new repertoires of evaluation in loyalties, memories, and dialogue. For this reason a concern with symbolic codes is not sufficient to account for new expressions of collective identity. Symbolic codes – such as those Eisenstadt and Giesen emphasize, namely primordial, sacred and civic or universal – relate to only one aspect of collective identity and presuppose a Durkheimian conception of culture as a moral totality (Eisenstadt and Giesen, 1995). Our account of identity, in contrast, draws attention to the socio-cognitive dimension of cultural identity as a pragmatic process of discursive construction through competing repertoires of evaluation.

In sum, European identity exists on different levels (personal identities, collective identities, and wider cultural models) which need to be carefully differentiated. It is possible to conceive of European identity as a cosmopolitan identity embodied in the cultural models of a societal or civilizational identity rather than as a supra-national identity or an official EU identity that is in tension with national identities. As a cosmopolitan societal identity, European identity is a form of post-national self-understanding that expresses itself within, as much as beyond, national identities. Post-national and cosmopolitan currents are evident within national identities and are given cultural form by what we have been calling new European repertoires of evaluation.

Unity in diversity – a new European repertoire of evaluation?

In recent years the question of the identity of Europe is coming increasingly to be defined around the idea of 'unity in diversity'.[2] This has become the most influential expression of European identity today as is evidenced by a wide range of documents, speeches, and publications (Taylor, 2001). It has rarely been the subject of critical studies (see McDonald, 1996). In many ways, it is a uniquely European discourse and the fact that it has become pronounced today is particularly interesting. This needs some qualification. The Indian Prime Minister, Nehru, used the term to define the national identity of India. Nevertheless, it has come to be a slogan to define the cultural and political identity of the EU. Although it is a bureaucratic expression, generally lacking philosophical depth, it has wider cultural resonances in the general crisis of other definitions of Europe. But a careful analysis of this discourse is warranted. In many ways it is a harmless, if rather pointless, conception of European identity as one of inter-cultural understanding. It might quite well be the case that this is the only way we can define Europe – not based on a single identity but on many. The idea of unity and diversity reflects a broader debate about universalism and relativism and, too, the much deeper philosophical theme in European thought of becoming and oneness – how something can change and still remain the same – has a certain resonance in it.

'Unity in diversity' can be traced back to nineteenth-century nationalism and cosmopolitanism. Wintle argues the idea of unity and diversity stems from the work of Guizot and romantic nationalism in the nineteenth century (Wintle, 1996: 4–5). It embodies two ideas – 'unity' and 'diversity' – but the key to it is the 'in' for the concept of unity that it indicates is to be found in diversity, not above or beyond it. It is in this respect that unity in diversity is a post-liberal construction and is influenced by a kind of postmodern communitarianism that has gained intellectual ascendancy today. On first appearances it suggests the liberal attitude, but closer examination reveals something quite different. Let us take each of these terms, unity and diversity, which are more than two terms in an equation. In fact each represents the hitherto dominant expressions of European identity, namely the Eurofederalist aspiration to a deep unity and the liberal respect of diversity within the limits of a broadly defined moral universalism. We can then consider more precisely the significance of the new discourse.

The notion of the essential unity of Europe is best associated with the Eurofederalist definition of Europe as resting on a civilization but whose highest expression is in culture. To a degree the Eurofederalist tradition sought to recover the idea of European civilization. For the greater part there is little doubt that this tradition, with had its roots in Enlightenment cosmopolitanism, lost out to the liberal doctrine, but it was for a time influential, leading to notions of a European federal order, the Pan Europe Union, the unification of Europe. The federalist vision, popular in the first half of the twentieth century, continued to be influential in the second half, but only in a more cultural direction. Many influential historians wrote works that aimed to be histories of Europe rather than of states, for example Daniel de Rougement. In such works the emphasis was on a higher unity that transcended the divisions of European history.

This civilizational idea was famously embodied in 'The Declaration of European Identity' of 1973, signed in Copenhagen by the then nine member states.[3] The declaration stated:

> The Nine member countries of the European Communities have decided that the time has come to draw up a document on the European Identity. This will enable them to achieve a better definition of the relations with other countries and of their responsibilities and the place which they occupy in world affairs.

The document is also interesting in that it suggests the idea of a unity in diversity, referring as it did to the 'diversity of cultures' in the plural. However, it did not express the version of this which has come into focus today. The Copenhagen Declaration was more explicitly concerned to elucidate the doctrine of unity than diversity. It referred to a 'common European civilization' based on a 'common heritage' and 'converging' attitudes and ways of life. The declaration strongly emphasized the notion of 'Identity' with a capital 'I' as an official identity – 'the European identity' – to define the political structure of what was then the EEC in its relation with the external world:

> The diversity of cultures within the framework of common European civilization, the attachment to common values and principles, the increasing convergence of attitudes to life, the awareness of having specific interests in common and the determination to take part in the construction of a united Europe, all give the European identity its originality and its own dynamism.

There are not many adherents to this idea of European unity today. Diversity and radical hermeneutics is the order of the day, but more importantly for a time it was the liberal idea of Europe that gained ascendancy and with this the liberal approach to diversity. This had two important dimensions, in politics and in morals. In Charles de Gaulle's notion of a 'Europe of Nations' the European project from the beginning was seen as a project of nation-states. As Alan Milward argued in a now classic text, the European Union rescued the nation-state from itself and from the problems facing it (Milward, 1993). While the momentum to greater integration did, as previously mentioned, lead to visions of a cultural identity emerging, there was rarely any assumption of integration leading to unity. Robert Schuman, the French Foreign Minister, perhaps more than Jean Monnet, looked to a higher unity and introduced the 'High Authority' of the Coal and Steel Community, which became the model for EU supra-nationalism. But there was no master plan for European unity in all societal dimensions. The French dominated project saw Europeanization as the culmination of those very republican values upon which the nation-state was founded. Catholic social modernism, to be sure, added another, more social and economic, dimension to this otherwise largely liberal project, but one that was easily contained within the liberal principles of the modern state. The principle of subsidiarity, borrowed from the Catholic states, was never seen as uprooting the national state and the republican principle of sovereignty. The term 'liberal' is used here in the sense of a project that was within the bounds of the political theory of liberalism, that is a conception of the state as limited in scope. The state as 'night-watchman' would not infringe on social and cultural questions. Beyond that role the 'founding fathers' had no vision of a unified Europe. They had no vision of culture as a binding force and they did not think much ahead of the prevailing liberal and republican ethos of the postwar decades. By the late 1980s this had changed in some key respects.

The liberal conception of the state had always presupposed some notion of the diversity of culture on the one side and, on the other, a basic commitment to universalistic moral values which were somehow beyond the reach of culture. The liberal position was characterized by tolerance of national cultures, which on the whole were untouched by Europeanization. This, in general, was a commitment to a thin European order of values, and which were not in essence specifically European but universalistic, if not merely western. In the context of the Cold War and the American-led west, this was not surprising. In this period the liberal ethos of European integration began to go into abeyance and eventually into decline. It declined simply because it could no longer be believed in, neither in theory nor in practice. In practice it ceased to be credible in face of the all too obvious legal might of the EU, which since Maastricht (1992) had handed over more and more power to the supra-state, which could no longer be seen in liberal terms. To a degree a kind of European civil society along with a European citizenship was emerging and which was not necessarily an extension of national civil societies but something quite different. In theory – in philosophy and in ideology – the liberal position lost out to a new way of thinking in which diversity would play a much stronger role. It was inevitable, in the age of postmodernism and globalization, that this would be a postliberal conception of diversity.

Official statements on European culture and identity are rare, but nonetheless indicative of the new cultural turn to what in effect has been a new repertoire of evaluation (Shore, 2000; Roche, 2001; Banus, 2002). Article 128 (now 151 in the amended Treaty of Amsterdam) of the Maastricht Treaty on European Union states: 'The Community shall contribute to the flowering of the cultures of the Member States, while respecting their national and regional diversity and at the same time bringing the common cultural heritage to the fore' (Commission of the European Communities, 1992). Influencing the intellectual and political shift towards diversity were the following developments.

The international climate, which might be seen as an expression of globalization, was one that led to a growing emphasis on a conception of diversity that could not be contained within liberalism. The influential UNESCO document, *Our Creative Diversity*, in 1995 (World Commission on Culture and Development, 1995) argued for a strongly relativistic conception of culture, although not one that rejected all the precepts of moral universalism (see Eriksen, 2001). More generally, developments in the area of human rights were leading more and more in the direction of cultural rights. Globalization increasingly seemed to be working towards a world order of multiple centres. With many parts of the world entering into a postdevelopmental phase, the idea of a universal world culture lost its hegemonic position and a new register of identity emerged.

Related to this was a socio-cognitive shift towards cultural relativism. From the 1980s onwards North American cultural relativism allied to radical hermeneutics reached new heights with radical communitarianism and its arguments for affirmative action and group rights. Postmodern thought, too, gave philosophical weight to cultural relativism.

Within Europe the major challenge facing the EU was the question of how to balance 'deepening' with 'widening.' The earlier enlargement projects of the European Union – the incorporation of the British Isles, the Iberian Peninsula and Scandinavia – did not challenge the basic assumptions upon which the EU had been built in the era of consensual politics. The eastern extension is a different matter, with the incorporation of ten states by 2004 and many more in the following years. The liberal assumptions have been challenged in two respects. Politically, the EU cannot avoid differential treatment of the new countries. The illiberal nature of the enlarged EU is, for the most part, an accepted fact. Culturally, given the diversity of languages, religions and societies, the recognition of diversity is an administrative necessity.

It was the creation of a regional policy from the late 1980s that was decisive in shaping the EU's cultural policy, which became an important basis of integration. Cultural programmes as the Capital of Culture Award moved the emphasis away from notions of unity to diversity. Regional policy thus tended to embrace notions of cultural diversity (Barnett, 2001; Pantella, 1999; Sassatelli, 2002; Schlesinger, 2001). Moreover, the older ideas of a Europe of nations had to adjust to the fact that Europe had become a land of significant migration from the rest of the world and that it is not any longer simply 'European' in terms of traditional assumptions about culture and identity. The socio-cognitive shift from homogeneity to diversity is at the core of all repertoires of evaluation on citizenship today (Bennett, 2001; Delanty, 2000b). For the EU, it marks a shift from a vague notion of unity to a clearer focus on integration.

Many countries within Europe have themselves national debates along the lines of unity in diversity. The best example of this is Germany where the emergence of the Berlin Republic has been accompanied by a debate on 'inner unity' (*innere Einheit*), a concept that reflects the wider European debate on unity within the limits of diversity. In the UK the debate on Britain as a multi-ethnic society has also appealed to the notion of unity in diversity, a concept that has also been implicit in the White Paper in 2002, 'Secure Borders, Safe Havens: Integration with Diversity in Modern Britain.'

Thus it came about that a new ideology of culture has emerged in Europe. Unity in diversity is the phrase that perfectly captures the cultural logic of Europeanization. It expresses too the political spirit of the age – to be equal but different (Touraine, 2000). The slogan differs from earlier conceptions of Europe in that the principle of unity is now posited less as a higher unity than one constituted in the fact of diversity, an 'inner unity'. The recognition of diversity replaces the older liberal notion of universalistic values which might be capable of loosely defining the basic normative framework of the European Union. In the case of the Council of Europe, which has a strongly human rights focus, the commitment to unity in diversity maintains a certain balance with a commitment to upholding universalistic values within Europe. 'Diversity lies at the heart of Europe's cultural richness, which is our common heritage and the basis of our unity', according to the official statement of the Council of Europe.

Moreover, unity in diversity makes a compromise with national and regional particularity. The EU is now caught in the contradictory situation of having to define a common European culture that is universal – but not so universal that it is global and thus not distinctively European – and at the same time does not negate national and regional cultures. On the one side, the condition of universality must be satisfied and, on the other, the principle of diversity must be upheld. The former President of the European Commission, Romano Prodi, in his book *Europe As I See It*, discusses this dilemma in an interesting way. Arguing that the cultural unity of Europe is in Christianity, from which it derives its univeralism, Europe can escape the Eurocentricism that it had become snared in. 'Europe's destiny is not inherently Eurocentric, but one of universality', he argues and goes on to say this universalism needs to be given a stronger position today in aspiring to 'a new cultural unity.' This new unity, which is based on an underlying unity, must, he argues, acknowledge 'otherness' and the ability of cultures to live together: 'This means the mutual acceptance among Europeans of their cultural diversity' (Prodi, 2000a: 46–7). In his preface to the compendium, *Unity in Diversity*, Prodi also refers to an 'underlying unity' that guarantees a European identity beyond the diversity of cultures (see Taylor, 2001).

The philosopher Hans-Georg Gadamer has also argued strongly for a conception of European identity as one based on unity and diversity. Faced with the diversity of Europe, he has argued for a conception of Europe that does not seek to overcome differences: 'To participate with the other and to be part of the other is the most and the best that we can strive for and accomplish' (Gadamer, 1992 [1984]: 235). Edgar Morin, too, argues the unity of Europe lies in the unique capacity to cope with differences without the need for an overarching principle of unity (Morin, 1987).

It is difficult to make theoretical sense of the these salutary and lofty proclamations of European identity and of the relationship between unity and diversity. However, it is possible to distinguish at least four arguments or repertoires of evaluation about the relation of unity and diversity. These are outlined in what follows.

Diversity as derivative of unity

This is the position that there is an underlying unity that comes from the historical heritage of Graeco-Roman and Christian culture. Although this has crystallized into different European traditions, the argument is that it constitutes the core of the European consciousness, which is one of centuries long tolerance, a spirit of compromise and a love of freedom. This is a position that is reflected in much of the older unity in diversity literature which identifies Europe with a spirit or ethos of liberty. In this way of thinking the older Euro-federalist influence is still strong. The basic idea here, then, is two-fold: (a) although unity may be incomplete, the foundations of it already exist and (b) diversity is not an obstacle to realizing unity because the principle of unity is in part one of tolerance and understanding for diversity.

Unity as derivative of diversity

In this sense unity derives from the overcoming of differences. This sense of unity and diversity is a more recent conception that abandons the assumption of an underlying unity. In the view of many EU policy makers unity – that is, a common

European identity – can be created by cultural policies. In this version of the unity and diversity argument European identity is a project to be achieved rather than simply an identity that exists in some form. This is a position that has some popularity with EU policy makers, but does not command widespread popular support, perhaps because it is associated with official culture and empty symbols. This model of cultural unity is quite explicitly European but seeks to accommodate national diversities on a symbolic level. Examples of this approach might be the Cities of Culture programme, or various cultural programmes supported by the European Commission (see Sassatelli, 2002; Shore, 2000). The 1973 Copenhagen Declaration, mentioned above, is also an example of this conception of unity over-riding diversity. Another example is the 1995 'Charta of European Identity'.[4] In all these cases unity is to be created out of the fragments of diversity, which suggests a weak kind of cosmopolitanism, such as inter-cultural understanding.

Unity as diversity

This is a more recent argument that moves the emphasis from unity to diversity. Hence the emphasis is on a unity that consists of the fact of diversity. In this view the unity of Europe derives less from a historical cultural heritage than from the interaction of the different European traditions. In this logic, the condition of diversity is given priority over unity – unity derives from diversity. Diversity, here of course, refers to the plurality of national and regional cultures and not to other expressions of diversity. European cultural policy has constantly oscillated between this position and the previously outlined stance (see Banus, 2002). With the official documents of the EU, it is this position that is becoming the more influential. It is also the broad stance of the Council of Europe. In this position, unity can only consist of the recognition of diversity and thus be based on values compatible with the fact of diversity. In this sense, European identity exists as a postmodernity identity (see van Ham, 2001).

A self-limiting unity

The unity of Europe is a minimal kind of unity formed out of an active engagement with diversity. In this case diversity refers not just to national and regional differences but to multi-ethnic differences. The diversity of Europe makes a strong unity impossible but does not preclude the possibility of a reflective kind of unity emerging. This is a position that is best associated with Jürgen Habermas who argues European identity must be related to values such as those that could be common to all Europeans (Habermas, 1992). In his view, because of the divisiveness of culture and the danger of nationalism, such values can only be constitutional ones, albeit ones that are formed out of processes of public critique and deliberation. This more explicitly post-national position thus sets up a tension between unity and diversity, positing a minimal but workable kind of unity that avoids essentialist cultural appeals to unity or to diversity. The recognition of diversity is essential, but it is also crucial, too, to see that diversity is not an overriding value in itself. In this view, unity is merely the limited universalism of modern values such as critique and reflexivity. The distinctive nature of Habermas's position is that these values go beyond the typical liberal ones of respect for others and tolerance for difference, etc. by giving a greater role to communicative structures than to an underlying cultural identity. This position and the previous one are not substantially different in that neither appeal to a strong sense of unity and seek to reconcile diversity with a workable kind of unity which does not see unity nor diversity as fixed principles. The Habermasian stance differs in arguing for a sense of unity that is stronger than the mere recognition of diversity and thus makes less concessions to diversity.

In another version of this argument, Massimo Cacciari offers an interpretation of European identity which captures a sense of unity emerging out of interacting discourses. In his book *L'Arcipelago* he describes Europe as an archipelago of spaces connected by various links (Cacciari, 1997). Europe in this view is a network of differences, a mosaic of overlapping and connecting diversities. There is no over-arching or underlying unity, but connections. A European identity thus might be seen as the recognition of differences and the capacity to build upon these links. In a similar spirit, Rémi Brague has argued that the uniquely European is to be found in the nature of the transmission of culture rather than in any specific cultural content (Brague, 2002). Europe is based on a particular cultural form that transforms that which it takes over, but it does not have a culture of its own. The essence of Europe is its capacity to transform culture. This is a reading of European culture as already decentred, 'eccentric' and containing alterity within it. For Brague, Europe cannot be defined by geography, by politics, or by a disembodied Platonic idea. It is not a place or a particular political order, but a mode of cultural communication. This capacity for self-transformation suggests that Europe does not belong to the Europeans, who do not as such exist: Europe is a culture, he argues, and cannot be inherited but only created. It is in this sense that Europeanization can be viewed as a project of social construction.

Neither the one nor many

The idea of unity in diversity has become an influential way of thinking about European cultural identity today, especially in the context of the enlargement of the European Union. It is an alternative to the two dominant positions, the strongly Euro-federalist notion of the essential unity of Europe as a largely underlying unity and the liberal influenced argument of a higher moral universalism over-riding the inconsequential cultural diversity of Europe. It thus offers an escape from the dilemma of universalism and particularism. With its suggestion of a unity that is shaped in an acknowledgement of diversity, many difficulties are overcome. But at what price? How coherent is this notion of a unity in diversity? Taking into account the different versions of this notion, discussed above, some problems can be mentioned.

One problem that needs to be addressed is why diversity should be a value in itself. It is not at all evident that the recognition of diversity will lead to a collective identity and indeed why a collective identity is desirable. This seems to be the assumption behind the phrase unity in diversity: a higher unity derives from an underlying one and will attain a degree of coherence out of the recognition of diversity and ultimately manifesting itself in a collective identity. Sociologically, it is difficult to make much sense of this beyond the suggestive level of a rhetorical commitment to a soft cosmopolitanism. Diversity exists on many levels in Europe and elsewhere.

There is the obvious level of polynational diversity to begin with, the numerous national cultures. Regional diversity both within and across national cultures is a further dimension complicating national diversity. Indeed, it may be the case that there is greater diversity within nations than across them. However these are two levels of diversity which are generally taken to be the only ones as far as defining the unity of European identity. Diversity also exists at the level of ethnic groups which does not have a geopolitical dimension to it. With most European societies being *de facto* multicultural, diversity has become the reality everywhere (Tully, 1995). On this level, diversity can be differentiated in several ways, as diversity is reflected in language, religion, national identity, customs, etc. We can add to this diversity on the level of lifestyles, taste cultures and forms of consumption, class and gender.

But diversity can also mean something beyond the simple fact of the plurality of forms of life. It can also indicate difference in the stronger sense of divisions. There is the question of diversity on the level of competing conceptions of morality, as in deep conflicts on life and death (abortion, euthanasia, genetic engineering, vivisection, etc.), between religions and between religion and secularism or many nationalist struggles where there is little if any common ground upon which, what John Rawls has called an 'over-lapping consensus' could be built (Rawls, 1987).

One of the problems with the unity in diversity argument is that it conflates these two senses of diversity: plurality and divisions. In the first sense the assumption is that unity is either the basis of the cultural differences – broadly the liberal position – or is something to be achieved on a political level – the position held by Habermas. The second sense is that diversity is an obstacle to unity. This leads theorists such as Habermas to argue that if unity is possible at all it can only be the recognition of difference or the capacity to stand outside a cultural tradition. In the case of Rawls, unity is possible where contending groups share a minimal common ground. What is at stake, then, is the degree of diversity, the extent of conflict arising from diversity and whether this conflict allows common ground to emerge (Rawls) or whether it facilitates a capacity for cultural transformation (Habermas).

Current thinking seems to point towards a view of unity in diversity as an accomplished fact and that therefore the only unity possible is that which is built on the basis of whatever common values can be found in the various European identities. A European identity is then not an over-riding identity but only the common expression of those values that presently exist. This might suggest that it is unlikely that European identity can rest on stronger values, in a way comparable to, for example, American values.

There is an interesting contrast here which is worth pursuing. American values have traditionally been defined in terms of meritocratic individualism and have mostly been moulded by consumer capitalism (Rifkin, 2004). More recently diversity has been held to undermine the possibility of defining shared American values, for culture has ceased to be universal. The language of debating diversity in Europe today leans too heavily in the direction of cultural divisiveness – culture is what divides, not what unites. In view of this it is difficult to see, from a normative perspective, how a European identity could be shaped. Identities, whether individual or collective, require more than the recognition of difference but shared values. The contradiction of the unity in diversity myth is that it denies the possibility of a European identity since this will always be in danger of undermining national diversity.

In addition to these levels of diversity there is the additional question of the relation of diversity to multiplicity, in particular to what is often called multiple identities. Diversity suggests the numerical condition of several identities which have to be chosen. It has in itself an unclarified relation to multiplicity conceived of as overlapping and entangled identities.

It might also be suggested that the appeal to diversity will legitimate xenophobic arguments, such as those now popular with the extreme right. It has been a pervasive tendency for the extreme right in several European countries to argue against migration, Islam and minorities precisely on the grounds of the need to respect cultural diversity. The ideological proponents of the new right argue that cultures are separate and cannot be reconciled to a unity (Taguieff, 1994, 1993/4). The diversity myth ultimately reinforces these extreme positions as well as more generally simply reflecting some of the positions nationalists have always argued, namely the autonomy of national cultures. Unity and diversity is, in essence, a doctrine of cultural relativism. To a degree relativism is an unavoidable dimension of any culture committed to the liberal values of pluralism, respect for the individual, tolerance, etc. But taken to an extreme it can be a legitimating ideology of cultural incommensurability. Interpreted in a less extreme way, it is a meaningless statement of the pluralism of a polynational Europe and does not explain how unity comes about. It certainly does not explain the nature of identity construction or account for existing kinds of unity that have nothing to do with diversity.

One of the major limits of the unity in diversity argument is that it confines European identity to very inflexible reference points. National and regional identities are thus static or rigid identities rather than interpenetrating identities and European identity can only be the expression of the common – in the sense of Rawls's (1987) over-lapping consensus – features of these identities, or in the more limiting case of the recognition of these differences. What is neglected is the critical and transformative dimension of identities and the capacity of Europeanization to bring about change as opposed merely to reflect existing identities.

In sum, unity in diversity is a deeply problematical concept where it is not a meaningless piece of rhetoric suggesting intercultural understanding. To the extent to which it corresponds to something tangible, it is close to a legitimation of xenophobic nationalism whereby the unity of Europe consists in the separation of peoples into different cultures. However a more nuanced interpretation is possible.

There is more unity than is indicated by the current appeal to diversity. This is not a refutation of the obvious reality of diversity on many different levels or of deep cultural divisions. Some of the deepest divisions in Europe are not in fact national or even cultural at all. There are major divisions on the level of political ideology for instance and the national polities themselves are fraught with huge differences that leave their populations largely indifferent to the wider question of Europe. Diversity exists on a European level in particular discourses, such as environmentalism, sustainability, anti-corruption, biotechnology, humanitarianism and anti-war. What is indicated by such examples is that a European identity is articulated in discourses that are concerned with neither unity nor diversity. The notion of diversity that underlies plurality can also be seen in terms of a limited universalism of cosmopolitan recognition of otherness. This will be discussed in more detail in Chapter 5.

Conclusion: beyond the diversity myth

The challenge for Europe is not culture but politics. Influential European intellectuals, including such prominent figures as Jacques Derrida and Jürgen Habermas, have argued in the wake of the controversial Iraq War in 2003 that the United States has betrayed the cherished ideas and ideals of modernity (Habermas and Derrida, 2003; Habermas, 2003a). Their argument is that the very principles of modern democracy and cosmopolitanism that the American Revolution embodied and that were a beacon to Europe and the rest of the world for some two centuries have been abandoned in a descent into empire-building. These intellectuals see the challenge of European identity to be the preservation of these democratic and cosmopolitan values. This is a view that prominent American intellectuals are also expressing (Rifkin, 2004).

Could this be the self-understanding of a European identity? Given the difficulties of defining Europe in exclusively cultural terms or by reference to a shared history or territory, quite different criteria will have to be found for Europe if it is to be meaningful as well as useful. Europe conceived of as a demos rather than an ethos accords with the political reality of contemporary European societies and the growing sensitivity to issues of global civil society. Undoubtedly, some people will see in this a danger that European identity may be defined as anti-Americanism. However, despite some cultural predispositions among the European intelligentsia towards anti-Americanism, this would appear to be more of an American invention than a current reality. Given the global presence and influence of American popular culture, science and technology, anti-Americanism is limited in scope, and European critical responses to American politics are not significantly different from opposition within the United States.

There is a strong case for linking European identity with the cosmopolitanism of European cultural and political modernity. It is important to appreciate that this kind of identity is not merely a collective identity in the conventional sense of the term. We are not talking about the collective identity of a particular group of Europeans or an official legitimating identity for the European Union, but of an emerging cultural model. Even without the European Union this would exist.

The European Union itself tries to take on the mantle of cosmopolitanism in order to assume a democratic identity it otherwise lacks. For instance, human rights have become an important expression of European identity, but a close look reveals a double standard. There is one standard for judging non-member states with regard to accession or development aid, and another for judging the conduct of member states. While this is undoubtedly the case, it is important not to reduce European identity to the political culture of the European Union or other institutions. Social actors, including the European Union, have to define their political projects by reference to the political and cultural legacy of European modernity. Examining this tradition, we may enquire what its defining tenets are and how the European political legacy can give form and orientation to Europe.

Of the wide range of political philosophies, ideals and movements that have characterized European modernity, the tradition that is most distinctively European is the aspiration for social justice. This is arguably more central to European political modernity than the republican tradition, although this must also be considered as constitutive of the European political imaginary (Friese and Wagner, 2002). The belief in a social project has been more a part of European political modernity than of political modernity elsewhere on the globe. The vision of solidarity and social justice has animated many of the major social movements in modern Europe, leading to the foundation of the twentieth-century welfare state, which is arguably the European political legacy. Social Catholicism, trade unionism and socialism have left an enduring mark on Europe, bequeathing a tradition that is the basis of its identity of social care, equality and the vision of a fair society.

This is particularly striking when Europe is compared to the United States. Whatever Europe is becoming, two things are clear: it is not Greater France and, critically, it is not a European version of the United States. It is no longer framed in the image of the French state and republican values, and nor is it a purely market society with loose federal structures. According to Will Hutton, there are three clusters of values that define Europe: the stakeholder view of property, belief in the social contract, and commitment to a vital public realm (Hutton, 2002). There is, he argues, a distinctive kind of European capitalism, which is based on uniquely European values and needs to be fostered so that it does not become like American capitalism with its veneration of the stock market and corporate economic freedom, and its acceptance of social marginalization. Europe's values entail a more responsible kind of capitalism held in check by the institutions of civil society. A European identity based on these values will be a modest Europe, which Goran Therborn characterizes as a 'Scandinavian' Europe (Therborn, 1997). These values are only weakly represented by the 'European social model', but they are a potentially viable basis for European identity.

Whatever the specific content of European identity, the important point is that it is not an identity rooted in a cultural form of life that might be the expression of a 'European People'. This communitarian and republican vision of Europe does not offer an alternative to the instrumentalist view of Europe based on the market and efficiency. A cosmopolitan identity suggests a collective identity beyond both values and interests. As a societal identity, it is a 'thin' identity and sustained by dialogic or discursive structures rather than a pre-established cultural foundation. I have earlier described this as a sense of collective identity closer to a cultural category than an identity of a specific social group. Identity in general, but specifically this sense of identity, cannot be seen as a 'thing'; it is a system of relations and a capacity for communication.

The argument of this chapter is that European identity exists on different levels, cultural and political, and is contested (Ifversen, 2002; Kohli, 2000). As a result of the ongoing process of Europeanization as well as wider processes of globalization and the cross-fertilization of cultures, there is an increase in the number of European personal identities within the populations of European societies; but there is less evidence of the existence of a European collective identity. Nevertheless, there are discernable signs of such a collective identity, which in general can be related to the cultural and political identity of the European Union.

A more diffuse kind of European societal identity exists on the level of a cultural model in which new forms of European self-understanding and self-recognition are expressed. It is only from the perspective of this societal identity that the shape of Europe can be discerned. European identity in all these senses – personal, collective and societal – and especially the latter, is not in competition with national identities; indeed, it is arguably the case that national identities are becoming more cosmopolitan, as are personal identities. Both national identity and European identity should be seen, like most collective identities today, as fluid or 'thin' identities rather than as hard or 'thick' identities that are rooted in pristine cultures or historical logics (see Chapter 4).

The implication of this view of collective identities in Europe as 'thin' is that cosmopolitan forms of understanding can take root in a variety of ways. Rather than an overarching, all-embracing collective identity reminiscent of the nineteenth-century nation-state, European identity should be sought in the cosmopolitan currents of European societies in which new forms of self-understanding are emerging. Whether a European societal identity will emerge and give shape to Europe – that is, to the constellation of elements that make up Europe – remains to be seen; but it may be suggested in conclusion that a decisive factor will be the creation of a social project in which some of the defining values of European modernity can be realized in a new order of recognition.

The critical implication of this for the European Union is that a future European post-national and constitutional order will have to reconcile itself with the fact that the identity of Europe is not easily codified in a cultural package. Identity is about giving voice, and this requires neither a clearly defined ethnos nor a demos but discursive spaces. This dialogic view of Europe seems to accord with the deliberative theory of democracy as a form of communicative power. For the European Union, therefore, the challenge is less to anchor its constitutional order in an underlying identity or overarching collective identity than to create spaces for communication.

4 What does it mean to be a 'European'?

The possibility of cosmopolitan loyalties

In asking the question 'what does it mean to be European?' we are not asking the thorny question 'what is Europe?' considered in Chapter 2. Europe as such does not exist, as Jean Monnet himself remarked; it has to be created. Europe does not exist as a subject in the sense of a subject that has sovereign power or a cultural essence. Europeans, then, are not like national subjects, who have to varying degrees political power based on the political subjectivity of the nation-state. As a political framework Europe has yet to be created. Although the current European Union has gone far in creating such a framework, a political subject that can be identified with the state does not exist. As argued in Chapter 2, it can also be stated that Europe does not exist as a clearly defined geographical territory and there are many tensions between the continental and civilizational dimensions of Europe. Our concern in the present chapter is with those elusive citizens, Europeans, who – if they exist – do so in a complicated relation to the political subjectivity of Europe and to the very meaning of Europe.[1]

There are approximately 450 million Europeans, if we take the population of the now enlarged European Union as constituting Europe. There are many more Europeans, such as those in the forty-three countries of the Council of Europe, which since 1996 includes Russia. Many Americans and Australians consider themselves to be European. What then does it mean to be European? For many it does not mean as much as it means to be French, Irish or British. But there is certainly an acceptable way of being European which does not set it against the primary loyalties of national or regional identity. To be European is, in a certain sense, optional or vague, lacking a clearly defined set of markers. There is no country called Europe, just a vaguely delineated geographical area so called and now a kind of supra-state that has created citizens in its name. In a more specific sense to be European is a lifestyle defined by the modes of behaviour characteristic of the people in the West (Borneman and Fowler, 1997). Almost anybody can be European in this sense, but consumption and identity are not the same. But the Europeanization of food, holidays and sport does not lead to mutual identification (Shore, 2000: 228–9). To be European, it might be said, is no different from being western or from being American. To ask the question 'what does it mean to be European?' concerns, rather, the nature of self-recognition in the designation 'European.'

Americans and Europeans

In an essay that provides a point of departure for the present chapter, Michael Walzer has argued that to be an American is to have a hyphenated-identity. American is a name that exists in relation to another identity, which it qualifies and expands upon in articulating a peculiar identity – Italian-American, Irish-American (Walzer, 1990). Is there a similar mode of self-understanding in the case of Europeans?

It would be tempting, but wrong, to conclude that this is also the case with Europeans. Clearly there is much that is similar. The United States of America is like the European Union, a union of states which have appropriated the adjectives 'American' and 'European' in denial of the wider territory and culture to which these names refer. It is easy to become American and even easier to become European. Moreover, the diversity of America is also reflected in the diversity of Europe. Diversity, then, does not exclude the possibility of a unity of purpose. The motto of the Great Seal of America E *pluribus unum* – 'From many, one' – could easily apply to the EU's identity as unity in diversity; but, of course, this is equally valid of the Republic of India with its 500 languages and democratic pluralism (Oommen, 2005). Both America and Europe are plural societies and there is widespread recognition of diversity as a positive feature of their societies. But the similarities end here.

The United States is a nation-state; Europe is not. Moreover, Anglo-Americans have generally thought of themselves as Americans in way that denied the hyphen, for the Anglo-Saxon category was not judged to be an ethnic category. There is no European equivalent to this group. Of course, the reality is that non-Anglo-Saxon Americans have become more numerous and these hyphenated Americans have shaped American pluralism. Americans settled for a cultural pluralism and political oneness. As citizens a measure of equality was found that did not question the reality of cultural diversity. How was this diversity in culture reconciled with equality in politics?

The hyphen was the solution Americans found. The very identity 'American' reflected this duality. The Irish immigrant could be Irish at the same time as being American. As Walzer correctly argued, they are not culturally Irish and politically American, but culturally and politically Irish-American. Walzer's point is that Americans are peoples with hyphenated identities – Irish-Americans, Italian-Americans. But what is particularly characteristic about American identity is the presence of non-white or non-European Americans. African-Americans, Caribbean-Americans, Chinese-Americans, etc. provide further illustration of a degree of diversity that has not been a feature of Europe (Kibria, 2002). There is no real European equivalent to American hyphenated identities. There are no Afro-Europeans as a self-consciously defined group, although we certainly have Black-British, Asian-British. The hyphen appears to stop beyond the nation. It is not inconceivable that some day there might be such groups of hyphenated Europeans – and already there is some indication of growing numbers of immigrant activists appropriating the designation European (Kastoryano, 2003: 76–7) – but the current reality is that they do not exist, except in those national contexts formed out of decolonization. It is difficult not to draw the conclusion that Europe does not have the same resonance as America as an identity construct.

The United States of America is a society that was formed out of successive waves of immigrants; it is a contrast to the relatively settled populations of Europe, which while experiencing waves of migration in recent times has on the whole not experienced the same degree of diversity. Moreover, the European experience greatly differs from country to country. Aside from migration as a formative feature of American history, there is the more or less total absence of a native or pre-migrant population in Europe. Most migration has been within Europe, with the largest wave being in 1946–9 in the aftermath of the westward advance of the Red Army. The result is that the term 'European' has tended to be more of an adjective than a substantive. As an adjective, it does not exist in a relation of equality but serves as a qualification or a description. Simply put, there are Europeans and there are nationalities. There are no German-Europeans or Italian-European, or Irish-Europeans, where the hyphen joins two identities and which designates a particular kind of self-recognition. Certainly there are Irish who consider themselves to be European, but not in the same way as the Anglo-Irish – those 'Protestant' southern Irish who are of English background – require the hyphen. To be European is not to reject nationality with which it may co-exist and possibly so in a relation of equality. But it rarely exists in a relation of duality in the sense of designating a specific category marked by a hyphen. It is doubtful that there are Irish-Europeans, while it is certainly the case that there are many Irish who are very European in terms of lifestyle and perhaps political inclinations. The same applies to almost every European national or ethnic group. In other words, most Irish-Europeans, to use this example, live more to the left of the hyphen than to the right. In this they differ from Irish-Americans.

Obviously, the appeal of Europeaness is stronger in some countries than in others and varies within countries. In the UK it is weakest, but distinguishing between England and Scotland we find a marked difference in European self-identity in the latter. Nordic countries, with the exception of Finland, see themselves only secondarily European and with a strong identification with a different model of society that is regarded as being threatened by transnational forces. This is probably true of most small countries overshadowed by a larger neighbour.

Europeans, then, are not notably characterized by hyphenated identities, which of course is not to say that they have only one identity. Europeans share with all other peoples multiple identities. The seventeenth report of *British Social Attitudes* documents that people in England, Wales and Scotland see themselves as both English and British, Welsh and British and Scottish and British, and thus having 'dual identities.' According to this report, there is an increase in dual identities in the United Kingdom (Jowell *et al.*, 2000: 157–61). This would suggest that to be European, unlike to be an American, is not a matter of ethnicity, but – as in the British example – an accommodation of a vague, national identity. Indeed, it is often suggested that rather than hyphenated identities, we are more likely to find Europeanness expressed in the form of a pyramid of identities, whereby the European component is at the top. This might be plausible but is too simple an account of identities, which while being indeed layered, or nested, are not necessarily ordered into a structure of allegiances that become progressively thinner and more anonymous as one departs from the 'secure' foundations of ethnicity and nationality.

If culture in the sense of ethnicity does not define the European, perhaps there is a broader and more inclusive cultural identity that is distinctively European. In the view of many this is Christianity. Giscard d'Estaing claimed as much on 9 November 2002 and argued that because it is not Christian, Turkey cannot join the EU. This is also one of the main arguments of Larry Siedentop, who claims Europe's democratic heritage has come from Christianity and Islam is based on a different cultural heritage (Siedentop, 2000). The most persuasive argument for a Christian Europe has been made by Joseph Weiler, who has argued that the proposed European constitution should contain a reference in its preamble to the Judeo-Christian tradition (Weiler, 2003). Weiler's position is based on two arguments. The first is a constitutional argument concerning tolerance, which does not require secularism or impartiality. In his view the secular tradition is only one constitutional tradition, represented by countries such as France and Italy and emulated by the EU today. In contrast, other countries such as the UK, Denmark, Greece, Ireland and Poland either have state churches or acknowledge in their constitutions a dominant religion. His thesis is that a general acknowledgement of religion is likely to increase tolerance for all believers, including non-believers. Second, Weiler argues the preamble to a constitution is the place where a society acknowledges its heritage. This is not a system of belief but a statement of a spiritual and civilizational inheritance. Moreover, without this deeper cultural commitment there is no alternative to the improvised mass culture of postmodern society. It should be stressed that this is not an argument for a confessional Europe or the establishment of an official church or religion, but an acknowledgement of a civilizational heritage that might be the basis of a European identity. Weiler defends this position against accusations of the undemocratic nature of Christianity, arguing that the Christian churches today have accepted democracy and that we are in a very different situation than in the first half of the twentieth century.

But once we look at this more closely we find that constitutional conservatism, the position that Weiler represents, creates as many difficulties as it solves. Christianity has been a divisive force in Europe. The greatest division in this regard is not the schism brought about by the Reformation – and the many divisions within the reformed churches – but the separation of Latin and Greek Christianity in the eleventh century (see Delanty, 1995a; see also Asad, 2002). In light of the incorporation of parts of Europe with large Orthodox populations into the European Union and the growing multiculturalism of Europe, which includes more than 15 million Muslims, this is a matter of not inconsiderable significance (Vertovec and Rogers, 1998). Although there can be no doubt that Christianity has been immensely important in shaping European history, as argued in Chapter

2, it is difficult to see how it offers a basis for a cultural identification and an orientation for European self-understanding. In this context the role of Islam in the making of European civilization cannot be neglected, as Jack Goody has argued (Goody, 2004). Moreover, Europe today – despite the existence of Christian monarchies, political parties and Christian commemoration days – has become predominantly secular even if there are state churches. Weiler is undoubtedly correct in his argument that secularism alone does not guarantee tolerance. The French obsession with banning religious symbols – the headscarf, the crucifix, and so on – has not led to greater tolerance. However, tolerance is not necessarily attained by conservative constitutionalism with a reference to the Judeo-Christian heritage. Moreover, there is a lack of clarity as to the relation between the confessional and the civilizational dimensions

It might be argued that to be European today is to identify with the European Union in much the same way that one aspect of being American – the political dimension – will invariably entail loyalty to the United States of America (Citrin, 2001). Clearly this cannot be taken to be a strong identity. It is evident that there is no strong identification with the EU, while also no strong opposition to it. The various cultural policies of the European Union have not led to significant expressions of European self-understanding, except for the euro professional class of administrators (Barnett, 2001; Shore, 2000).

There is also the problem of language. So long as Europeans do not share a common language the possibility of a common European culture is limited. The European elites once were educated to be multilingual and to master ancient languages. Today's Europeans are mostly monolingual, aside from the use of English as a lingua franca in the domain of work and consumption and bilingualism in Nordic countries. Nevertheless, the absence of a common culture does not mean that an interconnected culture is not possible. The ascendancy of English undoubtedly allows Europeans to communicate more, making Europe less of 'Babel' than might otherwise be the case (Schlesinger, 2005). However, political values certainly will transcend some of the divisions that language creates. There is a strong movement of European environmentalism, for instance, and there is a consolidating European public sphere around particular issues, such as anti-war. Cross-national solidarities cannot be underestimated, as is illustrated by the public acknowledgement placed in *Le Monde* by the Spanish Government thanking the French people for the support following the terrorist attack in Madrid in March, 2004.

There are clear trends indicating a certain attachment to Europe. According to Eurobarometer surveys (June, 2003) 54 per cent of EU citizens think that their country benefits from membership of the EU and in 2004 as many as 77 per cent approved of the draft European Constitution. People support the EU for pragmatic reasons (Christin and Trechsel, 2002) but they also increasingly support it for reasons of identification with the values they associate with it. Nevertheless, studies indicate that only a minority – Martin Kohli documents 11 per cent – put Europe before the nation as a reference point for their identity (Kohli, 2000: 125). Other research findings show that that while relatively few people (less than 10 per cent in this case) put Europe first, a significant and increasing number express equal attachment to Europe and the nation (Citrin and Sides, 2004). Thus, there are declining numbers who identify exclusively with the nation suggesting, according to Citrin and Sides in a major study, that Europe has become a viable and positive supplementary identity for many people who do not see it eroding national identity. In a study of national and European identities in football, King finds growing evidence of a European identity emerging amongst English football supporters (King, 2000, 2003). He argues there is increasing evidence of major football clubs, such as Manchester United, the focus of his research, cultivating a European identity based on an identification of the city as a champion in Europe.

In essence, then, there is an increase in dual identities, giving some support for the hyphenated conception of identity. However, this entails a different configuration than in Walzer's account of American identity. Europe means different things, depending on the national identity to which it is related. Thus the Germans see Europe as a means of relativizing national identity. The Irish see Europe as an alternative to a negative identity with respect to Britain. The French see Europe as an extension of French identity and Turkish Muslims see Europe as a multicultural alternative to the secular Kemalist state. A strong cognitive dimension to European identity can also be noted: the more the EU appears to exist as a real entity, the more identification with it occurs (Castano, 2004). Laffan argues that the EU is now a major component of the cognitive and normative structures in contemporary Europe (Laffan, 2004). The cognitive dimension is embedded in the symbolic culture of the EU. This leads to a transformative relation between the different aspects of the configuration of identities which act on each other. The relation is more than one of co-existence, for the various identities co-evolve. It is in this sense that Risse argues for the relevance of a constructivist approach (Risse, 2004a: 271).

The absence of a strong European identity does not mean that there are not weaker expressions of European identity which, moreover, are not necessarily focused on the EU but on civic values and which could be the basis of different kinds of loyalty. This is the sense that Habermas calls a 'constitutional patriotism', that is an identity with constitutional principles rather than with the actual form of the state or a particular set of political values (Habermas, 1994, 1998).

In this context an important distinction can be made between American and European identity. Where Americans are culturally plural and politically united by a shared liberal culture, as Walzer noted, Europeans in contrast are bifurcated in this way, which perhaps explains why they are not patriotic in the way that Americans are overwhelmingly so. Cultural identity and political identity are not part of a coherent collective identity that could be called European in any meaningful sense. Because of the mosaic of national, regional and political identities – coupled with different national traditions of immigration – there is no overarching European identity in the sense of a generalized categorical identity that includes all Europeans. Undoubtedly it is the intention of the European

Union to create such an identity, but it is unlikely to happen except as an official institutional identity.

Where Walzer's concerns were with the nature of political and cultural identity, Samuel Huntington argues that a new bifurcation is tearing America apart: America's elites are becoming cosmopolitan, while the people remain national (Huntington, 2004a, 2004b). Despite their hyphenated identities, Americans are overwhelmingly patriotic and proud to be American; but the elites are denationalizing America, he argues, and are out of touch with the people. Such polarities are misleading, but if there is any truth to it, it might be suggested the opposite is the case in Europe: the people are cosmopolitan and the elites national.

Cosmopolitanism and Europeanness

The point that is emerging from the foregoing analysis is that to be European is neither a matter of culture nor of politics as such. Instead the condition of being European is expressed more in an orientation to the world and which might be identified with the cosmopolitan spirit.

While not being exclusively identified with Europe, cosmopolitanism has a recognizable European character. In this there is a striking contrast with the history of Americanism, where the general tendency since the mid-nineteenth century has been towards nativism and, in recent times with the postmodern negotiation of ethnicities, with particularity and difference.

Some of the first visions of the European as a distinctive person emerged with the Enlightenment. In his *Consideration of the Government of Poland*, Rousseau, the champion of radical republican democracy, saw the coming of an age when 'there are no more French, German, Spanish, even Englishmen whatever one says, there are only Europeans. They all have the same tastes, the same passions, and the same way of life'. However, on the other side, when Edmund Burke said in 1796 in his *Three Letters on the Proposal of Peace with the Regicide Directory of France* 'No European can be an exile in any part of Europe' he almost certainly had in mind the elites of the Ancien Régime. This was a time when cosmopolitanism was identified with the French language and French standards of social behaviour. To be cosmopolitan was to be French and thus disguised a certain particularism and, where this was not the case, it certainly was a *European* cosmopolitanism, as was evident from the many cosmopolitan political projects to unify the continent of Europe. Nevertheless, the cosmopolitan idea contained within it a critique of European civilization and of the court culture of which in many respects it was a part, as is intimated in Hegel's comment in the *Philosophy of Right*:

> A human being counts as such because he is a human being, not because he is a Jew, Catholic, Protestant, German, Italian, etc. This consciousness, which is the aim of thought, is of infinite importance, and it is inadequate only if it adopts a fixed position – for example, as cosmopolitanism – in opposition to the concrete life of the state.

What is suggested in this is a conception of cosmopolitanism that goes beyond the particularism of national belonging. Europeans are citizens with a world outlook. What can this consist of? In the most basic sense it means that the citizens of one country consider the citizens of another 'one of us'; it means the recognition of living in a world of diversity and a belief in the fundamental virtue of embracing positively the values of the other. While this was once an identity of the European elites, there is some evidence that it has become a more general identity for all Europeans.

Cosmopolitanism is not the same as transnationalism or the fact of multiplicity, although they are not insignificant aspects of it. Anyone can be cosmopolitan, regardless of location and ethnicity or nationality. Cosmopolitanism does not require a hyphenated identity; it is rather a disposition characterized by a reflexive relation to one's identity. The reflexive relation is different from a hyphenated one as such, signalling a critical and transformative self-understanding. European identity does not rest on a secure foundation. The singular expression of Europeaness is to be found in critical and reflexive forms of self-understanding, rather than with an identity with 'Europe' or with the 'EU'.

It would be wrong to see this as the specific identity of Europe and to set up a distinction between Europe and America, as Robert Kagan (2003) attempts. To be European is not simply to be anti-American, as some recent tendencies might suggest. Anti-Americanism is certainly a part of the construction of Europeanization, but is not the only force sustaining it and positive positions on America have been important reference points in European modernity. The demonstrations against the war in Iraq in European cities in Spring 2003 certainly played a significant role in articulating a European identity based on constitutional values. However, it would be a mistake to read into this a new European anti-Americanism. Eurobarometer results (June, 2003) indicate that while the positive image of the United States has diminished as a result of the Iraq war and the record on environmentalism, Europeans are not in fact anti-American in the way Americans often think they are, although they are almost certainly more anti-American than Americans are anti-European, assuming that American anti-Europeanness is not equated with Francophobia (Ash, 2003). European anti-Americanism is a left and civic discourse, while American anti-Europeanism is right-wing and despite the rising tide of both currents, European identity does not rest on opposition to America. Most European governments – with the notable exception of France and Germany – supported the war against Iraq, and one has now paid the price for this. Anti-Americanism is not what is sustaining European civil and political values. Nor is there a basic political discord between a 'Hobbesian America' and a decadent 'Kantian Europe', as Robert Kagan would have us believe (Kagan, 2003).

Europeans are not particularly united among themselves. It is unlikely that they will unite against an Other. If there is not a European self or subject, there cannot be an easily defined Other. There is neither a European state nor a European people, although there do appear to be Europeans. The newly articulated European self-understanding that formed in the mass demonstrations in European cities in 2003 may be partly the expression of a political subject, but cannot be seen as a unified collective identity based on a pre-existing community linked by a hyphen to the shared political community of the liberal public sphere. Empirical studies suggest that European identity is often a pragmatic matter, rather than based on ethnocentric prejudices about other populations (Christin and Trechsel, 2002). In short, there is no European self-confronting an Other. It is now more evident than before that Islam does not fulfil this role, but nor does Europe. The opposition to the Iraq war reveals that Europeans are not hostile to countries with large Islamic populations and are more likely to see the greatest danger to peace coming from the American government. In this respect the Kosovo intervention was an important indication of a shift in European attitudes to what is included in the category 'European' (Balibar, 2004: 4–5). As Rémi Brague has argued, '[t]he danger for Europe cannot come from outside for the simple reason that it cannot conceive of itself as an "inside"' (Brague, 2002: 185). There is not a defining essence that is the basis of European culture. Derrida has made this point also with respect to Europe with the argument that

> *what is proper to a culture is not be identical to itself.* Not to not have an identity, but not to be able to identify with itself, to be able to say 'me' or 'we', to be able to take the form of the subject only in the non-identity to itself or, if you prefer, only in the difference with itself. There is no culture or cultural identity without this difference *with itself*.
>
> (Derrida, 1994: 8–9)

The upshot of this argument is that if a European self-understanding exists it is one that is not premised on an underlying identity as such or on the fictive myth of a 'people'. To be European is not to identify with something called Europe or have a common identity comparable to a national identity and for which the hyphen is needed. This is the principal difference between European and American identity. Nor does it require a negotiation of ethnicities. Europe does not exist except as a discursively constructed object of consciousness and Europeans also do not exist as a people with a shared past. To be European is simply to recognize that one lives in a world that does not belong to a specific people.

The possibility of cosmopolitan loyalties: is there a European loyalty?

Until recently the question of loyalty to the European Union was not an issue. The legitimacy of the EU rested on the prior legitimacy of its member states who could rely on the loyalty of their citizens. The EU thus profited from the alleged legitimacy of the nation-state. A second reason can also be given for the apparent irrelevance of the question whether citizens need be loyal to the EU. Since its origin in the period after the Second World War the primary justification of the EU – or the European (Economic) Community as it was then called – was cooperation between sovereign states, in particular France and Germany. Schuman and Monnet, its founders, regarded the European Union to be nothing more than an alliance of states for economic and political cooperation. Although the principle of unity that lay behind this was to grow in importance, it was primarily a community of interest, not of identity. If there was a higher principle of justification it was undoubtedly the need for peace in the aftermath of the devastation of the Second World War. Perhaps, too, there was a certain sense of loyalty to the values of European civilization. But this was not a very tangible category and in so far as the EU remained more like an organization than an institution loyalty did not matter.

We are no longer in this situation today. The memory of the Second World War is now distant for the majority of Europeans and the prospect of the western European states going to war among themselves is virtually unthinkable (although they may get involved in a non-European war, in which case loyalty will become divided, as has been the case with the Iraq war). With the obsolescence of these older justifications for European integration, we are forced to ask the question of 'what is the present justification of the EU?'. In a new century and millennium, the cultural and political heritage of the nineteenth century and its system of sovereign states, which cast its shadow over the twentieth century and its world wars, is also receding and new forces are emerging. Of these, and of particular salience in the present context, is the question of globalization and the alleged decline in the sovereignty of the nation-state. It is possible that the challenge of globalization is now replacing peace as the primary justification of the EU. Yet, we do not have a clear rationale for the EU in terms of a model of loyalty, though it appears that loyalty is increasingly shifting away from an identification with territory and the state and coming to rest on other more 'cosmopolitan' reference points, as Habermas and others have argued. Traditionally, political loyalty has been either to territory, state, party, ethnic group or the imaginary community of the nation. The EU fulfils none of these categories in an obvious way: it is not a specific territory, other than that of the member states, which is constantly changing as new states join and currently expanding into postcommunist space; it is not a state in the conventional sense of the term but a supra-national and regulatory agency; the parties that operate in its parliamentary space are largely juxapositions of national ones; and it clearly is not based on an ethnic substratum but is culturally highly diverse in terms of ethnicities, regions and nationalities. Indeed, much of 'Europe' contains the 'non-European' and diverse and often competing loyalties. With the enlargement project now underway, the diversity of the EU will increase and inevitably, too, conflicts over loyalty will increase.

Aside from the obsolescence in the idea of peace as a primary justification for the European Union, the other factors are also becoming increasingly questionable. The extent of the operations of the EU have gone beyond the model of inter-state cooperation. The EU has become something like a regulatory order which can undermine national sovereignty (Majone, 1996). This 'neo-functional' model is now more or less the reality of European integration. The inter-state level is, of course, still the main dimension but there is no denying the tremendous trans-formation of national sovereignty by the EU (Weiler, 1999). With respect to the first mentioned point, the nation-state itself is now under greater duress than in the period following the Second World War. Aside from the impact of globalization, the legitimacy of the state is also being internally eroded as a result of the rise of a new regionalism, various kinds of nationalist movements and, with the crisis of the welfare state, the apparent inability of the state to maintain the provision of collective goods.

There is also another reason why the question of loyalty is a major challenge for the EU. Loyalty today is becoming increasingly conditional and can no longer be regarded as durable resources to be tapped by political elites. Loyalties can be recalcitrant and unpredictable and this is especially the case where political elites are perceived as having betrayed democracy. In this respect the Iraq war was a major test of loyalties. Today more than ever loyalties are refracted through democracy and cannot be simply derived from the uncritical values of duty, patriotism or obedience. Again, the Iraq war was an interesting demonstration of cosmopolitan loyalties in Europe.

Under these circumstances the question of loyalty can no longer be confined to the prior legitimacy of national states or traditional kinds of patriotism but penetrates to the heart of the EU whose jurisdiction now touches individual citizens. In sum, then, the national states, on the one side, are losing their command over the loyalty of citizens and on the other the EU is forced to compete with the ailing nation-state for the diminishing resources of loyalty at precisely the time when democratization has become one of the major stumbling blocks of further European integration. The problem the EU faces is severe: to compete with the nation-state for the increasingly scarce resource of loyalty and at the same time build the foundations upon which democratic forms of loyalty can be expressed. We might quite well wonder, then, how can the EU – itself inherently undemocratic – achieve a sufficient measure of loyalty when the much better equipped nation-state is frequently unable to maintain the continued loyalty of its citizens. Will the legitimation crisis that Habermas (1976) in the early 1970s thought was endemic to late capitalism now extend to the supra-national? Or, to follow Niklas Luhmann, are loyalties irrelevant and anachronistic categories no longer relevant to the complex bureaucratic polity that the post-national state today has become (Luhmann, 1990)? Can the EU benefit from the emerging forms of cosmopolitan loyalty emerging in Europe and the rest of the world? A limited, or 'thin', kind of cosmopolitan loyalty is possible beyond the traditional class, ethnic and national loyalties but in the long run it will have to create 'thicker' forms of solidarity based on social values such as welfare. In the most basic sense, loyalty concerns the non-contractual ties that bind individuals to a community, in this case the political community. To speak of loyalty presupposes a degree of belief in the legitimacy of the political order, a trust in its institutions, and sense of community: legitimacy, trust and community are the defining tenets of loyalty.

According to Max Weber, in his classic account of legitimacy, power must be converted into authority if is to appear legitimate (see also Beetham, 1991). No political order can rest on force alone. States need the loyalty of their citizens. For Weber legitimate authority in modern society was almost entirely based on the formal rationality of legal procedure, a position which ultimately tends too much in the Hobbesian direction of law and order. However, we can, following Habermas, add to this that a belief in the legitimacy of authority must also rest on a principle of justification (Habermas, 1996). Authority must be capable of being rationally justifiable in the face of opposition. This communicative dimension allows authority to be challenged and always open to revision. In this sense, then, loyalty is more of a Lockean idea than a Hobbesian one since it recognizes the contingent nature of authority which is never final but revisable. Legitimacy is thus not more legality, but an essentially democratic process involving public deliberation. In this sense it rests on three conditions, which effectively define democracy: the rule or law (in this case, constitutionalism or liberal democracy); the representation of social interests (electoral or representative democracy); and citizenship in the sense of participation in civil society (republican democracy) (see Touraine, 1997). The claim that is being made in this chapter is that democratically achieved forms of legitimacy are becoming increasingly a condition of loyalty. Loyalty is thus not a residual category in citizenship, as it was, for example, in T. H. Marshall's theory of citizenship (Marshall, 1992). In Marshall's theory, the state earns the loyalty of citizens by bestowing on them certain rights and entitlements but beyond that loyalty is largely a passive quality of citizens. Today in contrast, as is reflected in many communitarian political theories, loyalty is less a passive condition as it was for Marshall and is more integral to citizenship as an active condition. The upshot of this is that legitimacy has become more and more contingent on a whole range of factors beyond the procedural dimensions of law and the state. It is thus difficult to be loyal to something that is not democratically legitimate. To a degree, too, legitimacy can be secured by efficiency – one of the major foundations of EU legitimacy – but in the long run this does not produce the legitimacy that can secure enduring loyalties.

Second, loyalty extends beyond legitimacy in that it is based on a belief in the basic reliability of the political system and this is ultimately something that goes beyond democracy. In practice no political order could function in a complex modern society if every action had to be democratically legitimated. With the growing complexity of organizational systems and the 'abstract' nature of society (Giddens, 1990; Luhmann, 1995), contemporary society is coming to rely on trust to an ever greater extent than in earlier societies where power could be more visible. This is something a wide range of theorists have recognized. Trust depends on the paradoxical suspension of the demand for constant legitimation but is not reducible to blind faith. We trust institutions because we feel our interests are best served by them. Trust and the pursuit of interests are thus closely connected. It was one of Durkheim's central arguments that solidarity in modern society can only be based on relations of cooperation between groups whose interests are best served by generalized rather than particularistic values. In earlier societies trust was confined binding masses to elites, but in our advanced societies trust is invested less in elites than in complex organizational systems. It may be suggested that trust is an essential ingredient, even a condition, of loyalty. Loyalty requires the existence of what might be called a responsible state. The state must provide for public goods, such as the social goods of welfare, education, and a basic infrastructure for society (e.g. transport, communications); ownership, in whole or in part, of certain natural endowments and of certain economic resources; and security for citizens against internal and external threats. It is a basic condition of loyalty to the state that the state is perceived to be a responsible actor, even if its opponents are irresponsible. The involvement of the British and American governments in Iraq in 2003–4 and the misuse of intelligence on weapons of mass destruction and mistreatment of prisoners is one of the most dramatic of recent examples of this principle of loyalty having been massively used against the state in widespread public displays of the withdrawal of loyalty.

Third, in addition to trust and the existence of democratic political institutions, loyalty is also articulated in the form of a sense of community or collective identity, here understood as belonging. Loyalties cannot be so easily secured without a sense of belonging. This can take weak and strong forms. Where group ties are very strong, perhaps underpinned by a dominant ethnicity or religion, a sense of belonging will be stronger and able to secure more durable forms of loyalty. As far as loyalty is concerned the idea of membership of a shared political community is clearly the most important dimension to community, but other factors too play a role, such as common cultural bonds. But most modern polities can at most rely on weak forms of belonging based on political rather than cultural community. In these cases political community cannot so easily be translated into a single culturally defined community. It may be suggested that the dimension of community in loyalty depends on the degree political community can be related to different kinds of cultural community. Thus different cultural communities, such as for example different ethnic groups or different regional communities, who may share little culturally, can in principle have a sense of belonging to the political community of the wider polity. This will depend partly on the kinds of values of the political community, whether they are inclusive or exclusive.

Loyalties are rapidly changing today and some of the existing loyalties are no longer reliable resources to be exploited by the state. Apart from the fact that loyalties are now multiple and frequently overlapping, they have become contested, volatile and can take radical forms. Traditional forms of loyalty are giving way to forms of legitimation and loyalties that are inseparable from democracy. This is one of the major changes in the nature of loyalty. Traditional loyalty was a sentiment that was largely outside the political culture of democracy, but today emotional content is entering more and more into the language of politics. Loyalties are emotional and subjective, and as such they have powerful resonances in the contemporary political culture. In view of these considerations what can be said about loyalty and the state? Can the post-national European 'state' command any loyalty? First here are a few remarks on the capacity of the state to exploit the discourse of loyalty.

There is no doubt that states can tap the loyalty of citizens, as the case of the final round of the French presidential election in 2002 demonstrated. Despite charges of corruption and disloyalty, Jacques Chirac won the support of virtually the entire opposition on grounds of loyalty to the democratic values of the French republic that his opponent, Jean-Marie Le Pen, was endangering. But while this was indeed an exceptional episode, it nevertheless demonstrates how volatile and indeterminate the category of loyalty is. In this case the extreme right were also able to claim the mantle of loyalty to the nation and secured one of the largest electoral mandates that an extreme right wing party has ever attained in recent times. Loyalty was central to all of this, demonstrating the argument made above that loyalty has become a fundamentally contested category in politics in today. But what is significant is not just the contested nature of loyalty, but that it has become to a very significant degree de-referentialized of any normative content. It is not easy to specify the nature of loyalty and whether it pertains to a category of the nation or to the state. Le Pen appealed to the nation, while Chirac appealed to the state. Especially in the first round of the election a significant number of anti-Chirac voters came from supporters of the left. Devoid of tangible referents, loyalty can be exploited by different groups to serve different interests.

The implication of this is that no group can control the fact that loyalty no longer has any clear meaning, but has become contingent. Chirac and Le Pen were not using the idea of loyalty in the same way and nor were those who voted for them; for each the other was disloyal and for the voters other kinds of loyalties played a role. It was not a case of one being more loyal than the other as might have been the case in more traditional contests in which patriotism was one of the stakes in the political game but in which the rules where relatively clear. This point is crucial for an understanding of the problem of loyalty and the EU since it demonstrates that there are no stable categories out of which loyalties can be made. The very category of the nation is no longer a clearly definable entity and in so far as a transnational and post-national polity such as the EU tries to emulate it, it will inevitably run up an even larger loyalty deficit.

The European Union and dilemmas of loyalty

Having outlined the general conditions of loyalty and the major changes in its composition, the problem of loyalty beyond the nation-state can now be discussed more specifically with respect to the EU. Let us now examine in some detail the extent of a disjuncture between the conditions of loyalty and the existing political culture of the EU.

First, taking the question of legitimacy and more generally democracy, it is apparent that the EU is at best a second-order democracy. The main institutions – the Council of Ministers and the European Commission – are not answerable to the citizens in the way national governments to a degree are. While having wide-ranging autonomy, especially the Commission, they are answerable to national governments, though this is rapidly diminishing. Thus the civic tradition of democracy does not apply to the political culture of the EU. Aside from the legal autonomy of the European Court of Justice, the only exception to this is the European Parliament, which has a direct relationship with European citizens. However, the Parliament is not comparable to national parliaments, having merely the power to influence agendas, which are effectively set by the Commission, but not legislate.

What has been a diffuse set of treaties is now taking a constitutional form, but the EU lacks a deep constitutional principle of sovereignty. As a result there is the much discussed democratic deficit (Siedentop, 2000), to be sure the EU can claim a degree of legitimacy based on legality. There is no doubt that this is the basis of the legitimacy of the EU but it does not extend into a deeper sense of legitimacy beyond legality. Especially since the Nice Treaty, it is increasingly being recognized that the formal legality of the EU is not enough to be the source of any significant commitment on the part of the public. The EU now needs stronger arguments to justify significant changes which the enlargement project will bring. Without a clear commitment to any specific values, the democratic deficit is now in danger of developing into a deeper crisis of loyalty.

Second, taking the dimension of trust the situation is less clear cut. There is nothing to indicate citizens do not trust the EU or that the EU is not a responsible state. In fact, this might be a source of strength, particularly given the historical reputation of the nation-state. The EU has been a leading voice in the institutionalization of sustainable environmental policies and has done much to enforce civil rights in many of the member states, especially in the area of work and the rights of women (Meehan, 1993).

But it is in the dimension of community that the most severe problems arise. There is no substantive basis to Europe as a cultural community in the view of many critics (Smith, 1992). Lacking the crucial asset of a shared language, the diversity of national and regional culture in Europe, it is argued, makes a shared sense of a culturally rooted identity impossible. There is of course the historical memory of Christendom but this is more likely to be an obstacle to loyalty than an asset, given the fact that the European countries are now committed to some degree of multiculturalism and that the cleavage between confessions is becoming less salient than that between all religious beliefs and secularism. At the most if we use these conventional yardsticks, perhaps Europe can claim some loyalty from intellectuals and the professionally mobile. But for the majority of citizens, who are not polyglots, there is little in the ideal of a common European cultural identity as an aspiration. The diverse nature of the populations of the EU make any simple appeal to community impossible. But this does not mean that there cannot be a European identity that might be the source of loyalties. Before taking this point up in the following section a few further remarks can be made.

In the transnational context of the EU loyalties are no longer based on conservative values such as duty, deference to authority or obedience, but have become more and more discursively articulated. Until recently, as noted earlier, loyalty expressed fairly conservative values of patriotism as a moral and affirmative resource for the state to secure basic obedience. The dominant language of loyalty today in Europe is not one of conservative values but of liberal and democratic demands of solidarity and legitimacy. Moreover, the fact that loyalties have also become more and more conditional is evident in the way European publics are becoming more sceptical of political elites who are having to contend with loyalties that are volatile and can easily be withdrawn if conditions change. This is evident, for instance, in the very variable nature of public opinion as monitored by the Eurobarometer.

Euroscepticism is now a major public discourse in virtually every European country (Tiersky, 2001). Originally in the formative period of European integration it expressed the anti-European values of the major social democratic parties, it became increasingly in the course of 1980s and 1990s, as the left embraced European integration, an ideology of the nascent neo-right, which in many countries moved against Europe. Today it is a wider and popular discourse that does not easily fit into any one political position. No longer an ideology of specific political elites, the Eurosceptic discourse expresses the concerns of many groups in almost every European society that the project of European integration is losing its connection with basic loyalties. While the Euro elites blame the masses for not being loyal to Europe, the truth is that it is the elites who are now being portrayed as disloyal. As Christopher Lasch has argued in the American context, the betrayal of democracy is now being blamed on elites, while in the past it was the elites who blamed the masses (Lasch, 1995). Europe, in short, has now become a focal point for all kinds of discourses of loyalty, from environmentalism, nationalism and humanitarianism to right and left ideologies.

In sum, it would appear that the EU is unable to tap the power of loyalty which is still a major resource of what remains of the nation-state but which also extends beyond the limits of national governance. With respect to the three components of loyalty mentioned early – legitimacy, trust and community – the EU is able to score high on legitimacy, in so far as this is based on formal procedural legitimacy in the Weberian sense as well as on efficiency but is weak on deeper democratic forms of legitimation; it is low on trust, except in relation to the condition of responsible government, and especially so with respect to social commitments; and is weak on community and collective identities. But does this mean there is not something like a cosmopolitan kind of loyalty that might correspond to a post-national polity such as the EU?

Conclusion: post-national loyalty?

The analysis in this chapter is indeed pessimistic: the EU cannot realistically be based for the foreseeable future on a significant sense of loyalty comparable to what the embattled nation-state can still command. The EU will have to secure different kinds of loyalties than those to which the nation-states typically appeal. In so far as loyalty is seen as a pre-existing resource there are no chances of the EU gaining much of it, given the problems outlined in the foregoing. Traditional forms of loyalty will in any case be more likely to be used against the EU than for it. Instead one must see a series of trade-offs operative in the loss of some kinds of loyalties but a gain in others. What are the chances of a post-national, cosmopolitan form of loyalty emerging?

It can hardly be denied that there are identities that are not nationally specific and in many ways are quite European rather than British, French, German, etc.

These may not take the 'thick' forms that the Eurosceptics assume must be the defining characteristic of collective identities. Undoubtedly there are 'thick' kinds of European identity, although it is difficult to see them having a role to play in shaping loyalties of significance. The idea of a European cultural heritage commands only minimal loyalty, and not to a degree that can be easily mobilized. Euro-elites, such as the Euro-federalists and many champions of European integration, have frequently made appeals to the cultural achievements of European history to forge a collective identity for the culture bereft EU. Such attempts have found their way into European cultural policy, but are not the basis of strong forms of loyalty (Shore, 2000).

However, looking beyond these official attempts to forge a European collective identity, the Eurosceptical criticism neglects certain forms of identification and cultural codes that are increasingly taking shape and which might be termed transnational, in the sense of being specifically European. There is growing evidence that more and more people are identifying with Europe, which is becoming a focus for identity. The euro and other examples from material life, such as sport, education exchanges, architecture and city scapes and tourism, point to a tendentially European way of life in the sense of common patterns of life, symbolic structures and transnational discourses across Europe. A sober look at the prospects of a European identity might indicate that a European society is emerging in a slow and very diffuse way and producing new kinds of attachments and loyalties.

In sum, while a 'thick' European form of loyalty remains unlikely, as the Euro-sceptical critics claim, this does not preclude the possibility of viable 'thin' kinds of loyalty to emerge in European public discourse. There is no reason why concrete reality of many cosmopolitan expressions of loyalty, such as loyalty to humanity, to the earth, future generations, and justice cannot be a basis of a distinctively European identity, in the sense of one that is not derivative of national identity but based on more generalized reference points. These are forms of loyalty that are being constructed in public discourse and do not simply reflect an already established loyalty. In the multicultural societies that now exist in Europe many people have several loyalties – loyalties to different groups and even to different societies – but this does not mean that these loyalties are not reconcilable. Loyalties, like the identities upon which they are based, can be negotiable and flexible and, moreover, they are rarely fixed for long but can shift along with generational change. Thus loyalties in Europe today are less likely to be ranked in a hierarchy of allegiances from family and kin to friends and colleagues to the national community. The state no longer commands an exclusive demand on loyalties as other more cosmopolitan kinds of loyalty come into play and yet the state is more and more dependent on loyalty as a form of legitimacy.

Thin forms of loyalty exist on the European level and are very different from national forms of loyalty that generally presuppose a pre-existing loyalty. The specifically European forms of loyalty identified in this chapter do not operate on this assumption. These forms of loyalty are highly contingent on certain conditions being fulfilled and take the form of a processual discourse. While thick loyalties will take a long time to consolidate, for the moment thin forms of loyalty are more in evidence. These new European forms of loyalty should not be exaggerated, but they should also not be denied as many of the Eurosceptics try to convince us.

It may be speculated in conclusion that dialogic forms of loyalty as described by Habermas will be more and more relevant to the EU in the context of the enlargement project. The prospect of military conflict has not entirely disappeared from the EU, as the enlargement project demonstrates. While the present composition of the EU has more or less solved the problem of war, this may not be the case in a not too distant future with a possible twenty-seven (or more) member EU. The Turkish–Cypriot conflict is one obvious example of a potential military clash and where major issues of loyalty are involved. Aside from the question of major military clashes, there are many other examples of potential conflicts of loyalties which the EU will have to address. As the EU expands into quite different kinds of societies it is unlikely that simple appeals to 'unity in diversity' will suffice to resolve potential clashes over loyalties. It is not too far-fetched to propose that the strengthening of dialogic and reflexive kinds of loyalty along with social solidarites will be crucial in the future. Whether Europeans will succeed in making a positive virtue of their diversity rather than seek unity or a common collective identity will depend to a large extent on whether they can create a culture of debate in which different views can be articulated.

5 The new cultural logic of Europeanization

Citizenship, memory, and public discourse

The assumption that citizenship is defined by nationality has been widely questioned over the past two decades. The separation of citizenship from the condition of membership of a specific state has been one of the major themes in recent social and political theory (Delanty, 2000b). New conceptions and practices of citizenship point to something considerably more differentiated and multifaceted than nationality. If, in the most general sense, citizenship entails membership of the political community, it is apparent that many of the legal and cultural assumptions inherited from the previous two centuries are questionable. The very status of membership has become highly contested as a result of new conceptions of rights and new expressions of belonging. Where citizenship was once confined to a passive condition as a legal status based on rights and duties, today in the view of many it has become a condition of empowerment.

In addition to the conventional rights of citizenship as described by T. H. Marshall in his classic essay – civic, political and social rights – there is now a growing emphasis on cultural rights and questions of participation (Marshall, 1992 [1950]). This has led to two major changes in citizenship. First, it has led to the recognition that some degree of group rights are necessary in order to extend citizenship to minorities, especially ethnic minorities, migrant groups or disadvantaged groups, and that consequently citizenship cannot be entirely reduced to the rights of birth. In this respect, citizenship must be capable of a certain flexibility, for example in reconciling individual and group interests. Second, partly as a result of the need for the legal recognition of minorities but also because of the growing sense that citizenship entails the right to express one's identity, culture has entered more and more into the politics of citizenship and democracy, as in for example debates about forms of commemoration, heritage, minority languages, religion, special rights or dispensations from certain duties, etc. A key dimension of this, and of particular salience to Europeanization, concerns consumer rights (Cronin, 2002; Stevenson, 2003). In sum, citizenship as membership of a political community now extends into a much broader notion of participation than was previously the case.

However, the implications of these new conceptions of citizenship extend beyond issues of rights and the identity of minority groups to the very self-understanding of national identities (Povinelli, 2002). It is a fact of great significance that the debate on rights is occurring at a time when the national polity is itself being challenged as the primary location of citizenship and of national self-understanding. No account of citizenship today can neglect the wider transformation in the very nature of political community understood in terms of a sovereign and territorially defined polity based on an underlying cultural identity (Castells, 1996). As a result of the growing impact of global processes and world cultural concepts, political community itself has become open to new definitions, some of which point to the contemporary salience of cosmopolitan community (Stevenson, 2003). There are enough empirical indications to make the claim that political community cannot be codified as a national community in which political identity is based on a prior cultural identity. The nation-state is no longer the primary reference for loyalties, identities and democracy. This does not mean that the nation is an exhausted category or that the state has ceased to be an effective agent of justice and democracy; what it means is that the nation has become pluralized and open to new imaginaries about belonging, community and identity. The nation is now a fragile, liquid and contested category. Nowhere is this more evident than in responses to multiple cultural identities and cosmopolitan self-understanding.

One of the most important developments in recent times as far as citizenship is concerned is the cultural transformation of national identity as a result of what may be broadly subsumed under the category of globalization. National identities are not immune to the growing sense of the interconnectivity of the world, the emergence of global civil society, world ethics, planetary problems and, within its member states, the European Union and the emergence of a European public sphere. These expressions of political community have had an undeniable impact on the capacity of national identity to define political community exclusively in particularistic terms. It is widely agreed that globalization is not simply bringing about a new global and homogenized order as such or that the universal is replacing the particular; on the contrary, the global and the local complement each other (Appadurai, 1996; Robertson, 1992). Nations are perfectly capable of appropriating and adapting to globalization, producing new national imaginaries and that something like 'nations without nationalism' is possible (Kristeva, 1993). The imagined community of the nation now extends far beyond the borders of the nation-state. In sum, cosmopolitan political community has become a reality both within and beyond the nation and no national polity can define itself in exclusively particularistic terms (Delanty and O'Mahony, 2002).

In this chapter the emerging condition of post-national membership is discussed around issues of citizenship, commemoration and the politics of memory, and the nature and limits of the idea of a European people. The major claim that is made is that while a distinctive European public sphere is emerging around particular forms of public discourse, there is as yet no European people as such. The most striking expressions of Europeanization in terms of political subjectivity are in public discourse rather than in a particular expression of peoplehood.

European post-national citizenship

The idea of citizenship as distinct from nationality is a departure from the older traditions. In civic republican theory citizenship has been largely associated with the idea of the participation of the public in the political life of the community. This has given rise to a strong association of citizenship with civil society and in general with a definition of citizenship as an active condition. In liberal theory, which has tended to stress the passive dimension of citizenship, what is important is that it is a legal status, based on rights and duties. In these conceptions, despite their differences, citizenship is something that presupposes a strict definition of insiders from outsiders and, moreover, has a strongly territorial basis to it: citizenship defines the rights and duties of the members of the polity. In general, most modern nation-states have determined a legally codified citizenship as a set of rights incurred by virtue of birth in the territory of the state. Citizenship, enshrined in the passport, thus served as an instrument of state control over its population and as a means of cultural homogenization (Mann, 1987; Hindess, 1998; Torpey, 2000). For several reasons citizenship and nationality have become blurred today. The following brief list will suffice to indicate the degree of bifurcation.[1]

First, notably in the countries of the European Union, residence rather than birth is increasingly coming to be an important factor in determining citizenship rights. Although still based on a prior national citizenship, a legally codified European citizenship now exists as a post-national citizenship albeit one that is based on prior national citizenship (Lehning and Weale, 1997; Wiener, 1998; Hansen and Weil, 2001; Eder and Giesen, 2001). Most civic and social rights are determined by residence rather than by birth. In this respect nationality is not the decisive feature of rights.

Second, in addition to the blurring of citizenship and nationality, the older distinction between the rights of citizenship and human rights is also becoming more and more blurred. In many countries minorities, migrant groups and refugees can claim various kinds of rights on the basis of appeals to human rights, which are now part of the legal framework of most European nation-states (Cesarani and Fulbrook, 1996; Soysal, 1994; Jacobson, 1996). In general, legal pluralism is becoming more and more important. Legal systems are increasingly overlapping, as in the recognition of indigenous law in Canada, New Zealand and Australia. European integration is itself an example of legal pluralism, whereby national and European legal systems are inter-penetrating.

Third, new kinds of rights arising from technology are becoming more important (Frankenfeld, 1992; Zimmerman, 1995). As a result of new technologies, such as communication and information technologies, new reproductive technologies, the new genetics, biotechnologies, surveillance technologies, and new military technologies aimed at populations rather than states, technology has transformed the very meaning of citizenship, which can no longer be defined as a relation to the state. The new technologies differ from the old ones in that they have major implications for citizenship, given their capacity to refine the very nature of society, and in many case personhood.

Fourth, one of the traditional assumptions of citizenship, namely the separation of the private from the public, has been undermined. Feminist theorists have shown how citizenship must be seen as something that extends into the private (Lister, 1997, 1998). In this respect, the politics of citizenship cannot be separated from identity politics. The focus on production and social class, which informed Marshall's account of citizenship, has given way to greater interest in subcultures based around leisure pursuits and consumption. Citizenship is increasingly about the right to express one's identity, as in for example gay marriages or rights for disabled people, developments that suggest a move beyond a liberal notion of cultural protection to stronger demands to articulate new identities (Lurry, 1993; Stevenson, 2000).

Fifth, as mentioned earlier, the rise of group or cultural rights is replacing the previous concern with individual rights and more generally is displacing the older aspiration for equality as the primary aim of citizenship. It is now generally agreed that citizenship is also about the preservation of group differences (Parekh, 2000; Touraine, 2000). Multiculturalism cannot be reduced to policies designed to manage in-coming migrant groups (Hesse, 2000). Migrant groups have become more and more a part of the mainstream population and cannot be so easily contained by multicultural policies and, on the other side, the 'native' population itself has become more and more culturally plural, due in part to the impact of some four decades of ethnic mixing, but also due to the general pluralization brought about by postindustrial and postmodern culture (Delanty, 2000a). The growing salience of culture has implications for Europeanization in the domain of consumption (Cronin, 2002). It is in issues relating to consumption and consumer rights that citizenship is expressed for many people. These new 'cultural' freedoms deriving from the citizen as consumer challenge the traditional assumptions of citizenship in bringing a political dimension into the market.

In view of these developments we can say citizenship has entered the domain of culture which has become both a sphere in which legal rights are mapped out and at the same time a realm in which in major shifts in identity are occurring (Isin and Wood, 1999; Turner, 1990, 1993). There have been several theoretical responses to this trend towards post-national citizenship within political philosophy. Charles Taylor's essay, 'The Politics of Recognition', is one key work in this direction (Taylor, 1994). Taylor's essay established the argument that citizenship must take account of the need for cultural recognition. In this respect his work has been a major statement of what has become known as liberal communitarianism, that is a liberalism that is modified by the desirability of granting official recognition to cultural identities, or in more general terms the need to modify a politics of citizenship based on individualism with one based on community (Mulhall and Swift, 1996). Taylor argued an essential feature of democracy must be the right to protect a cultural way of life. However, Taylor's position has generally been seen as a limited one and confined to the recognition of large-scale national minorities.

In this respect the work of Will Kymlicka offers an alternative, but also from a broadly liberal position (Kymlicka, 1995). His contribution to the communitarian debate has been to argue for the recognition not just of the cultural claims of large-scale subnational groups, but for the recognition of the claims of minorities. According to Kymlicka, the recognition of cultural differences does not endanger democracy. He argues that groups rights can be defended for some kinds of national minorities such as indigenous minorities (who at the time of their incorporation into the state possessed a distinct cultural way of life and territory). However, he does extend this to groups created by migration (who voluntarily gave up their cultural way of life and entered a new society). In fact, Kymlicka's arguments make only very limited concessions to diversity and, like Taylor, are heavily influenced by factors specific to Canada.

Departing radically from Taylor and Kymlicka's adherence to liberal communitarianism, Iris Marion Young has made the case for a differentiated concept of citizenship (Young, 1990, 2000). Her position – in effect an argument for radical pluralism – is one that defends the necessity for group rights in order for minority groups to maintain their autonomy against the mainstream society. Of principal importance in her view is the practical necessity that the rights of citizenship be differentiated in order to make justice possible. Universal citizenship rights fail to secure the practical efficacy of justice, she argues. While her concern is not merely with ethnic groups or large-scale national minorities but of all socially disadvantaged groups, radical pluralism ultimately leads to the implication that citizenship is entirely a matter of justice as such. Although it is not Young's aim, radical pluralism has given legitimation to a politics of cultural difference in which equality is now firmly challenged by difference. Here the aspiration is not simple equality but the right to remain or be different.

The implications of radical pluralism, when taken to the extreme, would undermine the possibility of a shared political culture. However, although largely rejecting the universalistic premises of liberal communitarianism, Young's concerns are mostly confined to specific issues of justice and democratic multiculturalism. Nevertheless, the problem of how to balance universalism with particularism remains a central challenge for post-national citizenship. Jürgen Habermas and Alain Touraine can be mentioned as two leading social theorists who have tried to do precisely this (Habermas, 1998; Touraine, 2000). In their work the universalistic idea of citizenship must be able to accommodate the recognition of particular cultural claims. But this does not entail a compromise as much as a creation of a common civic culture. In Habermas's formulation, the only universalistic normative framework possible in culturally diverse societies is one that is grounded in the constitution and the norms of democratic deliberation. He rejects as not viable the idea of a common ethos underlying the demos and, moreover, rejects the relativistic scenario of extreme pluralism.

The idea of constitutional patriotism advocated by Habermas is not without problems (Habermas, 1994). It has often been criticized for being too minimal in its demands and for making the assumption that all cultural obstacles to citizenship can easily be overcome (Delanty, 1997a). It has been more recently criticized for being a product of the German domestic postwar political culture (Turner, 2004). As a response to these limits within Habermas's position several critics, such as

Gutmann and Benhabib have argued for a stronger cultural dimension to democratic citizenship (Gutmann, 2003; Benhabib, 2002). In these approaches culture is itself a site of democratic explorations, translations and dialogue suspended between particularism and universalism. Where Habermas thinks culture can be transcended and a culturally neutral civic citizenship created, these critics suggest that democratic citizenship is constituted in deeper levels of cultural dialogue.

The dialogic model has gained increased support in much of recent writing. Several studies show that there are costs and benefits in granting minority rights and it is important not to overstate the dangers (Kylimcka and Norman, 2000; Cowan *et al.*, 2001). There are some very convincing arguments that minority rights do not involve a zero-sum game between citizenship and minority rights and that a balance can be achieved between conflicting conceptions of the common good. The view of culture in these studies is far from the culture wars of the 1980s and early 1990s. Culture is not divisive and can be a basis of citizenship. It is unlikely to be a basis of common citizenship in the classic liberal sense, but it is essential to the working of a democratic order and the costs will be greater by not granting minority rights, as there is likely to be increased resentment and hostility stemming from exclusion. Insofar as democracy rests on citizenship – along with representation and constitutionalism – and to the extent that citizenship entails participation in political community, then minority rights are essential. With some 5,000 to 8,000 ethnocultural groups in the world and only 200 states to accommodate them, clearly democracy must find a way of dealing with the reality of ethnoculturalism, as very few states are, or can be, monocultural. The problem is not the validity of special minority rights but establishing their limits. If one group's rights are accepted, we will be pushed more and more into conceding other rights to a point that may make the political unit non-viable. There are also problems of reconciling the rights of different groups, and even in defining what constitutes a group in the first instance, and in problems in reconciling the conflict of the autonomy of the individual with the rights of the ethnocultural group. Yet, there is common ground between cultures and moreover there are few ethnic cultures that are untouched by the critical and reflexive values of modernity (Ong, 1999; Povinelli, 2002; Smelser and Alexander, 1999).

A general conclusion that can be drawn from these developments is that citizenship has been inextricably drawn into cultural issues over identity and belonging. As a result of these developments the form of citizenship is no longer reducible to nationality. It is unlikely that the EU or any transnational body or polity will be able to reproduce nationality, but this does not mean that other kinds of group membership are not possible.

Globalization and the nation: cosmopolitan imaginaries

It was not the aim of the preceding discussion to suggest that the category of the nation has been overcome by a post-national order or that national identities have been rendered obsolete. The decoupling of citizenship and nationality has been reflected in another decoupling process, namely the decoupling of nation and state. While there is no evidence that nations and states are disappearing from the allegedly global age, it is arguably the case that the nation-state as such is undergoing major reshaping, not least as a result of globalization. But globality can be understood only in relation to locality and what is decisive is the way the local appropriates the global. Globalization, itself a multi-faceted process, in fact offers national cultures many opportunities for new expressions of nationality to be codified, ranging from extreme right wing to cosmopolitan projects. The upshot of this is that the local global nexus will not necessarily result in the continuation of state codified conceptions of the nation. Few states today can claim to rest securely on the shoulders of a unitary nation. Exactly what constitutes the nation, where its borders lie and who belongs to it have become major issues in recent years. This means that states cannot simply attempt to secure the political identity of the polity in an underlying cultural identity. National identities are constituted in multi-centric ways and cannot be reduced to unitary or homogenous projects (Jenkins and Sofos, 1996; Preston, 1997; Westwood and Phizacklea, 2000). It is important to recognize that national identities are themselves open to new codifications.

Cosmopolitan currents are evident both within and beyond the nation and can be related to various processes of globalization (Archibugi *et al.*, 1998; Breckenridge *et al.*, 2002; Cheah and Robbins, 1998; Vertovec and Cohen, 2002). As argued in Chapter 1, globalization can be analyzed under various headings, economic, legal, political and cultural all of which can be related to processes of differentiation and integration. Political globalization refers to the new politics of governance on a global scale, that is the growing importance of non-state actors in politics, such as NGOs and global civil society. Legal globalization refers to the growing importance of international law and changes in the nature of sovereignty, but also relates to the increased interdependence of nation-states, which are increasingly embedded in international legal contexts. Economic globalization refers to the interconnected world of global capitalism, markets, information and communication technology, etc. which have all created increased economic interdependencies. Cultural globalization refers to the growing role of transnational culture, societal interpenetration, hybridity and multiculturalism; it refers also to the expanded interdependence of cultural identities. Taking each of these in turn we can see how cosmopolitan influences have reshaped the imaginary of the nation and thus presented new challenges for national identity.

Political globalization has marked a significant turn in politics from the nation and the state to civil society. This is the domain of politics that is distinct from the institutions of the state, such as parties and government, and which is also distinct from the idea of the nation in so far as this is conceived of in terms of an undifferentiated notion of the people or an ethnos. With the growing consolidation of global civil society, national civil societies are increasingly forced to address global concerns. This has clear implications for national identities and for the established conceptions of the nation and prevailing forms of political legitimation. New loyalties challenge older ones and in the ensuing shift in identities and values, reactionary nationalism can be as much the result as a cosmopolitan reorientation of the nation.

Legal globalization is frequently a product of political globalization and is most evident in the growing importance of international law. As discussed in the previous section, international laws, tribunals and treaties are now increasingly embedded in national legal systems. The result of this legal pluralism is a blurring of human rights and citizenship rights. In a wider sense, too, globalization has led to new regulatory regimes in a wide variety of areas – environment, markets, crime, health – resulting in what is often called a crisis of national sovereignty. However, this alleged crisis can also be viewed as the expression of a cosmopolitan sovereignty whereby sovereignty is shared rather than residing exclusively in the state.

Economic globalization is generally seen as the most extreme kind of globalization, often equated with global Americanization. Where the political and legal forms of globalization are multifaceted, economic globalization is 'top-down' and driven by the pursuits of global markets. In the extreme, as in 'McDonaldization', it is a process of standardization and rationalization in which all parts of the world are subject to homogenization determined by capitalism, but a homogenization that does not produce social integration or even system integration. The information revolution is often seen as consolidating this process which leaves little room for the heterogeneity of national cultures.

Cultural globalization in contrast to economic globalization is a process by which globality is appropriated by the local and given new and more heterogeneous meanings. Such processes can be described in terms of hybridity or indigenization. Theorists who stress the cultural dimensions of globalization stress the role of agency and tend to see globalization in terms of global local links. In this view, information and communication technologies and other processes of globalization offer opportunities for national cultures to reinvent themselves.

From the perspective of globalization, nations and nationalism are far from being erased, although they are certainly on the defensive. The nation has indeed lost its capacity to provide a model of social integration based upon cultural cohesion. This is possibly one of the greatest changes occurring in the role of national culture. As many authors have argued, most notably Gellner, nationalism and national identity since the mid-nineteenth century has served to provide modern societies with a uniform system of communication to offset the differentiation – and with it the dislocations – brought about by modernization, such as urbanization, industrialization and migration (Gellner, 1983). The creation of a national culture, achieved through national education, capital cities and architecture, forms of commemoration, state churches, a legally defined citizenship in the form of passports, etc., provided modern societies with a common system of communication and identity. By creating a cohesive cultural order, a degree of social integration was possible. What is different today is that national culture no longer fulfils this function of social integration. Globalization has unleashed numerous processes of differentiation, as well as of de-differentiation, and which cannot easily be resisted by recourse to nation building or nationalism. The nation has ceased to perform an integrative function not just because of the changing role of the nation-state but also because culture in general has lost its integrative function. One such site of the dislocation of culture is memory.

Spheres of memory: commemoration and the politics of peoplehood

Throughout Europe today one of the major sites of symbolic contestation over belonging in the public sphere is memory. Almost every society that has ever existed has had forms of commemoration by which the political community symbolically represents itself, connecting the present with the past. Commemoration, the social construction of time and collective memory are closely linked (Le Goff, 1992; Gillis, 1994; Halbachs, 1980; Giesen and Junge, 2003). Commemoration has been the basis of collective memories, national identities, modes of political legitimation, and re-enchantment. Central to such forms of commemoration are narratives in which collective memory is produced and frequently given a spatial and public dimension. Since the creation of the republican state in Europe and the consolidation of national states from the early nineteenth century the symbolic forms of commemoration have become closely linked with national identities and the projects of the state (Nora, 1996). They have been codified in national holidays, national festivities, marches, and the pageantry of the state and have been encapsulated in material forms such as in national coinages, stamps, monumentalities, and museums. In these forms of commemoration the polity relives its history. Until now most of these acts of commemoration have been the remembrance of the foundation of the nation or state or a major and formative episode in the constitution of peoplehood. Is there a European commemorative event? In one of her last essays, Gillian Rose concluded with the words: 'the victim's resentment is not a memorial legacy of the holocaust still to be "settled", but, I would argue, a foreshadowing of Europe's memorial future' (Rose, 1998: 267). This will be explored in what follows.

In Europe a particularly potent act of commemoration has been the festivities and monumentalities associated with the republican tradition, which has often been related to nationalist liberation wars. Although many of these practices are not the product of the enduring traditions they are often believed to be, and are in every sense of the term, invented traditions, they have the function of enacting history in the present and crystallizing collective identity in symbolic forms. Commemoration is one of the ways the state is able to anchor itself in the everyday world of citizens (Navaro-Yashin, 2002). To achieve this, there are many symbolic forms of mediation by which commemoration is performed and imagined, central to which are forms of commodification (heritage as an industry) but also democracy.

It is of course true that forgetting has been central to many national foundations, as in the example of the Act of Indemnity and Oblivion, passed by the English republican government after the ending of the English Civil War. The Irish Civil War in the 1920s ended with the repudiation of history and there are numerous examples of how states commenced with declarations of oblivion, which should not be equated with the amnesia that Ernst Renan argued is a feature of all acts of remembering: they were expressions of the modernist spirit to renounce the past and commence with a clean slate (Renan, 1990). We can think of such examples as the Nazi book burnings, the Cultural Revolution in China, the Soviet purges of intellectuals. Commemoration occurs only when the political community seeks to know itself. But this presupposes a political subjectivity. States that had a sudden violent origin generally do not seek to commemorate themselves through remembering/selective amnesia: they prefer to resort to the oblivion of memory. That a surge in commemorative debates is occurring today in Europe is particularly significant, suggesting that the era of oblivion is over and a new age of memories is beginning. But what kind of memory is involved? Is it possible to speak of what Margalit has called a European ethics of memory (Margalit, 2002)?

There is much evidence that the symbolic forms and repertoires of commemoration are undergoing major cultural transformation in the present period. The crisis of representation in all of culture has had its impact on the symbolic practices of commemoration which is no longer able to appeal to authoritative memories. These have become more contested and open to new interpretations in recent times. At the same time there has been a huge expansion in commemoration and popular interest in memory throughout Europe which can be seen as an expression of the democratization of the past. As a result of more expansive modes of democratization, multiculturalism, inter-cultural encounters, and authoritative forms of cultural representation are giving way to more reflexive, ambivalent and critical expressions of cultural belonging.

Until recently monuments and memorials were in effect proclamations of the virtues of heroes and leaders, but increasingly they have come to represent ordinary people and forms of life (Lowenthal, 1985: 322–3). Since 1945 war memorials have tended towards abstraction and therefore indicating a democratization of memory, as in the memorials to the Unknown Soldier (Turner, 2005). The myth of the heroic war is now a thing of the past: war is seen as a universal disaster (Mosse, 1990). In Britain, for example, how commemoration should be undertaken has been the subject of wide-ranging debate and has led to new symbolic forms, as is evident in controversies and debates over commemorative forms as different as the role of the Poet Laureate, Orange marches in Northern Ireland, state funerals, the role of the monarchy, the continued significance of the Second World War, and public memorials to Princess Diana.

In 2004 the twin commemorative events of the sixtieth anniversary of the Normandy Landing and the Warsaw Ghetto uprising had a cosmopolitan dimension in a more inclusive mode of commemoration than was previously the case. National monuments and museums now rarely remember triumphant victories, but recall the victims of the past, as Bernd Giesen has argued (Giesen, 2003: 31).

In Ireland the pivotal significance of the 1916 Easter Rising in popular memory and its mythic role in the foundation of the modern republic has been questioned. The seventy-fifth commemoration in 1991 was a low-key event, a contrast to the triumphant fiftieth anniversary in 1966. Fearful of appearing to legitimate republican terrorism, the government distanced itself from the romantic cult of the martyred nationalists. The resulting repudiation of this founding event was a significant turn towards a post-national position on history, effectively announcing its end.

In a similar way the Spanish Prime Minister, Felipe Gonzalez, declared on the occasion of the fiftieth anniversary of the beginning of the Spanish Civil War that the civil war was history and Spain had become 'European'. In 1993 the handshake between Rabin and Arafat in Washington marked a point at which Jewish memories will have to include Palestinian experiences (Young, 1998: 220).

In addition to these developments, there is also a new privatization of memory along with its political neutralization. The solipsistic commemorative events relating to Princess Diana are, in addition to their commercial purpose, indicative of a shift in the nature of public mourning towards post-national acts of personal redemption. The continued public controversy over memorials to the princess, too, is a reflection of the impossibility of a single authoritative, or official, commemoration. The past is not only in ruins, but so too are its heroes.

The crisis of representation has not led to the decline of commemoration, but to new forms and to new discourses about it. Inescapably such discourses are centrally about the changing form of the state and the political community of the nation. Commemoration is now inseparable from the wider question of cultural citizenship, for to commemorate is to make a symbolic statement about belonging. Who and what is commemorated is also a performative act in which the commemorating subject symbolically constitutes itself in an act of commemoration. Public debates today about commemoration are about the meaning such events have for particular groups, rather than just for the state; and for this reason they are related to different subject positions – the subject as a victim, a spectator, a perpetrator (Gray and Oliver, 2001). But fear of contestation is also part of the perpetuation of particular forms of commemoration (Spillane, 1997). The result can be a political neutralization of memory. Another result can simply be a proliferation of subject positions, with more and more demands for a commemorative recognition of suffering. One of the major debates in recent times in Germany indicative of this trend concerns the question of memorials for expelled peoples.

Commemoration in Europe has also changed in another major respect beyond the role of unitary national memories; more and more it has to address the problem of divided loyalties and frequently major national traumas and catastrophes such as war and the persecution of minorities and the implication of large numbers of the population as collaborators (Ashplant *et al.*, 2001; Bodei, 1995; Evans and Lunn, 1997; Huyssen, 2003; Samuel, 1994; Müller, 2003). In this context the question of commemoration as collective memory has to relate forgiveness with mourning.

It is widely recognized that public mourning has changed in recent times, as the examples of the funerals of Princess Diana and the Queen Mother illustrate; it is no longer a mode of political legitimation in which collective expressions of national grief are inseparable from the pagentary of the state. Public mourning is taking more diverse forms, including commodification, but can also take cosmopolitan forms, as the example of new expressions of the holocaust memory indicate (Levy and Sznaider, 2002; Young, 1993). Underlying these changes in the nature of commemoration is a new emphasis on 'cultural trauma' (Alexander *et al.*, 2004).

In an application of the theory of cultural trauma to the question of a European identity, Bernd Giesen has argued that the memory of collective trauma is becoming the hallmark of European identity and having a role comparable to the role that the memory of revolutions had in the past (Giesen, 2003, 2004a, 2004b). But for Europe today, there is no European wide memory of a heroic uprising that includes all Europeans. Instead of the heroic revolutionary tradition of modernity, there is a new European culture of apologies, mourning and collective guilt for national crimes such as the Holocaust and acts of violence against minorities (Cunningham, 1999). This culture of forgiveness is epitomized by the former German chancellor Willy Brandt's famous symbolic act of kneeling in front of the Warsaw Ghetto memorial in 1970. This new cultural development could indeed be seen as more profound than a constitutionally based 'thin' European identity.

But how significant is the rise of the cultural trauma? Can it be the basis of a European identity or is it simply an expression of the therapeutic culture of the age? According to Giesen, the shift from triumphant to traumatic memories has a distinctively European character, as opposed to a national character, in that only in Europe is there official recognition for victimhood and, moreover, he argues, this is the expression of the Judeo-Christian tradition of the confession of guilt through which the individual is purified of wrong-doing. In Giesen's terms this might explain why the Turkish government has so far not made a public apology for the 1915 massacre of Armenians.

This, however, is too simple. It is undoubtedly the case that there has been an increase in the public expression of guilt for the past and in this respect Europe may be different from other parts of the world, where the trauma of genocide has not resulted in the same degree of official acknowledgement. But whether this is the result of the Judeo-Christian repentant tradition alone is doubtful. In terms of a religious explanation, the Christian liturgical cult of the commemoration of saints is as equally persuasive as the confessional culture of guilt. A more plausible explanation is simply a more advanced degree of democratization. The incorporation of more perspectives into the public sphere inevitably results in a pluralization of memories. In any case, atonement for the collective guilt of the past could offer only a very limited kind of European identity. As Andreas Huyssen argues, to collapse memory into trauma unduly confines memory to pain, suffering and loss: 'Memory, whether individual or generational, political or public, is always more than only the prison house of the past' (Huyssen, 2003: 8).

In essence, the thesis that cultural trauma might be the basis of a collective identity for Europeans generalizes from the German postwar experience where there were only victims and perpetrators (Fulbrook, 1999). This is a collective identity for perpetrators and may paradoxically be in contradiction with a genuine multicultural collective identity in so far as it both privatizes memory and increases group competition in a 're-sacralization' of memory (Mistzal, 2004). For such a project to become inclusive it would have to include memories that are not only cultural traumas, which in the cultural trauma theory is a trauma only for the guilty perpetrators in their attempt to create a new national identity through a coming to terms with the past. But this coming to terms with the past can also be an act of political neutralization, with the victim coming to take on the role and function of the subject who can now only know itself through the eyes of the Other. This is not to deny the importance of memory as trauma, but questions its exclusive priority over other expressions of memory.

There is also the danger of overgeneralizing the Holocaust memory. In the postcommunist countries trauma takes an entirely different kind than in the Holocaust memory. The latter may indeed serve as a kind of post-national identity for Germany, but the negotiation of memory in postcommunist societies is more complicated. In the postcommunist countries commemoration has become tied to new definitions of the nation and in many countries it has led to a crisis in the naming of buildings, streets, squares, and monuments. Decades of complicity with the Communist Party and the secret police have ensured that the line between perpetrator and victim is a fine one. Rather than perpetrators, it is a case of collaborators. Not everyone was a perpetrator, but almost everyone was complicit in the Stasi operations. The result is that commemoration will inevitably entail greater self-implication and amnesia may be more likely the result than post-national atonement. In Freudian terms, to recall may be an act of emancipation, but it can also produce new problems, as the debate about collaboration reveals. The post-national repertoire of commemoration as reflected in holocaust memorials in contrast is paradoxically more cosmopolitan in its focus on the victim than on the nation which can exist only in seeing itself from the perspective of the vanquished other. Thus it is not easy to speak of a Europeanization of commemorative repertoires except in the sense of an emerging discourse about the ethics of memory.

It is certainly the case that there are few European-wide memories and much of what is now being called European is devoid of memory. Most memories – including in Foucualdian terms 'counter-memories' – are national ones or ones that are specific to particular groups. One of the major expressions of a tacit Europeanization of memories is in conceptions of peoplehood as expressed in school textbooks. According to Yasmin Soysal, ancestral tribes are increasingly depicted not in heroic terms but in cultural terms. Thus, the Vikings are being reinvented as long-distant traders rather than as Nordic warriors and the crusades are taught not as holy wars but occasions for cultural exchange (Soysal, 2002a: 275). An example such as this one illustrates to a degree a Europeanization of memory, the significance of which lies in a growing public discourse about commemoration and the ethics of memory. Another example is the Europeanization of the holocaust memory. Until recently, this was a German memory, but according to Levy and Sznaider it is becoming the reference point for a European cosmopolitan memory (Levy and Sznaider, 2002). In this respect the politics of commemoration has been reflected in a European-wide change in language. The German term *Vergangenheitsbewältigung* – the overcoming or the past/coming to terms with the past – is one of the best examples of a reflexive and critical approach to the semantics of past in the present. It appears a political community must first be able to distance itself from the past in order to re-imagine itself.

There are also some indications of an emerging culture of memory associated with the EU, although such tendencies are weak. As an administrative and legal framework, the EU is itself relatively memory-less (Schlesinger, 1992; Shore, 2000; Smith, 1992). Moreover, it is unlikely that the EU will be able to create powerful memories, given the absence of a 'European people'. The founding events of the EU – the Treaties of Paris (1951) and Rome (1957) and the more recent ones of Maastricht (1992) and Amsterdam (1997) – have been relatively undramatic events that had little if any symbolic content. The EU's official day, 9 May – the fateful day Robert Schuman launched the plan for the Iron and Coal High Authority – is hardly noticed as the symbolic founding event of the EU polity. The 'founding fathers' were not charismatic figures, but pragmatic functionaries whose experience of war in Europe predisposed them to forget rather than remember the past. There were no revolutionary episodes or programmatic ideologies in the formative moments of the EU, just piecemeal organizational expansion unconnected with ideology and the zeal that had been a characteristic feature of nation-building. Despite the myth around him, Jean Monnet had no great belief or interest in cultural matters.

Yet there is an emerging official commemorative culture, as is reflected on the seven Euro banknotes, each of which displays an architectural style of a period in European cultural history. These designs are non-representational in that they do not refer to a particular building, but to what are obviously symbols of openness and access, bridges, windows and gateways. The central motif of the bridge is a universalistic one devoid of history and memory (Delanty and Jones, 2002). Habermas's constitutional patriotism is the cultural expression of this attempt to construct a new European consciousness; however, it is based neither on memory nor on forgetting, but on discourse. In short, in place of the heroes, fallen soldiers and monumentalities of the past, there is now only the twin alternatives of a memoryless culture focused at best on constitutionalism or the memory of guilt. It is unlikely that there will be a trans-European memory.

While eurosceptics dismiss Europeanization as a project that is by its very nature memory-less, there are dimensions of memory that have been neglected in this debate and which are also not merely the post-Christian traumas of perpetrators. One example is the memory of popular rebellion. While there in no pan European popular movement based on a single people rising up against an aggressor, it is possible to see in this some of the major struggles in modern times, the signs of what Axel Honneth has called a 'struggle for recognition' (Honneth, 1987). From the anti-fascist resistance movement during the Second World War to the revolutions of 1989 and 1990, which brought about the demise of authoritarianism in central and eastern Europe, to the anti-war protests in European countries in 2003, a modern version of a long tradition of public protest can be found. This popular tradition to a degree constitutes a European phenomenon, the cultural significance of which consists of a polyvocal struggle for recognition by different social groups. Cultural traumas are only one dimension of the ensuing transformation and crisis in memory that comes when the secure reference points of the past are unsettled. However, despite their post-national form they are largely associated with the rebuilding of national identities and often reflect official state policies (Young, 1993). There is unlikely to be a new European historical memory based on trauma, although to varying degrees this will continue to be a feature of different national contexts for at least another generation or two. Instead, it may be speculated that the kind of collective memory that there is room for on a European level will be related to other struggles for recognition within the public culture that are not related to the crisis of the grand narratives of nations and the attempts of states to reinvent themselves within a post-national repertoire. The tsunami in the Indian Ocean on 26 December 2004 was marked by a three minute commemorative silence in the countries of the EU on 5 January 2005. It is significant that this was instigated by the EU which requested its member states to remember the victims. This was not the first injuction of the EU for its member states to instigate acts of commemorative silence. In March 2004 the victims of the Madrid bombing were also commemorated in this way. Such forms of memory are neither guilt driven nor triumphant. What is at stake is an ethics of memory and an uncertain notion of peoplehood which is being articulated in the interface of the European and the global context.

To sum up the foregoing discussion, there are four main repertoires of memories that constitute the cultural landscape of the new politics of commemoration in Europe today. First, there are the traditional nostalgic forms of national commemoration, such as the rituals associated with the state and foundational events in the making of a people. In these cases, which are epitomized by marches and the official commemorative acts of the state, the main development that has occurred in recent times is that such commemorative events have become more and more contested along with growing contestation over the political subjectivity of the people who are being commemorated.

Second, marked by a shift from triumphant to traumatic memories, are new kinds of post-national commemoration based on forgiveness and the recognition of victimhood. The holocaust memory remains the paradigmatic instance of such forms of traumatic commemoration.

Third are amnesiac forms of memory, which are best associated with postcommunist countries where the crisis of memory cannot be so easily translated into acts of public commemoration.

Fourth, are cosmopolitan forms of commemoration which aim to give expression to common bonds, as in the example discussed above of the Vikings as a European people or transcultural icons, such as the myth of Europe. Such forms of commemoration often tend towards sentimentality and lack the potency of state based memories. In addition, in this context, the allegedly memory-less repertoires of commemoration associated with the EU can be mentioned under this category.

Whether these forms of memory will be able to express what Adorno and Habermas called a 'critical working through of the past' remains to be seen (Adorno, 1986; Habermas, 1988). Commemoration in Europe has entered a post-historical moment: the political subjectivities that were the basis of collective memories of the nation have become questioned, while new expressions of peoplehood have not yet become fully articulated and may never. While some critics are sceptical that memory can be extended to large groups who have little in common (Margalit, 2002), others believe that a politics of cosmopolitan memory is possible (Adorno, 1986; Derrida, 1994; Ricoeur, 2004). For the moment all that can be said with certainty is that throughout European countries the ethics of memory have become a major site of public discourse on the nature of peoplehood. We are certainly talking about an ethics of memory here but not a collective European memory as such (Margalit, 2002; Hacking, 1998). The European quest for an ethics of memory goes to the heart of issues of democracy, justice, and citizenship.

Is there a European 'people'?

In the present time there is no 'European people' in any of the three senses the term can be used: the people as a *Volk* or *ethnos*, that is a culturally constituted community of memory and descent; the people as a national community defined by the political boundaries of the state and its territory; and the republican or Kantian notion of a people defined by the civic consciousness of a *demos* as opposed to a state. The EU has solved the problem of defining the European people, as Balibar has argued, by simply stating that only those who already possess national citizenship belong to it. In this way the notion of peoplehood is reduced to a legal category that is based on exclusion rather than inclusion (Balibar, 2004: 1991). The first sense of peoplehood as an ethnos is also clearly absent and there is not a desire to create it. Peoplehood is constituted in stories and narratives, according to Rogers Smith (Smith, 2003). Nothing like this has yet been articulated on a European level. The Treaty of Rome (1957) set out the aim of the European project in lofty terms as nothing less than to 'to lay the foundation of an ever closer union among the peoples of Europe'. Jean Monnet said the goal was the unification of 'peoples', not states. Presumably 'ever closer union' would produce *a people*, but the reality is that widespread racism, xenophobia and discrimination against migrants along with national hostilities undermines the possibility of an inclusive European people emerging. To a degree, there is an emerging civic consciousness in different national contexts and which might be said to be close to a distinctively European consciousness. However, a clearly defined sense of peoplehood as a demos is weak.

Yet, many conceptions of post-national community from Rawls to Habermas assume the existence of such a notion of peoplehood. Rawls simply states in his 'law of peoples' that the term 'peoples' is meant to emphasize the 'singular features of peoples as distinct from states, as traditionally conceived, and to highlight their moral character and the reasonably just, or decent, nature of their regimes' (Rawls, 1999: 27).

The problem with the Habermasian cosmopolitan vision of identity, on the other hand, is that it is not rooted in a European people in anything but a minimal sense of accepting otherness and insubstantial notions of a 'common European way of life'. The notion of a constitutional patriotism, when taken out of the German context, loses its symbolic power on a European level where it must distance itself from substantive expressions of peoplehood. According to Charles Turner, it is rooted in the German experience of overcoming the legacy of the Second World War and has only a limited application to Europe (Turner, 2004). The idea of a cosmopolitan European people is thus caught up in the paradox of having to appeal to notions of commonality while denying the existence of an underlying 'We' as a community of fate. If all that binds Europeans together in the post-national constellation is the renunciation of history, there is nothing left to define them as a people in the three senses mentioned earlier: ethnos, demos or nation. This presents the double danger that cosmopolitanism will be unable to defend itself against racism and other extremist movements, on the one side, and on the other will itself end up defining itself by reference to an outside and thus taking the form of a 'Euro-nationalism' (Varenne, 1993). As an illustration of the latter, there is the example of how one of the first and major expressions of European peoplehood consolidated itself in anti-Americanism in 2003. Habermas and Derrida's own declaration of a cosmopolitan European identity was also significantly couched in the language of European anti-Americanism (Habermas and Derrida, 2003). In a newspaper article published in Germany in 2003, Habermas explicitly stated: 'Let us have no illusions: the normative authority of the United States of America lies in ruins' (Habermas, 2003a). According to Cris Shore, fear of Americanization is a recurring motif in EU discourse (Shore, 2000: 52).

For a genuine European sense of peoplehood to be possible there is a need for a language to be created, but the EU has found it easier to create a common currency than a common language (De Swaan, 2001: 144). This need not be a language in the sense of English or French or even a lingua franca, but a medium of discourse. What evidence do we have of a European public discourse?

An interesting example of the new cultural logic of Europeanization is the emerging European public sphere. This is not a public domain that can be compared to national public spheres, in the original Habermasian sense (Habermas, 1989), but rather takes the form of discourses that are common to many societies (Eder, 2000a; van de Steeg, 2002; Perez-Diaz, 1998; Trenz and Eder, 2004). It is not located in a particular public space. What is distinctive about this European public sphere is not so much the existence of a transnational forum – although such spaces are not insignificant – but the emergence of European-wide forms of communicative competence, discourses, themes and cultural models and repertoires of evaluation within different national contexts. The rise of transnational governance in Brussels and the emergence of new networks for the mobilization of opposition and of organized interests, etc. has been of major importance in shaping inter-societal exchanges – and which in turn have also had an impact on transnational governance – but what is really significant is the inter-societal cross-fertilization that is occurring on the social and cultural level in the institutionally unique circumstances of the EU. It is on this level of public discourse that loyalties of a quite novel kind can be generated. The European public sphere differs from conventional public spheres, whether national or transnational, in that it is polyvocal, articulated in different languages and through different cultural models and repertoires of justification, and occurs in very different institutional contexts. But what makes it unique is that it is based on certain common issues and inter-connecting debates in which the community of reference becomes increasingly diluted and, as it does so, reconfigured. However, this has not yet given rise to a European people as such. Yet, it is a medium in which new expressions of cosmopolitanism are taking shape.

Conclusion: Europeanization and public culture

Rather than being integrative and based on an underlying consensus, culture must be seen as fluid and negotiable; it is not fixed or rooted in immutable principles, and is not defined by reference to territory, the state, an elite, a church or a party. Culture consists of different forms of classification and evaluation, cognitive models, narratives, forms of evaluation, collective identities, values and norms, and aesthetic forms. Some of these will be shared, others will not. Culture is primarily a system of communication rather than a form of integration and is always open to different interpretations and to new codifications (see Eder, 2001). We have only to consider the role of the internet and more generally information and communication technologies to see that culture cannot be separated from its modes of communication.

As noted in the previous section, culture is also a medium in which citizenship is articulated, in addition to the classic social, civic and political rights, and cultural rights relating to language, information, heritage, memories, and what in general concerns symbolic expression has increasingly become a focus for citizenship. But social integration cannot be understood solely in terms of agency and culture. The picture of culture that emerges from these theories is one that sees culture as articulated in identity politics: culture while being separate from agency is continuously transformed by agency which is in turn shaped by culture. In Ann Swidler's (1986) view, culture is a tool kit of beliefs, values, norms, symbols, arguments, etc. which can be used in different ways depending on the kinds of situations with which agency is confronted. Like Bourdieu she argues for a performative theory of culture, a notion that is also reflected in Bauman's (1973) concept of culture as praxis or the notion of culture as practices, as in repertoires of evaluation (Boltanski and Thévenot, 1991, 1999).

Integration today more than ever before is sustained by forms of communication rather than by a stable system of cultural values and norms. The cultural form of modern society is responding to globality by becoming more and more discursive.

Societies must evolve the cognitive capacity to cope with the increasing volume of communication. According to Jürgen Habermas no society can simply opt out of the critical and reflexive forces at work in modern culture which has 'rationalized' societies' modes of legitimation to a point that communication is now the cultural form of societal reproduction. The result is that a 'post-national' polity can only be based on cultural forms of commonality that can accept certain basic principles, such as procedural rules for the resolution of conflicts, the need for communicative solutions, and the limited patriotism of an identification with the constitution – a 'constitutional patriotism' – rather than with territory, cultural heritage or the state. It shows how cultural forms of identification and loyalty are still possible and that therefore culture is reconcilable with diversity and is not threatened by conflict but in fact is sustained by the constant negotiation of conflict.

National culture is not to be identified with the state: the nation has become considerably entangled in wider cultural processes to be easily tied to the project of the state. The globalizing world has brought about a new situation for the nation and which is especially evident in the areas of authority and loyalty, conceptions of territory and sovereignty; and national narratives and symbolic structures. The traditional forms of authority have been undermined and new loyalties are emerging, as argued in the previous chapter.

National identities are increasingly taking on a post-national form; they are compatible with multiple identities and require identification only with the limited values of the demos. As Habermas has argued a result of the diversity of the cultural forms of modern societies and the accelerated rate of change, cultures will survive only if they adapt themselves to the principles of discursivity and critique. In these terms, then, national cultures and cosmopolitan values are not entirely antithetical. In this regard a really central question is exactly how divisive is cultural identity. Does the deepening cultural differentiation of Europe necessarily lead to deep cultural divisions that might make a cosmopolitan form of loyalty impossible? As is suggested by some recent American debates, culture may in fact be less divisive than is often thought because there are also powerful integrative forms of communication going on (Smelser and Alexander, 1999). Of course the European situation is different, but the question of the actual extent of the divisiveness of culture cannot be avoided. The critical issue thus is whether the European public sphere can provide a new kind of political community for citizenship based on pluralization and which need not necessarily lead to 'culture wars'. In this view, conflict is not necessarily always adversarial. Despite the apparent rise of nationalism and xenophobic sentiment in Europe, there is much to suggest that other kinds of identity, along with cognitive and symbolic models, are also operative, diluting the resurgent nationalism which is now entering a post-national phase in which nationalism is no longer the dominant force in the state project.

6 The European Social Model
From welfare state to learning society and beyond

The European Social Model (ESM), the EU's projection of its values, norms and core social policy concerns, links many of the themes developed in the earlier part of this book with questions concerning the relationship between European Union integration and the processes of Europeanization. The idea of the European Social Model, a much contested term it should be said at the outset, resonates with debates on the fundamental values, shared history, and political identity to which Europe can lay claim. EU concern with its social model can be interpreted as an attempt to come to terms with the difficulty of establishing a true social dimension to the post-Maastricht integration project. Alternatively, it can be read as an attempt to project an image of the EU as fully orchestrated, possessing the requisite social, civic and welfare dimensions deemed lacking in more critical narratives of EU development. Interestingly, the debate on the European Social Model has arisen at a time when enlargement and the EU's role as a global player have further complicated the question of European identity. In this sense, the ESM can be read as an attempt to construct a coherent identity, not primarily to resolve internal disputes about the nature and direction of the EU project, but to present a united front to the rest of the world.

The ESM connects to debates on societal transformation through, for example, its association with managing the transition to an information or knowledge-based society. It also links debates on the EU's strategy towards its 'near abroad' to wider concerns with globalization: the EU sees its social model as both a defensive reaction to global pressures and a central plank in promoting a 'moral framework for global governance'. Despite its potential for stimulating debate on the meaning and future of Europeanization it has to be acknowledged that the ESM remains seriously underdeveloped as a coherent policy domain – consisting of little more than a number of existing social policy objectives corralled together for convenience or an aspirational account of political community through which to channel newer initiatives, depending upon your point of view – and its relevance and significance are contested by both EU scholars and policy-makers alike. So we start with a paradox: the European Social Model hardly exists, except in EU rhetoric, yet it is exactly what we should be studying.

The EU needs a wide-ranging debate on its social model: to what extent it can lay claim to possess one; the nature and content of the ESM; and its origins and trajectory. In the context of Europeanization, consideration of the European Social Model can be justified on the grounds that if the EU is determined to formulate a social model then it should be the outcome of the broadest possible debate on the nature of the European project. At present, the interpretation of the ESM preferred by the EU can be too easily dismissed as another attempt to secure legitimacy through an appeal to a powerful political signifier in the absence of any compelling link to the lives of Europeans: file alongside European civil society, the Constitution, and a Euro-welfare state. The debate on the ESM provides an opportunity to rethink the functionalist framework within which the social model has emerged and align the ESM and its policy regimes with the more normative idea of a 'good society'. In other words, the recent interest in the transition to a knowledge society not only means that the debate on European society is future-orientated, but invites a much needed injection of social theory into the field of EU studies.

The ESM is an important new direction in EU studies, made more so by its provisional and contested status. Any development in EU studies which focuses on society rather than institutionalization and policy-making is to be welcomed, and it is not difficult to see how the ESM has the potential to place questions of European society at the heart of contemporary European studies. It is particularly relevant to a study of Europeanization and societal transformation as it connects many key themes: globalization, EU governance, external relations, civil society, citizenship, democratic legitimacy, education and learning, European identity, and external relations. However, there is a sense in which consideration of the ESM takes EU studies in a direction in which it is reluctant to travel. EU scholars appear comfortable with the idea that social integration follows economic and political integration and is dependent upon them. This unease is manifested in the tendency for the ESM to be studied less in terms of societal dynamics and more as an instance of the EU-as-state or a reorganization of EU governance. The social model tends to be interpreted as a means through which society can be organized by the state rather than evidence of the potential for society to drive European transformation.

The emergence of a European Social Model

> The European Social Model: many claim that it is not really a 'model', it is not only 'social', and it is not particularly 'European'.
>
> (Diamantopoulou, 2003)

Opinion is divided on the existence, nature and future prospects of the European Social Model. The notion is derided by some commentators for being little more than a wilful projection of an idealized EU self-image and criticized by others as an over-optimistic interpretation of the EU-as-welfare-state. At the same time, many believe in its existence and issue calls to arms to defend Europe's workers' rights, welfare provision and social policies from the perceived threat of globalization and/or Americanization. The idea that Europe possesses a distinctive social model took shape in the 1990s at a time when the impact of globalization on the EU began to be taken seriously by students of EU integration. However, it would be a mistake to view the ESM only as a reaction to the external challenges represented by globalization: it is also very much an attempt to provide the EU and its member states with a future orientation. From the perspective of this book, what is most interesting about the ESM is the way that it has been framed by the EU and its deployment by the European Commission, particularly in terms of a vision of a European society of the future and in its dealings with non-members and the wider world.

Interpretations of the EMS are many and various. One major issue to have emerged is the tension between a multiplicity of national social models and the construction of a unified European social space. Alternatively, rather than a single social model it is possible to identify a number of European variations. Hay, Watson and Wincott (1999) draw a distinction between a generic ESM based on social protection and the institutionalization of class divisions, and an emerging supra-national model propagated by the EU on the one hand, and the survival of a variety of national models, on the other. Other commentators lean towards the view that each member state has its own social model and these can conflict with EU attempts to harmonize aspects of social policy.

The tension between the national and the supra-national runs deep in EU studies and is linked to the way the European project is theorized. The tension has its origins in the assumption that originally there was a Europe of nations which decided, in the latter part of the twentieth century, to come together in a project of integration. Whilst few would dissent from such a straightforward historical account the case can nevertheless be overstated. For example, Le Gales (2002: 114) writes that '[w]ithin western Europe, each national society has followed its own trajectory and undergone its own form of development, contrasting with others'. This superficially plausible narrative can be used to explain national variation in social models and also frames integration as a process which has led to the convergence of disparate societies. However, a case can be made for the convergence of European societies over a much longer period (pre-dating EU integration), and rather than having reinforced differences in culture and social structure it is possible to argue that European nation-states have long been implicated in the dissemination of broader European and world cultural values (Jepperson, 2000). In integrationist accounts of postwar Europe what often gets ignored is the possibility that the mutual interdependence of European nation-states may long ago have contributed to the Europeanization of nation-state society.

Another major axis of the debate is whether we should talk of a European Social Model or a European Model of Society. This may seem a rather pointless distinction, particularly so in view of the rather arbitrary way the terms are often employed by EU commentators, but there is an important distinction, at least historically speaking. The idea of a European model of society was popular with the Delors Commission in the 1980s and denoted the unity of economy, politics and society that was presumed to follow from the accelerated integration associated with the single market. In contrast, the idea of the ESM is more recent and tends to refer to the values which are supposed to underpin the EU project. However, this rule of thumb is not followed consistently in the literature, and in order to establish the lineage of the ESM it is necessary to draw upon sources which refer also to the European Model of Society.

Within the context of a drive for greater economic integration in the late 1980s and early 1990s the European Commission, under the Presidency of Jacques Delors (and later his successor, Jacques Santer), advanced the idea of the European Model of Society as a way of countering criticism that in striving for growth and competitiveness the EU had become dominated by market considerations while downplaying its welfare commitments. Delors' European Model of Society, comprising redistributive policies, social cohesion, and economic liberalization, aimed to balance economic integration with social harmonization and the single market with social protection. Moreover, it was envisaged that economic integration would promote a wave of cooperation resulting in social solidarity and harmonization across Europe. This was a vision of European society as an organized social space, distinct from an aggregation of national societies, and foresaw the EU as a coherent political entity or a Euro-polity. Delors' vision of the European model of society embraced a civilizational unity of economy, politics and culture. It is this which distinguishes it from the idea of the European Social Model which is best thought of as representing a cluster of policy priorities centring on welfare, social partnership and a mixed economy, although the EU is held to be increasingly constrained in its choice of social model as a result of the external pressures brought by globalization.

Contemporary understandings of the European Social Model vary enormously. For instance, the ESM can stand for European labour regimes and their relation to the welfare state (Martin, 2001; Martin and Ross, 2004). Another overtly welfare state interpretation emphasizes the distance between Europe and the US. Europeans have welfare states, Americans do not (Wickham, 2002). According to one commissioner, 'the difference between the European model and the American model is that, for us in Europe, social policy is a permanent concern of the state' (Diamantopoulou, 2000a). More commonly, it refers to either a mixture of employment and social policies, or a basket of principles and values promoting human rights and human development. This distinction corresponds, to a large extent, to another set of concerns which animate discussion of the social model. The ESM is thought to be either under attack, and therefore in need of defence, or a useful vehicle for managing social change. In turn, this schema is associated with the question of whether the ESM is seen as a matter internal to the organization of the EU or an important element of the EU's external relations. Interestingly, the majority of approaches to the question of the European Social Model ignore one very important dimension which deserves serious consideration: the role of education and learning in the construction of a unified European space. This is rarely alluded to in the commentaries, even though the EU makes the connection explicit. One likely explanation for EU studies discounting the learning dimension of the ESM is that education is rarely placed alongside welfare provisions in studies of EU social policy (for example, Geyer, 2000; Kleinman, 2002). In this chapter it is argued that the ESM is best understood in the context of European citizenship, lifelong learning, and the governance of European space.

As indicated above there are two broad interpretations of the ESM, the first emphasizes welfare policies, the second focuses on European values (this is not to say that the two approaches are mutually exclusive, however). Will Hutton (1997: 96) provides a useful summary of the first approach. 'There is a broad European model. There is a commitment to an inclusive social security system, public health and education systems funded from progressive taxation of incomes in all European states'. This vision places great emphasis upon employment, both as the prerequisite for taxation and as a means of social inclusion. It is no coincidence that the ESM was formulated strongly during a period when unemployment in the EU became identified as a major problem (it is worth noting that the Lisbon European Council in March 2000 combined a call for the modernization of the European Social Model in order to manage the transition to the knowledge society with setting the goal of full employment in Europe). As identified by Hodge and Howe (1999: 179), concern for the ESM in the 1990s emerged from within an EU dominated by neo-liberal policy preferences and a general reduction in public spending in EU states. There was a concern that one of the main legitimating mechanisms of the European nation-state – the welfare state – was being undermined by the drive to create new markets and boost competitiveness. As such, the ESM 'embodies both the drive towards a minimal welfare state and the imperative to defend welfare-state functions as important symbolic and practical supports for the further development of the EU'.

Welfare state interpretations of the ESM risk creating an artificial national/supra-national distinction in EU governance (a trend encouraged by the popularity of multi-levelled models): member states have welfare systems, the EU does not. This view is reinforced by the tendency to see economic policy as supra-national while welfare policies remain national (Scharpf, 2002). This is an unhelpful way of viewing the EU at work. For example, Alan Milward (2002: 25) advances the view that 'the EU's inheritance of national welfare states is usually described by scholars, and seems also to be thought of in Brussels, as an intractable problem for supranational governance'. However, this is only so if one insists on seeing social policy as the preserve of the state, which is then viewed as safeguarding society against the depredations of the market. Many advocates of the ESM emphasize that it is not antithetical to the market.

> The European social model is not a barrier to economic objectives. It is not an obstacle to the work of building an open and dynamic market economy … It is a productive factor in achieving strong economic performance. In the European social model, social policy is economic policy.
>
> (Diamantopoulou, 2000a)

On this reading, the ESM aids economic development by creating the environment in which companies can adapt to change, invest in new skills, and promote equal opportunities.

The ESM can also be interpreted as comprising a system of values and principles which are demonstrably European. While this interpretation tends to draw upon a rather tired narrative of a European cultural lineage stretching from ancient Greece to the Renaissance and beyond, it does locate the ESM within a global discourse of rights, justice and world peace. According to former French Finance Minister Strauss-Kahn (commissioned by Romano Prodi in January 2003 to establish a round table to investigate the viability of a 'European model of development') the ESM consists of four components: the inviolability of human rights; culture as a means of emancipation; a model of sustainable development; and a vision of a peaceful international order (Strauss-Kahn, 2004). What is most interesting about this formulation is that it works to establish the ESM in terms distinct from the productivist model preferred by welfarist interpretations: employment and redistribution are displaced by rights and justice. Strauss-Kahn's account of the ESM aims to establish balances between human development and economic prosperity, between economic growth and environmental protection, between wealth creation and welfare provision. Significantly, this vision of the ESM has a marked global dimension: it connects with a world of justice based on the indivisibility of human dignity, and most importantly 'defends the dignity of all human beings, not just of Europeans' (Strauss-Khan, 2004). However, this global dimension is also a source of potential threats, as a result of which the future of the ESM is in doubt.

In recent years, the EU has linked the development of the ESM, globalization, and the EU's relations with the wider world, particularly the near abroad. The idea that the ESM is an aspect of the EU's internal development, mainly associated with welfarist interpretations, has yielded to a vision of the ESM as something that can be exported. The ESM has thus been deployed by the EU as a foreign policy instrument, particularly in its dealing with the near abroad or the 'European Neighbourhood' as it is increasingly referred to (see Chapter 7). The EU stands for peace, stability, prosperity, democracy, human rights, the rule of law, and social solidarity. In this context, the key coordinates of the ESM are formulated in universalistic terms rather than in the specifics of welfare targets and redistributive mechanisms (Prodi, 2004). The European model of regulated capitalism and social justice is held to constitute a model which can be of benefit to the rest of the world. Equally, the EU is increasingly concerned to manage globalization, to give it shape and direction and have it conform to 'European values'. The EU wishes to promote a 'moral framework for globalization based on solidarity and sustainable development'. Announced at the Laeken summit in 2001, this encourages the opening of markets and adoption of EU norms of democracy, governance, respect for human rights, and the rule of law in all the countries with which the EU deals. For Lamy and Laidi (2001), Europe's main collective preference is arguably the pursuit of global governance in order to defend non-market social policies and social solidarity. In other words, the EU believes that under proper management globalization becomes the most appropriate means of safeguarding and promoting the European Social Model and its blend of market and non-market values, which would otherwise be under threat from the expansion of unregulated capitalism.

It is common to encounter the idea that the ESM is under threat. This threat can either come from within the EU, or from external pressures, usually grouped under the rubric of globalization. For Strauss-Kahn (2004), 'the crisis of the European model is primarily endogenous', and consists of a lack of growth, slow adaptation to economic change, and a failure to engage with the needs of citizens (equal opportunities, social exclusion) and the needs of an aging population, as well as a failure to grasp the importance of environmental issues. The external threat stems from the globalization of neo-liberal values and the abandonment of the European model that this could entail. The EU is vulnerable because the ESM has not been institutionalized: the EU's primary concerns are still business and economics, and, as such, 'there is no political embodiment of the European model by the European Union' (Strauss-Kahn, 2004).

Not everyone sees globalization as a threat. According to Kleinman (2002: 58), we should proceed with caution if we wish to push the argument that globalization can threaten the ESM. As there are a range of different social models in existence (in Europe) 'it logically follows that the idea that European Social Policy is about "defending" a European Social Model against, say, globalization, is logically inconsistent'. Rather than defend existing arrangements European social policy in fact seeks to create a European Social Model by imposing one model on all. In this sense, the ESM can be considered to be a 'founding myth' (Kleinman, 2002: 58) of European integration, creating the very notion of Europe which it is then called upon to defend. This is what Tony Judt, writing about European integration more generally, described as the invocation of an 'ontological ethic of political community … adduced to account for the gains made so far and to justify further unificatory efforts' (Judt, quoted in Holmes, 2000a: 95).

There is another dimension to the external threat. It is alleged that the European credentials of the social model have, under pressure from globalization, become Americanized. The concern is that in the desire to harmonize and coordinate social policy across member states the EU runs the risk of privileging the development of the market over social priorities in such a way as to erode the welfare commitment on which Europe prides itself. Majone (1996: 55), for one, sees the rise of a US-influenced 'regulatory state' replacing the more traditional forms of welfare state in Europe. Wincott (2003: 299) concurs: 'the impact of European policy on national regimes has been to introduce and/or reinforce a "new" policy style – of social regulation – that has been influentially identified as "American"'. In the name of the European Social Model the EU, it transpires, has moved Europe in an 'American' direction.

The subordination of social solidarity and welfare policies to the need to consolidate and stimulate markets is advanced by Offe (2002) as a key reason why the EU has not engendered a European society. The association of European integration with markets rather than liberation is one reason why Europeans remain unconvinced as to its legitimacy. In other words, Europeans are aware of a disjuncture between the economic agenda of the EU and its commitment to solving social problems such as unemployment, poverty, and inequality. One consequence, according to Castells (2000c: 357–9), is that European integration has spawned divisive nationalism not European federalism. For Bornschier (1997) the EU represents a compromise between nationalism and liberalism, the latter being the driving force behind growth and development, the former the inherited principle of social solidarity. The problem with these formulations is that they tend to polarize the debate on the ESM, reinforcing the idea that welfare is national and vulnerable, while markets are transnational and predatory (hiding behind the cosy belief that naked capitalism, like fascism, is somehow not authentically European). This in turn fuels the notion that the 'Europeanness' of the ESM is rooted in statist models of social protection rather than in terms of universal values and principles.

What is needed, as an additive to the debate on the ESM, is a sense that the ESM has been shaped by the global context that is increasingly important to the EU's self-identity, and in particular by the increasing competitiveness that is characteristic of the world economy. As it stands, the deployment of the ESM by the EU is an attempt to provide a coherent discourse of social solidarity in a Europe characterized by social diversity, plurality, contestation and fragmentation, on the one hand, and the break-down of previously rigid divisions, such as state/ market, state/society, domestic/foreign, on the other. On this interpretation the ESM is a palliative for a populace which requires the reassurance of policies couched in the familiar language of the welfare state.

Addressing these concerns, Wolfgang Streeck (1999) has developed the term 'competitive solidarity' to capture the ways in which 'national communities seek to defend their solidarity, less through protection and redistribution than through *joint competitive and productive success* – through policies, not against markets, but within and with them, gradually replacing *protective* and *redistributive* with *competitive* and *productive* solidarity'. Equality is to be achieved through access to opportunity rather than redistribution of wealth, balanced economic development through growth rather than redistribution, and social cohesion through competitiveness rather than compensatory mechanisms (Rumford, 2000a). Neo-liberalism induces policy-makers to 'frame policy in terms of competitiveness rather than social goals such as equality or solidarity' (Hooghe, 1998: 463). Put bluntly, this reinforces the logic that 'social policy is economic policy' and invites the conclusion that for many EU policy-makers and politicians markets are the new welfare state.

The ESM has also been associated with the management of social change, particularly in the context of the transition from industrial to the knowledge or information society. This has assumed a greater importance since the Lisbon Summit committed the EU to the goal of creating a competitive and knowledge-based economy, which also involves the modernization of the ESM by investing in people and combating social exclusion. Since this time, the Commission has adopted a future-orientated view of the ESM which is deemed 'central to our ability to manage change' (Diamantopoulou, 2000b). The Commission now prefers to think of the ESM as a combination of minimum standards for the workplace coupled with a set of principles and policy guidelines designed 'to help Member States to reform employment policies, pension policies, anti-poverty policies and healthcare policies' (Diamantopoulou, 2003). What is needed, it is argued, is a dynamic social model which is responsive to changing circumstances. There is another important dimension to managing change and orientating European society towards the future. This is the notion that the EU is becoming a learning society, a development which has particular implications for the relationship between the individual and society and the orientation of the ESM.

The learning society and the European Social Model

> The society of the future will therefore be a learning society.
>
> (Commission of the European Communities, 1995)

The Presidency Conclusions of the European Council meeting held in Lisbon in March 2000 stated that lifelong learning was a basic component of the European Social Model. Curiously, the role of learning and education, although discussed readily enough in the context of increasing competitiveness and meeting the demands of living in a knowledge society, is not usually seen as a key element of the ESM. This is unfortunate as EU interest in lifelong learning reveals an important link between education, work, citizenship and transnational governance. The EU has appropriated the nation-state's functional discourse of education and has evolved the idea of lifelong learning as a way of building Europe (Lawn, 2003). In doing so the EU has constructed a European education space – a European area of lifelong learning – within which citizenship is enacted through a commitment to learning. This betokens a new role for the individual (the responsibilized learner as citizen) in the construction of European space, and a new form of European governance. The addition of lifelong learning as a key element in the social model has shifted the ESM further away from its national and statist origins and placed fresh emphasis on its social and transnational dimensions. It can be argued that the European Social Model finds fullest expression in the European education space.

Modernizing the European Social Model, also identified as a priority by the Lisbon Summit, was a strategy designed to contribute to making Europe the 'most competitive and dynamic knowledge-based economy in the world'. The Lisbon declaration codified the view that knowledge is the key to industrial competitiveness and combating unemployment: education and learning more generally are the keys to economic growth in the knowledge society. This 'educational turn' is significant not least because throughout the development of the EU educational policy has been left in the hands of member states, although there have been 'semiclandestine' attempts to promote supra-national regulation of education policy (Novoa, 2001), and the Commission has been active in promoting both networks of educationalists and a European agenda in teaching and learning (Lawn and Lingard, 2002: Soysal, 2002b). It has also coincided with changes in the way both society and the individual are viewed, speaking from the perspective of EU policy, and a move towards the construction of a European educational space as a governance objective.

The EU now places far greater emphasis on society comprised of individuals rather than a more traditional reliance upon organic notions of society as a 'people' or a nation of citizens. Education is no longer seen simply as a public good but is deemed to be a necessary life project for the individual. As Lawn (2003: 330–1) explains, the individual is encouraged to take responsibility for his/her own learning and contribute to the creation of the knowledge economy. Europe is a vision of the future in which knowledge, economy and society are brought together through a commitment to lifelong learning located in the individual. As envisaged by the Lisbon Council, Europeans are charged with delivering the future. The European educational space becomes the centre of a project to create Europe, and this is to be achieved through combining the citizen, the learner and the employee – citizen as worker no longer: citizen as decision-taking, lifelong-learning, economically mobile individual. 'New citizens will be integrated, successful, responsible and mobile … They will carry with them the obligation to upgrade their learning, a learning related to knowledge and citizenship within a vision called the European educational space' (Lawn, 2003: 332).

Europe as an educational space comprises 'learning territories', particularly cities and regions within which the EU is developing its educational policies and learning initiatives (Lawn and Lingard, 2002). Europe's citizens inhabit these learning spaces and find mobility within the knowledge society. This is not traditional mobility, of either the upward or the geographical kind, but is premised on the necessity for Europeans to move between jobs during their working life, or become 'portfolio' workers commuting between various part-time or temporary jobs. Workers need to be constantly involved in the upgrading of their training and the acquisition of new skills. They have responsibilities to lifelong learning and knowledge acquisition, in addition to commitment to nation or place. Education is less and less the business of state provision (or the state's role is limited to only certain kinds of learning provision) and more and more a project to be realized by the individual. Lifelong learning promotes active citizenship and active citizens make European countries not only more competitive and inclusive, but also more tolerant and democratic (European Council, 2002). They are also more reflexive, having a greater awareness of their role in European decision-making and the rights and duties of both other European citizens and those further afield. Learning societies are reflexive societies.

The emphasis placed on the individual in the construction of Europe as a knowledge-based economy and society marks out Europe as a learning society, a designation which captures the responsibilization of the individual regarding education and learning better than, say, the notion of knowledge society. It also captures the changed nature of society, at once more individuated and geared to managing change. The term 'reflexive society' suggests not only that individuals are more aware of their roles, responsibilities and opportunities but also that the institutions and agencies within society are more capable of acting upon it to bring about change. This kind of society is not fixed or static but highly contingent and provisional, and as such it cannot easily be apprehended in knowledge. As society changes it is imperative that citizens update their knowledge of its goals, workings, and priorities. As Jarvis (2000: 349) points out, 'society has become reflexive and the knowledge that people acquire is no longer certain and established for ever – its value lies in its enabling them to live in this rapidly changing society'. On this view, learning is necessary, not only for professional life, but as a means of coping with an ever-changing social environment. To succeed in the knowledge society, learning has to be part of the individual's daily round and an expression of lifestyle and identity, rather than a calculation based on a rationalization of future needs: lifelong employability has replaced a 'job for life'.

Gosta Esping-Andersen somewhere makes the point that we now live in aging societies in which social policy is directed at the young. The EU conforms to this picture; public policy is very much future orientated. The ESM's alignment with the future has become very noticeable in recent times, particularly in the context of managing the transition to a knowledge society, the importance of lifelong learning, and the transformation of EU governance. As many commentators have noted the construction of the EU is best seen as a process and in terms of becoming rather than as a completed project. While this is undoubtedly the case, it is also true that a new and more urgent appreciation of the future has emerged in EU discourse in recent times. This can be illustrated by the way the EU has used future-orientated imagery in official documents and policy debates: 'Building our common future'; 'Towards a learning society'; the Convention on the Future of Europe; and Strauss-Kahn's working party on 'a sustainable project for the Europe of tomorrow', are all examples. Lifelong learning is key in this context, signifying both the continuous nature of individual development (a project that is never complete) and the investment in the future that this represents, and the ever-changing nature of European society to which the individual must constantly adapt (learning for life).

Enlargement has long been a future-orientated process. This is now joined by the need to develop sustainable models of economic development as a way of expressing solidarity with future generations. The need for the EU to modernize and update its modes of governance has become widely acknowledged, the Strauss-Kahn group concerning itself with the need to promote a 'new Europe' with the competences to be effective both in a post-national Europe and in the wider world. The White Paper on Governance (European Commission, 2001b) highlighted the need to reinvigorate the community method as a model for the future, and warned of the problems associated with applying short-term thinking to long-term problems. Investing in the future, through promoting competitiveness and lifelong learning, helps 'society to anticipate and manage social change' (European Commission, 2004c). Debate on the ESM has revealed that the EU is not only concerned to develop a coherent vision of the future, but that the future itself has become an object of governance.

Conclusion: Europe in search of a society

Despite its increasing relevance to EU integration the European Social Model has not risen to the top of the agenda in EU studies. At times it is ignored altogether, individual social policy issues such as welfare regimes, unemployment, poverty, women's employment rights, and social exclusion being deemed more pressing areas to investigate. When it is addressed directly there is a preference for a welfare state interpretation of the social model, and for some commentators social models and welfare states are synonymous (Hemerijck, 2002). EU studies have a history of assuming that the EU has welfare ambitions. Understandable enough perhaps at a time when it was assumed that the EU would become more like the nation-states that brought it into being, the preference for seeing the EU as a putative welfare state has not diminished with the advent of multi-levelled or network polity interpretations of the EU-as-state. For example, some authors view the Common Agricultural Policy (CAP) as an extension or variant of the welfare state. In some formulations the EU's welfarist ambitions are limited and specific, the CAP representing 'something which could be called a welfare state for farmers' (Rieger, 1996: 104). In contrast, Hix (1999: 252–3) interprets the post-Maastricht reforms of CAP as evidence of a new type of welfare policy which seeks to work in the 'general public interest rather than the narrow interests of the farmers'. The interpretation of CAP as a component of a wider welfare regime is certainly not shared by all commentators, and some have rejected out of hand any suggestion that the EU is developing a welfare state (Pierson, 1998).

Nevertheless, welfare imagery has reinforced the notion that the role of the ESM is to transcend the state/market distinction that has structured nation-state societies throughout the modern period (Rifkin, 2004: 234). The development of the ESM, prior to the turn towards lifelong learning, implicates a discourse of European society which rests on some very questionable assumptions. First, that state, society and economy are distinct realms. Second, that society ameliorates the negative effects of the economy, and that in order to perform this role social policies and welfare protection have to be provided by the state. Third, state and market have privileged roles *vis-à-vis* society in terms of social transformation. The ESM is thus predisposed to see society as a state-sponsored project. This statist vision of the ESM sits uneasily alongside recent interest in other aspects of European society, particularly the positive vision of civil society as a governance partner in a multi-agency networked Europe developed by the Prodi Commission. At the same time, it should be recognized that the EU's interest in society is largely instrumental, and organized civil society is seen as another way in which an integrated Europe can be constructed (Chapter 10).

The idea of the European Social Model as a learning society, although outlined by the EU in many strategy documents, has failed to inspire EU scholars to reconsider the role of society in the grand architecture of European integration. It is perhaps tempting to dismiss the idea of Europe as a learning society as yet more EU rhetoric and/or wishful thinking on behalf of a commission for whom a coherent vision of European society has remained consistently out of reach. The Commission's insistence on subordinating the learning society to the drive for competitiveness deprives it of autonomy and according to one critic, the idea fails to develop much beyond an awareness of the benefits of lifelong learning and technological competence (Field, 1997). However, couching the ESM in terms of a learning society is very valuable from the point of view of aligning EU studies' appreciation of contemporary European society with recent work in sociology and social theory. For a start, the learning society is future orientated and does not seek to locate the ESM in terms of civilizational or historical-cultural commonalities. It also accords society its own dynamics rather than seeing it as dependent upon state or economy. The learning society puts the social back in the European Social Model.

There are four dimensions of European society which are highlighted particularly well by the notion of learning society. First, the global dimension to European society is recognized; namely, that it is one part of a wider global society, and the values upon which Europeanization rest are, in large part, cosmopolitan values. Also, the dynamics of European society are placed in the context of globalization, from which the ideas of learning society and knowledge society take their meaning. It is not possible to conceive of the learning society being something specific to Europe or as a development that can be appropriated, sequestered and managed by European institutions: as the Commission has acknowledged, the knowledge society is a universal society (European Commission, 1995: 10). The question then becomes 'to what extent can Europe claim a stake in a globalized learning society?', rather than the extent to which the learning society has European origins or a peculiarly European configuration. Interpreting the ESM in terms of a learning society emphasizes the extent to which Europe can be woven seamlessly into global processes (which in part constitute it and which the EU in turn may be influential in propagating) rather than the specificity of a European model.

Second, the heightened role of the individual is foregrounded. The learning society is not a society which administers to its citizens in the ways associated with nationally-constituted societies. Citizenship in the European learning society, which in any case has acquired cultural and post-national dimensions as one aspect of Europeanization, is acquired through a commitment to lifelong learning rather than loyalty to a state. The individual is encouraged to view learning as a life project for which he/she has responsibility. Educational aspirations and goals can no longer be measured according to benchmarks of excellence etched into a main pillar of the welfare state. In the words of the European Commission (1995), '[i]t is clear that the new opportunities offered to people require an effort from each one to adapt, particularly in assembling one's own qualifications on the basis of "building blocks" of knowledge acquired at different times and in various situations'. A commitment to lifelong learning requires flexibility and the ability to re-skill in order to maximize the benefits that the knowledge economy can offer. In a Europe in which a return to full employment is not a realistic target (Commission rhetoric notwithstanding) the access to skills provision is a putative welfare state. In the words of former Italian Premier Massimo D'Alema, 'skills are the highest form of social protection' (quoted in Marshall, 2000).

Third, the learning society captures the incomplete and ever changing nature of European society, an idea which is further reinforced by its projection into the future: a society to come. This conforms to the idea that a society must be constructed and reconstructed and that failure to generate, adapt to, and manage change is a major problem. The learning society discourse also emphasizes the role of external pressures (referred to as 'internationalization' rather than globalization in the Commission's 1995 White Paper on Education and Training: Towards a Learning Society) and the formative role of new ideas and challenging visions in bringing forth a new society. The ambivalence contained in the designation 'learning society' points to the role of ideas in forging a new society. Society is geared up to provide learning opportunities for its citizens who must embrace opportunities for lifelong learning, and, at the same time, society itself must learn, it must become reflexive and constantly reassess its needs and the needs of its citizens and organize itself accordingly.

Fourth, the notion of the learning society should serve to increase the importance of society in EU studies' accounts of contemporary European transformation, and encourage EU scholars to look beyond integrative accounts of European society generated by the recent interest in the possibility of European civil society. In fact, the idea that the EU has developed a European education space requires us to investigate the governance role of the learning society. The governance of the EU is best conceived, it can be argued, not in terms of the EU as a form of state but in terms of the way in which the EU constructs European realms through which to extend its networks of power and influence, and the ways in which these networks work through society rather than more formal and hierarchical modes of institutionalization (Chapter 8). In fact, the most important conclusion to draw from this investigation of the European Social Model is that what we need to study in order to understand European society and its role in processes of Europeanization are the nature of European space as a tool of EU governance, the non-state qualities of the EU polity, and the globalized institutional moorings of European (civil) society. These are the topics under investigation in the remainder of this book.

7 Organizing European space

Borderlands, 'undivided Europe' and spatiality beyond territory

Europe is unfamiliar territory. That is to say, Europe conceived as a unified political space is a novelty, and thinking about it requires us to reconsider the territorial assumptions which guide conventional thinking about the spaces of European politics. We are accustomed to think about places as discrete, bounded and nationally-constituted and, in the case of Europe for much of the twentieth century, these places were divided from each other by state politics which sought to affirm the importance of national borders. In addition, the Iron Curtain further divided European countries into antagonistic political blocs, or, in the case of Germany and Cyprus, from themselves (the latter division remaining in place despite EU membership for one part of the island). In a Europe in which governance no longer necessarily coincides with national borders, and peoples, politics and societies are not constrained by territory to anything like the former degree, space can no longer be taken for granted. Invoking the idea of Europe as an integrated and harmonious entity requires new ways of thinking about the spatiality of politics.

The need to understand European space is an important task for social theory: a renewed interest in questions of space over the past decade or so coinciding with a recognition that the spatial organization of society has undergone a dramatic transformation (Urry, 2000b, 2001). In addition, the spatial dimensions of Europeanization (and broader questions of European space) have, until relatively recently, remained at the margins of European Studies. This is changing, partly due to the popularity of the idea of the EU as a post-national polity, and the concomitant reflection on the political spaces of the EU that accompanies it, and partly due to the European Commission's interest in constructing European spaces as part of its governance portfolio, as was seen in Chapter 6. Moreover, the issue of European space has been projected into public consciousness by the efforts of the European Union to forge new and more wide-ranging dimensions to the project of European integration: the 'borderless Europe' represented by the single market and the Euro-zone, for example.

A new spatial vocabulary has emerged with which to understand the nature of European spaces; networks, variable geometry, and multiple 'levels' the most important of them. This lexicon is rooted in a territorial imaginary which works to apprehend the reorganization of space internal to Europe and the efficacy of new external borders. In one sense, the idea of the EU as a networked or multi-levelled polity is no great departure from more conventional approaches to European space. The assumption is of an aggregation or increasing connectivity of pre-existing national spaces (or alternatively as a 'Europe of the regions': the aggregation of sub-national spaces). In consequence, approaches to European space tend to reflect and reinforce the presumed internal coherence of the EU, and the idea of European space has become synonymous with integration and unity.

The network metaphor has come to dominate contemporary accounts of European integration. It has made it possible to rethink the political structure of Europe and to some commentators it has heralded 'the possibility of an ordering of political space which bypassed the nation-state' (Barry, 2001: 90). The idea of network Europe has come to stand for a European Union characterized by connectivity and mobility: a networked polity able to stake its claim in a networked and globalizing world. It is argued here that the network offers only one take on the question of the relationship between globalization and the transformation of European space. Network Europe approaches, with their functionalist emphasis on internal coherence and integration, tend to ignore a number of other pressing issues. First, we should consider ways in which networks do not only 'work' to secure internal coherence but also provide an interface between the global and the local, and break down barriers between EU and non-EU countries. Internal and external developments are not necessarily separate. Second, there is the ability of networks to acquire agency and pursue agendas which may or may not correspond with EU objectives. Rather than assuming that the EU initiates, directs and manages the networks operating within its territory we need to allow for the fact that European networks may possess non-integrative capacities, or may lose their European orientation as they extend to the world beyond. Third, there must be consideration of the nature of the EU's borders. Paradoxically, at the same time as EU borders have become more important in an enlarged union they have also become more differentiated and less unitary. Borders should be seen less in territorial terms as firmly delineated and fixed and more in terms of new spaces ('borderlands') within which the impact of the global on the residual territoriality of the EU can be accommodated. We are witnessing a blurring and reconfiguration of EU borders: from the markers of Fortress Europe to topographical borderlands which reduce the separation between Europe and the rest of the world. Fourth, the novelty of European space should be taken into consideration. It can be argued that we are witnessing the creation of new cosmopolitan (and other) spaces alongside the more conventional aggregations of national spaces (Beck, 2003). On this view, globalization has disrupted traditional nation-state imaginings to such an extent that there now exist a plethora of groups, institutions and individuals who think and act in ways which owe no necessary allegiance to nation-states, for example diasporic communities, transnational social movements, and global advocacy networks. Europe has become a space within which cosmopolitan attachments can generate new networks and new communities. On this reading, new European spaces are not necessarily the outcome of the activities of the EU, nor are they limited to a European scope of operation.

In a number of fields the EU has pursued policies which have sought to constitute Europe as a governable space, and more especially Europe as a space where Europe-wide issues can be acted upon by agencies of the EU (we will consider this further in Chapter 8). Of particular note are attempts by the Commission to construct a European education space (Lawn, 2003), a European planning space (Jensen and Richardson, 2004), a European information space (Axford and Huggins, 1999), and European technological zones (Barry, 2001), in addition to the more obvious attempts at constructing economic space: a Euro-zone for the single currency, and the Europe-wide mobility (four freedoms) associated with the single market (Emerson, 2003). This interest in the construction of European space has been matched by a similar interest in the EU's borders, partly as a result of the recent round of enlargement and partly due to the realization that in a world of global flows and mobilities maintaining a strict demarcation between inside and outside and the policing of external borders is increasingly problematic. This chapter takes as its theme the relationship between the construction of European space as a technique of EU governance and the changing nature of EU borders. To this end it focuses on the recently developed idea of 'undivided Europe' and associated policies towards non-members in the 'near abroad'. Whereas previously the EU was interested in the development of harmonized internal space, its attention is now also directed to the management of non-EU space and new 'borderlands'.

Social theory and space

Space occupies an ambivalent position in accounts of social transformation. On the one hand, space is a defining characteristic of society, given the territorial imagery central to a world of nation-states which Scholte (2000) terms 'methodological territorialism'. However, as Urry (2000b: 416–17) notes, the social structures of national societies have been viewed as uniform to such an extent that they have been rendered aspatial. Beck *et al.* (2003: 12) concur, pointing out that the nation-state depends upon 'the identity of space and people' where territory and citizens become one. On the other hand, some approaches to globalization have suggested that space is 'annihilated' by global networks and flows and the greater interconnectivity of the world. On this view, communities exist without the need for geographical contiguity, and the influence of actors on each other and institutional structures is indifferent to the distance between them. At the same time, many writers have suggested that globalization has resulted in the production of new spaces (Beck, 2002; Robertson, 1992), and that space and place do still matter in a globalizing world (Amin, 2004; Massey, 1993; Sassen, 2000).

Despite past ambivalence, space is becoming recognized as an important dimension of society. Moreover, space has emerged as a crucial dimension of much contemporary sociological enquiry. For example, space is a vital component of studies of mobilities, consumption, tourism, embodiment, nostalgia, community, culture, citizenship, technology, and cosmopolitanism. It is possible to identify a number of key themes emerging from recent studies of the spatial dimensions of society. First, there are the tensions that exist between new social and political spaces and older, territorial arrangements. This can be seen in the case of the European Union where geographically bounded forms of national regulation can clash with pan-European attempts at harmonization. Second, the blurring of borders and the erosion of the importance of the inside/outside distinction can be considered. Territorial space presumes fixed borders which can be policed and defended. The impact of the flows and movements associated with globalization has necessitated a rethinking of the function and meaning of borders and boundaries in the contemporary world. Third, experiential space no longer coincides with that of nation-states. The interconnectedness of individuals cannot be simply mapped onto national territories and cross-border mobilities and supra-territorial solidarities are commonplace. Fourth, and following from the above, a new understanding of relations between individuals, their societies, and the world is required. It is not necessarily the case that local communities can be aggregated up into larger equally cohesive entities. In short, the spatial dimensions of society cannot be taken for granted but need to be studied afresh.

We can identify two key spatial dynamics at work in contemporary Europe (and elsewhere). The first, as identified by Castells (2000a and 2000b), reveals a tension between a space of places and a space of flows; between fixity and mobility. This is the dynamic associated with Castells' reading of the impact of globalization on Europe and embodies the 'network Europe' approach to understanding European space. The second dynamic, seen as less important in much of the EU studies literature, is the tension between autonomy and fragmentation, or in the European context between integration and 'fragmegration' (Jönsson *et al.*, 2000). As we have seen, conventional accounts of the relation between EU integration and globalization see the latter as a catalyst for the former. What is left out of this account is the way in which globalization can work to fragment as well as to integrate. The argument advanced here is that the tendency in the literature to focus on the contradictions between a Europe of places and a Europe of flows (which assumes the integration of Europe) masks more fundamental dynamics which reveal the complex and contradictory nature of Europeanization.

Fixity and mobility

The first spatial dynamic is a tension between an emphasis on territoriality, places marked out by established geographical coordinates, and the fluidity represented by 'network Europe'. In theoretical terms this is the tension between fixity and mobility, foregrounded by an increasing awareness of the impact of globalization on European space – the logic of places versus the logic of networks and flows. The nation-state understanding of space has provided us with a certain imagery of territoriality – boundedness, cohesion, social solidarity, functional integration of administrative levels – which still exerts a powerful influence on the way we think about European space. However, territory is no longer the main or central organizing principle for European space. There is widespread recognition that a distinctly European space (as opposed to the agglomeration of member-state spaces) is emerging, but that the properties, dynamics and potential of this space are not sufficiently understood. To understand European space a new range of images have been introduced: networks, flows, scapes – all of which emphasize the fluidity, mobility and interconnectedness which is characteristic of contemporary Europe.

Castells holds that the network society is constituted by the space of flows which exists in tension with a space of places. The space of flows refers to 'social practices without geographical contiguity' (Castells, 2000b), a world of mobility and networked connections, while the space of places refers to the 'historically rooted local spatial organization of human experiences' (Jensen and Richardson, 2004: 217). Financial markets, transnational production networks, and media systems are organized according to the logic of flows, as are social movements and personal networks. For Castells, the network society signals the advent of the information age and the decline of industrial society: the former relying on a space of flows, the latter on a space of places.

There are two major issues raised by Castells' intervention. The first is the supposed incompatibility between these two logics, which 'threatens to break down communication channels in society' (Castells, 2000a: 459). Castells voices the concern that the two forms of space may lead to polarized experiences of social existence – 'life in parallel universes' – where networks impose themselves 'over scattered, segmented places, increasingly unrelated to each other, less and less able to share cultural codes' (Castells, 2000a: 459). This rather bleak vision is founded on a particular reading of global–local relations, which tends to equate networks and flows with the global and a space of places with the local. For Castells, the global and the local are at opposite ends of the spatial spectrum and therefore can never engage meaningfully: we can see this in his idea that capital is global while labour is local and therefore no longer pitted in struggle, for example. The local cannot challenge the global and the communities of faith, social movements, minorities and other representatives of the politics of identity cannot bring about generic social change. As Friedmann (2000: 119) points out, for Castells local struggles are not sufficient to bring about social transformation (see Rumford, 2002: 20–4 for a discussion of this aspect of Castells' work).

The second is the way in which the idea of spaces of flows has been deployed in EU discourse to sustain a narrative of integration in the context of the relationship between globalization and the EU. To investigate this further we can draw upon the work of Jensen and Richardson (2004). The project of European integration, according to their study of the European Spatial Development Perspective (ESDP), is fundamentally concerned with the construction of a single European space, what they term a 'monotopia'. The single market and single currency are examples of a concerted attempt to create Europe as 'one space' made possible by 'seamless networks enabling frictionless mobility' (Jensen and Richardson, 2004: x). This is a Europe which has removed constraints to the physical movement of goods and people (national boundaries). The trans-European transport networks are emblematic of these developments and represent 'homogenous EU territory linked by a single transport network which seamlessly crosses the borders and natural barriers between member states' (Jensen and

Richardson, 2003: 17). The key words are mobility, accessibility and connectivity: a Europe of global competitive flows has become hegemonic over the alternative idea of a Europe of places. Greater mobility is seen to be the answer to a range of social and economic problems – exclusion, peripherality, uncompetitiveness – and the key to the EU being a player in the global economy (Jensen and Richardson, 2004 : 223–4).

Autonomy and fragmentation

The second dynamic is the tension between the need to maintain sovereign nation-states (and/or the construction of an entity sharing sovereignty at the European level) and the rise of a multiplicity of legitimate actors – regions, cities, localities – independent of national or EU control. In theoretical terms this is the tension between autonomy and fragmentation, central to the dynamics of modernity (Delanty, 1999). This dynamic, generally seen as less important by EU studies scholars, is well represented by Beck's (2002) idea of 'cosmopolitanization' or globalization from within societies. Beck emphasizes that the nature of state and society is undergoing change as a result of globalization and that inside/outside, domestic/foreign assume new meanings. The tension between autonomy and fragmentation also suggests a different relationship between spaces and borders: they are mutually constitutive, and borders exhibit spatiality.

Nation-states have been traditionally considered as the repositories of collective autonomy, and as such have freely entered into the pan-European project of cooperation of unprecedented scope and ambition represented by the EU. However, despite progressive integration (and determined attempts to promote the success of the EU project) the EU exhibits a heightened potential for fragmentation in addition to unity. This fragmentation is manifested in various ways. On the one hand, continuing concerns about the EU's democratic deficit, the widening rather than deepening resulting from wholesale enlargement, persistently high unemployment figures and social exclusion, and the absence of a European public sphere or civil society all point to the incomplete or fractured polity resulting from integration, and, on the other hand, the fact that regions, localities and cities are increasingly empowered to act independently of each other, of their nation-states, and indeed, of Brussels (Albrow, 1998). Such freedoms do not only stem from EU policy: they have extra-EU origins too. One impact of globalization on Europe has been to destabilize traditional social and economic hierarchies and reorder relationships between regions, cities, localities, and the nation-state. This stands in marked contrast to narratives of the relationship between globalization and the EU which emphasize ways in which the former has catalysed integration.

We need also to question the assumption that autonomy or fragmentation is best measured against the coherence of the nation-state. Too often the autonomy-fragmentation question is mapped onto a subnational–region–national state–supra-national continuum which reinforces an integrative and statist reading of the EU polity, all of which works to keep autonomy and fragmentation on a tight rein.

On this reading, fragmentation entails 'breaking down' EU member states into constitutive parts (subnational regions) out of which a new project of integration can be constructed (Jönsson *et al.*, 2000). The position advanced here is that it is necessary to recognize diverse forms of autonomy and fragmentation, many of which cannot easily be domesticated by the EU. Moreover, the tension between autonomy and fragmentation is characteristic of the Global Age, and individuals, social groups, political actors, cities, governmental institutions, policy-makers and many others are all implicated. One of the arguments to be developed is that while conventional accounts of EU integration and globalization concentrate on the shifting dynamics of flows and places, Europeanization also requires an awareness of the (possibly more important) dynamics of autonomy and fragmentation.

To demonstrate these points we will look at the EU's recently developed 'proximity' policies concerning relations with the near abroad centred on attempts to stimulate closer cooperation between the newly-enlarged EU and countries to the east and south. The focus will be on the way in which the construction of 'wider Europe' requires an understanding of the global dimension of EU policy framing, and how EU attempts to construct European space increasingly blurs the distinction between Europe and non-Europe. We will also look at the ways in which the spatial dynamics identified here are manifested in contemporary developments, particularly in the idea of European borderlands. The argument, in brief, is that the idea of the EU as a network society only captures one dimension of contemporary European space, which is characterized by discontinuity rather than uniformity, connectivity rather than unity, and contestation rather than harmonization.

'Undivided Europe': proximity and neighbourhood politics

> An 'undivided Europe' cannot be a united but inward-looking European Union that does not care about what happens beyond its borders.
> (Günter Verheugen (European Commission 2004b))

The European Neighbourhood Policy (ENP) is the clearest manifestation to date of the EU's desire to disseminate its market, democratic, and governance norms beyond its immediate sphere of influence, and forms one dimension of the 'moral framework for global governance' announced at the Laeken summit in 2001, where it was stated that: 'Europe needs to shoulder its responsibilities in the governance of globalization.[1] The role it has to play is that of a power ... seeking to set globalisation within a moral framework, in other words to anchor it in solidarity and sustainable development' (European Council, 2001). To achieve this, the EU decided, it needed to export its social model (see Chapter 6).

There are two features of ENP which are especially significant. First, it represents an extension of EU governance beyond EU borders. It signals that the EU is increasingly concerned to manage non-EU space, particularly that of its neighbourhood or near abroad. Success in constructing European spaces as realms of governance which the Commission can then promote itself as being best suited to managing has led to the idea that non-Europe can also be constructed as a space of governance: countries who are not likely to become official candidates for full membership can be brought within the orbit of the single market and other pan-European projects. The distinction between members and non-members has been replaced by a notion that integration can proceed in new ways. As such, in the wider Europe envisioned by the ENP a large number of countries of the former Soviet bloc and North Africa would be integrated (to differing degrees) within the single market but would not necessarily move closer to full membership of the EU. 'Neighbourhood policy is different from enlargement. It neither prepares for enlargement, nor rules it out at some future point. For the time being the accession of these countries is not on our agenda' (European Commission, 2004b). According to former Commission President Romano Prodi, the EU and its neighbours can share 'everything but institutions'. In short, the EU envisions integration without enlargement.

Second, it represents a blurring of the EU's external borders. The latest round of enlargement has brought with it a renewed concern with borders, not least because the EU's land borders with the rest of the continent have increased from 1,300 to 5,100 kilometres (European Commission, 2004b). The Commission is increasingly aware that one consequence of globalization is that in terms of financial flows, communication networks, and common markets, rigid borders are a source of potential instability rather than a guarantee of security. Internal dynamics and external relations are increasingly interrelated. Fortress Europe has given way to undivided Europe. It is also worth pointing out that ENP has revealed a new vocabulary of spatial politics: 'zones of prosperity', 'proximity politics', 'new neighbourhood', 'wider Europe', 'borderlands', and 'ring of friends' contribute to the construction of an 'undivided Europe', brought together by the EU's initiatives in the fields of economics, security, governance, and human rights. This indicates, amongst other things, that the Commission recognizes the value of constructing new political spaces through which it can extend its governance portfolio. Previously it was the construction of European spaces (single market, single currency, education, etc.) which were the priority, but now it has turned its attention to non-EU spaces.

Managing non-EU space: integration without enlargement

Following enlargement, the EU's attention has turned further east and south. The EU is concerned to promote stability and economic wellbeing beyond the limits of the EU, to create a new zone of prosperity within its neighbourhood. To this end, in March 2003 it published a communication entitled 'Wider Europe – Neighbourhood: A New Framework for Relations with Eastern and Southern Neighbours' (European Commission, 2003). The communication signalled the EU's intention to 'develop a zone of prosperity and a friendly neighbourhood – a "ring of friends" – with whom the EU enjoys close, peaceful and co-operative relations' (European Commission, 2003: 4).

The key to this initiative is the offer of participation in core areas of EU activity in return for opening markets and adopting EU norms of democracy, respect for human rights, and the rule of law. The ENP is more than another initiative to engender greater cooperation on the EU's outer limits. 'The European Neighbourhood Policy's vision embraces a ring of countries sharing the EU's fundamental values and objectives, drawn into an increasingly close relationship, going beyond cooperation to involve a significant measure of economic and political integration' (European Commission, 2004a).

While this would undoubtedly be a welcome development from the EU's point of view we can identify a potential problem: the normal incentives for countries to align with the EU are absent. The Commission acknowledges that 'the incentive for reform created by the prospect of membership has proved to be strong – enlargement has unarguably been the Union's most successful foreign policy instrument'. The EU has no intention of offering Moldova, Armenia, Egypt and the rest the prospect of full membership, thereby diminishing its attractiveness. Moreover, the EU has firm ideas regarding the areas in which it wishes to cooperate. These coalesce around the single market and security measures, and means that the Commission is 'unable to grant neighbouring countries the two benefits that they really want: visa-free access to the EU and free trade in agricultural products (Grabbe, 2004).

Interdependence is seen to be the key to security, stability and sustainable development and the integration of wider Europe is seen to be the best way of promoting EU objectives in the near abroad. Moreover, it is deemed to be in the interests of Europe as a whole to extend the benefits of the enlarged Union to its new neighbours (European Commission, 2004a). What is notable about ENP is that it seeks to blur the distinction between candidate, member and non-member by opening up access to EU programmes to a greater extent than ever before, while at the same time ensuring that agenda-setting and policy-making remains the preserve of the EU. A suitably motivated neighbouring country could participate in EU networks, markets and common policies without the prospect of a formal accession framework. In brief, 'all the neighbouring countries should be offered the prospect of a stake in the EU's Internal Market and further integration and liberalization to promote the free movement of persons, goods, services and capital (four freedoms)' (European Commission, 2003: 10).

The ENP is also significant in that it seeks to promote regional cooperation between neighbouring countries which are not part of the EU. In other words, the EU aims to foster regional cooperation and promote its policies for security, prosperity and stability amongst countries of the Middle East and the Maghreb, even though its direct involvement in these regions is limited. In the words of Commissioner Verheugen, 'I strongly believe that the basic principles of European integration can be applied in those regions to bring about a strong interdependence between neighbouring countries by means of integrating policies and institutions in order to make conflict highly unlikely or even impossible' (European Commission, 2004b). This is in marked contrast to the EU's strategy for the former Communist countries of Eastern and Central Europe following the collapse of the Soviet Union. At this time the EU developed a 'hub and spoke' relationship with each country, one element of which was to deter them from organizing regionally (Gowan, 1995).

Its recent promotion to accession country status notwithstanding (Turkey is due to open accession negations with the EU in October 2005), the emergence of ENP may prove to be bad news for Turkey, the EU's most dogged candidate country. The 'half-way house' solution represented by proximity politics would satisfy many European politicians who see Turkey as a problem. Too large, too poor, and too Muslim to be easily assimilated by the EU, a situation which recent enlargement to the East has brought into sharper focus. Wolfgang Schäuble, deputy head of the CDU in Germany, is one politician who has advocated that the EU should offer Turkey a 'special relationship' that amounts to less than full eventual membership (BBC News, 21 November 2003). There is little doubt that Turkey's recent dealings with the EU conform to the 'proximity politics' model: incorporation into the single market (via the customs union approved in 1995); systematic adoption of the *acquis communautaire*; progressive alignment with EU norms of democracy and human rights as codified in the Copenhagen criteria; and piecemeal participation in pan-European networks (educational mobility, etc.). The recent debate about the possibility of Turkey becoming a member of the EU sometime in the next decade and the opposition to this outcome voiced by some European politicians (notably in France where a referendum is likely to be held before Turkey's membership could be supported) has led to a Commission proposal that the accession negotiations should be 'open ended', in other words that Turkey's eventual accession to the EU is not assured. Thus, the shadow of 'proximity politics' looms large for Turkey, and although anything less than full membership would be extremely difficult to swallow in Ankara, less-than-full membership is a distinct possibility and made more likely by the existence of ENP. Whilst the progress towards fulfilling EU expectations regarding human rights and protection of minorities made by the current government in Turkey has been impressive, and a decade or more of social, political and economic progress should result in eventual accession, the availability of the ENP – which will itself be more developed in ten year's time – offers the EU a potential escape route should one be needed.

Blurring of borders

As mentioned above, the EU's recently evolved interest in global governance in conjunction with the 2004 round of enlargement has led to a new appreciation of the importance of the EU's lengthening borders. This interest does not simply revolve around the need to construct barriers to the outside world: on the contrary the EU displays an awareness that rigid borders are extremely problematic and that the key to security and stability is not to create impenetrable frontiers but to increase the permeability of borders and to encourage a range of institutional and other actors to take responsibility for them.

There are four main aspects of this recent interest in and new perspectives on borders. The first revolves around the tension between the need to maintain 'hard' external borders, as represented by the Schengen area (which does not map exactly onto EU space), and the abolition of internal borders represented by the 'four freedoms' associated with the single market: capital, goods, persons and services (Zielonka, 2002). It is common to encounter the idea that borders are becoming less significant between EU member states at the same time as the EU's external border is heavily policed, leading to a defensive shell designed to prevent seepage of the economic gains made by the EU in the face of economic globalization, and the unwanted influx of migrants from the near abroad. A more complex account of Europe's borders has arisen from this tension, and in particular an awareness that the EU's borders are becoming differentiated and can vary in scope and tightness (Hassner, 2002: 43). For example, the EU's security borders are more rigid than its economic, telecommunication and education borders. In brief, the EU's borders are not singular, clear cut and fixed.

The second, and closely related, aspect is the way in which the EU acknowledges the interrelationship between internal development and the external environment, coupled with a realization that it is not possible to conceive the EU as having a rigid internal/external division (for example, demonstrated by the ways in which the single market or trans-European networks already extend to non-member states). According to the Commission (2003: 3), 'Over the coming decade and beyond, the Union's capacity to provide security, stability, and sustainable development to its citizens will no longer be distinguishable from its interest in close cooperation with its neighbours'. This appreciation stems from the EU's interpretation of globalization, which emphasizes both open borders and the interconnectedness of internal and external developments. For example, the European Council's 'European Security Strategy' (European Council, 2003: 2) emphasizes that in a world of open borders, 'the internal and external aspects of security are indissolubly linked', especially in a world in which global terrorism is a particular threat.

The third aspect relates to the way EU borders are perceived to be problematic in a variety of ways: in terms of potential negative consequences for countries on the other side of the border; in terms of the difficulty of policing them; in terms of barriers to trade; and in terms of the creation of disadvantaged regions. In short, the EU is concerned that the recent round of enlargement could create instability on the EU's new eastern borders by exacerbating the difference between rich and poor regions, between the interconnectedness of EU members and the relative isolation of non-members, between a new core and periphery. In the original 'Wider Europe – Neighbourhood' document the Commission made it clear that the EU was determined 'to avoid drawing new dividing lines in Europe' (European Commission, 2003: 4). As such, there are attempts to strengthen cross-border relations between the enlarged EU and its 'circle of friends', focusing on cross-border trade. In recognition of a long tradition of cross-border interchange in the eastern regions the Commission is developing a proposal for a 'local border traffic regime' for the EU's external land borders, thereby facilitating the movements of local inhabitants and maintaining 'people-to-people contacts'.

The fourth aspect is the coordinated management of the EU's external borders, and promoting awareness amongst new member states that national borders with third countries have, after enlargement, become more than national borders: they are also external borders of the EU. New members, 'are in fact now guarding the borders of the Member States of the European Union' (European Commission, 2002: 9). These European borders need to be managed in a common European fashion. The Commission's role is to ensure that the EU has a single external border with non-members, rather than a collection of national borders. There is an understandable concern that the internal security of the EU – an area without internal borders – can be compromised by lax security at its external borders. But the issue here is not just one of border controls, policing, anti-terrorist measures, and security checks of persons crossing at border points. Rather it is focused on the (lack of) coordination between different national practices. 'The current difficulty resides in the need for much greater operational coordination and much greater complimentarity of action between the national services which are responsible for the external borders' (European Commission, 2002: 22). The Commission (2002: 5) has identified several possible weaknesses, 'the purely national management of borders or management under agreements between neighbouring countries' foremost among them. Of course, the management of border controls is one important interface between the enlarged EU and its neighbourhood, and coordinated arrangements can help ensure that productive relations with new partners can be engendered.

In conclusion, we can say that the EU sees borders less in terms of dividing lines between individual nation-states and more in terms of a zone of (potentially) unstable countries: the new borderlands of the EU (Batt, 2003). In the Council's security strategy document (European Council, 2003) it is written that: 'It is in the European interest that countries on our borders are well-governed ... Our task is to promote a ring of well governed countries to the East of the European Union and on the borders of the Mediterranean with whom we can enjoy close and cooperative relations'. It is the EU's wish that its 'ring of friends' reinforce their border controls with other non-EU countries beyond the ENP, such as Russia. This suggests a shift away from Fortress Europe in which border lines must be policed vigilantly towards the idea of borders as buffer zones, comprising a ring of well governed and compliant states.

Borderlands and European space

The metaphor of the network has dominated thinking about European integration in recent times. In addition to academic discourse the idea has found favour with policy-makers and politicians. Former Commission President Prodi (2000b) talks of 'network Europe', a fluid, dynamic, and interconnected Europe in which civil society plays an active role in governance. The recent enlargement of the EU and the accompanying discourses of 'new neighbourhood' and proximity politics have reinforced the idea that the EU is a network polity, increasingly interconnected with its near abroad. The popularity of the term, which can be read as an attempt to come to terms with the new spatial politics of the EU, has worked to reinforce the idea that what is occurring in Europe is integration. The idea of the network has become synonymous with integration and the question of European space has been answered in terms of a new connectivity of existing places. Europe has been narrated as a multi-levelled and networked polity which has undergone a successful internal reorganization as a result of the external threat of globalization.

The argument advanced here is that the question of European space is more complex. The tendency for Europe to become networked has to be set alongside the tendency for globalization to create dynamics of autonomy and fragmentation which cannot necessarily be held in check by the EU. Whereas the construction of networks furthers the cause of integration, particularly where the networks are constructed or sponsored by the EU, other spatial dynamics are less amenable and lead to greater uncertainty in European affairs. Emerging EU policy towards its near abroad has pointed to the need to go beyond the network metaphor in order to understand the question of European space. Put simply, a network-based approach is very good at accounting for the integrative capacity of the EU in its dealings with its near neighbours and broadening European space, but remains blind to ways in which the EU is increasingly blurring the inside/outside distinction in order to manage its near abroad, and misses important dimensions to the question of Europe's borders.

We suggest that the idea of borderlands is an important one in the context of the recent enlargement of the EU and the new-found interest in developing a ring of friends. It also speaks to the complex spatial arrangements which characterize contemporary Europe and acknowledges the autonomizing potential of globalization. The notion of borderlands has both a social theory and an EU studies provenance, usage in the latter case being more descriptive than analytical. The EU's concern not to create rigid boundaries where the newly enlarged EU meets the former Soviet Union has prompted EU scholars to suggest that the identification of common policy spaces, coupled with the promotion of the idea of integration without enlargement, has led to the construction of the EU's eastern edges as 'new borderlands' (Batt, 2003).

A good deal of social science literature on globalization has accorded centrality to questions of borders and boundaries. In one formulation (economic) globalization is creating a 'borderless world' in which capital, information, goods and people increasingly move unhindered across a world of nation-states. As Kofman (2003: 19) points out, a number of theorists, Castells and Ohmae amongst them, 'have been seduced by the allure and simplicity of a world without borders, places and states'. Further, the idea of the borderless world is closely associated with the connectedness of places, and draws upon the image of the network to emphasize the transformative power of the flows which make territorial jurisdictions redundant (Axford, 2001: 115). While there is a certain predictability to 'hyperglobalist' accounts there is no doubt that it is a commonly held assumption that borders are amongst the first victims of globalization.

Other approaches to globalization suggest a more productive relationship, and for some borderlands are examples of the new spaces created by the contradictory logics of globalization. World-systems theorists, for example, place great store by the power of globalization to de- and re-produce borders. The expansion of the world capitalist system creates frontiers and boundary zones which are the 'locus of resistance to incorporation, ethnogenesis, ethnic transformation, and ethnocide' (Preyer and Bos, 2001: 5). However, these are not issues which trouble the EU's attempts to incorporate its near abroad. More relevant to the case of Europe are the ideas on 'analytical borderlands' developed by Saskia Sassen (2001). Borderlands, for Sassen, require borders to be thought of, not as dividing lines, but as circuits which cut across two or more discontinuous systems. In other words, borderlands draw out the commonalities shared by neighbouring regions. In a world of continuous border crossings represented by globalization, borderlands modify and transform spatial identity and undermine the territorial integrity of all parties. Borderlands represent a new spatiality: 'discontinuities are given a terrain rather than reduced to a dividing line' (Sassen, 2001).

The notion of borderlands captures an essential dimension of European space and is more useful in the study of contemporary Europe than the rather over-worked ideas associated with networks. There are four aspects of borderlands and European space which are particularly noteworthy. First, borderlands are 'places where the local, regional, national and international come together' (Hakli and Kaplan, 2002). Whereas network explanations assume that the local, regional, national and supra-nation are separate 'levels' ideally resting upon and sustaining one another in an integrated Europe, the idea of borderlands is suggestive of dynamic spaces which contain all these 'levels' simultaneously, with all the conflicts and contradictions that this co-habitation can generate. In a Europe shaped by globalization it is not possible to simply recast the idea of a bounded polity at other 'levels'. Borderlands are global spaces which can neither be fully integrated or entirely domesticated by the EU. Borderlands contain both core and periphery, members and non-members, global and local, networks and discontinuities. Borderlands can be thought of as spaces in which older territorial arrangements are being dissolved yet co-exist with provisional and shifting orderings of space.

Second, borderlands extend to both sides of the EU border. This differentiates the notion of borderlands being developed here from the more conventional application of the term in EU studies: Batt's (2003) notion of the new borderlands of the EU, for example. The blurring of inside and outside associated with the interpenetrating flows comprising globalization means that the EU's borderlands are not simply on the 'other side' of the EU border. If borderlands are seen as spaces within which the EU attempts to accommodate global processes then Europe can be conceived of as a continuous borderland perpetually engaged in an attempt to fix its territorial and spatial arrangements into coherent patterns while global processes continually disrupt older geographical certainties.

Third, borderlands signify the fragmentation of spatial units previously thought robust. European Union space is not simply constructed out of pre-existing territorial units (regions, national-states) which have been combined in new patterns to create a new supra-national entity. Globalization makes the survival of these units more difficult by, on the one hand, disrupting them from the inside

– Beck's (2002) idea of cosmopolitanization – and, on the other, eroding their ability to sustain themselves as discrete geographical entities. At the same time, the EU works to rescue the nation-state, in the way that Milward (1992) suggested, and also promotes the sub-national region. The EU is caught in a contradictory position *vis-à-vis* its spatial components. In order to counter the threat posed by globalization to the survival of discrete, bounded territories the EU works to sustain both the nation-state and regions. However, regions are not simply building blocks of integration created and deployed by the EU to defend territorial integrity. The EU long ago calculated that regions were the places where globalization could best be accommodated (Rumford, 2000b). As such, they can be identified as conduits of 'globalization from within' and have also been animated by forces beyond the EU.

Fourth, borderlands do not necessarily divide places from one another but can also work to unify (Hassner, 2002: 40–1). As was mentioned earlier, borderlands exist on both sides of the EU's borders, thereby linking what would otherwise be separate or divided realms. Borderlands suture spaces which would otherwise remain separated. Thus, we can identify another logic of integration in Europe, one which derives from the inability of the EU to constitute itself as a supranational polity unifying economic, political and social realms. Borderlands also suggest that the European Union is becoming less divided from the rest of the world: globalization has led not to the separation of the EU from other regions of the world but to their interpenetration. Europeanization suggests both that there are processes at work which are configuring Europe in particular ways and also that Europe is becoming increasingly globalized. This can be seen, for example, in the ways that European citizenship cannot be understood without taking into account the global regimes of personhood rights which inform it, or in the ways that asylum as a site of contestation in European countries links popular politics in European countries to global issues concerning restrictions on the movements of persons.

Conclusion: the 'dynamic space' of the European Union

The EU project has a concern with space at its very core and questions of spatiality and territory are key to understanding EU integration (Berezin and Schain, 2003a: vii). It has been argued in this chapter that in EU studies there is a tendency to see territory as the most important dimension of spatiality. In particular, the idea that European space can be explained in terms of networks has taken hold in EU studies. It has been further argued that networks have been seen as synonymous with integration and, as such, more far reaching discussions of European space have been foreclosed. To correct these tendencies, the network metaphor and its integrative logic needs supplementing with a more developed sense of autonomous and dynamic space. The idea of 'borderlands' is particularly useful in this context as it signifies the indeterminacy of European space and highlights the problems associated with viewing the EU in terms of bordered and integrated territory and undifferentiated, uniform space.

To understand contemporary Europe and the meaning of Europeanization we need a new spatial context. We need to view the spaces and borders of Europe, not in terms of territory and fixed spatial units, but as dynamic zones in which various forms of connectivity (including networks) and discontinuity are continually shaped and formed. Dynamic zones exist where borders between inside and outside are eroded, and where global processes interact with more static territorial arrangements to constitute new local, regional and transnational spaces. European spaces, whether local, regional or supra-national, are forged by the co-existence and connectivity of a diverse range of 'spatial entrepreneurs' for whom creating new European spaces is a major goal: regional government; the European Commission; educationalists' fora; business associations; advocacy networks; and asylum seekers and migrants, twinning committees.

There are three key features of Europe's dynamic space that can be contrasted to a territorialist version or 'network Europe' mapping of the spatial dimensions of Europeanization. First, borders and territory do not have to be coterminous (cf. Berezin, 2003: 4). Borders no longer only demarcate a bounded territory: increasingly they designate emerging spaces – borderlands – best seen as regions of connectivity and interpenetration between neighbours. The latest EU project for constructing European space as a realm of EU governance, going under the name of 'proximity politics', concerns the creation of borders, not as lines or frontiers but as spaces to be governed. Borders have long been a preoccupation of EU member states, one of the few things that they share in common. Indeed, the history of the EU can be read as an ongoing project to come to terms with the problems associated with shifting borders, and at the same time apprehend the meaning of borders (external and internal) in a globalizing world. Through the EU's European Neighbourhood Policy organizing European space has become indistinguishable from managing borders.

Second, and following on from this, space can be represented as discontinuous. This has two dimensions: discontinuity between separate realms and discontinuity within unitary regions. First, we have seen how Sassen's idea of borderlands replaces a more territorialist idea of geographical borders. Borderlands represent forms of connectivity between discontinuous systems. One advantage of this idea *vis-à-vis* the European Union is that borderlands are internal to the EU (as well as external) and the internal space of the EU does not have to be seen as continuous and integrated. This means that it is no longer necessary to account for European space in terms of internal uniformity and coherence. There are obvious discontinuities in EU space. For example, Greece shares land borders with no other member state. Second, one feature of the EU's approach (and that of EU studies) to the sub-national region is the emphasis on internal harmony and coherence. Regions are projected as homogenous, even natural, when they also possess internal differentiation and rather arbitrary boundaries: the 'discontinuous region' as studied by Allen, Massey and Cochrane (1998). Differentiation, variation, heterogeneity and diversity do not necessarily inhibit the creation of dynamic spaces: this is in fact the nature of global/local relations. Dynamic spaces are porous: they allow diversity to be funnelled into locality without requiring the outcome to take the form of a territorially continuous or geographical contiguous region.

Third, dynamic spaces do not distinguish between networked and non-networked places, as Castells does. His idea of 'parallel universes' suggests that a big gap has opened up between networked Europe and those places not on the network. This is akin to suggesting that there can be globalized and non-globalized spaces, an idea which derives from a reading of globalization which suggests that the global 'level' connects activities and processes which span the global or which have global reach. These can be contrasted to local activities or places which are recipients of globalization. The ideas of dynamic zones suggests that spaces and places can be situated within a new framework of connectivity. Ideas associated with discrete 'levels' need to be replaced by a notion of spaces interpenetrated by the global, local and national, in the context of which the conventional idea of inside and outside, domestic and international, no longer holds.

This chapter has sought to understand the changing relationship between European space and European borders and how these have been articulated with EU discourses of governance. It has been argued that the dynamic nature of European spaces is a central component of Europeanization. The chapters that follow utilize the insights on the spatial dimensions of the EU project developed here in order to better understand the nature of the EU state, in terms of modes of EU governance (Chapter 8), and the possibility of constructing a European polity (Chapter 9) or civil society (Chapter 10). As we shall see, the organization of space is integral to both creating European forms of governance and constructing a European society.

8 The European Union as non-state

The spatialization of EU governance

There exists no satisfactory account of the EU as a form of state. Indeed, the question of the EU-as-state has proved to be an intractable problem for social scientists. This is not because social science has been unable to develop concepts with which to attempt to understand supra-national state forms. In fact a great number of novel approaches have been developed to capture the nature of the Euro-state: multi-level governance, network polity, transnational state, infra-national state, metagovernance, regulatory state, quasi-federal polity, etc., all of them at least partially successful in capturing some aspect of the state-like properties of the EU. The problem lies not in the inability of social scientists to construct new models of the state but in that they find it impossible to think of the EU in terms other than that of a state. As such, if the EU must represent *some* kind of state then the task becomes one of finding the most appropriate designation. This has led to a situation where important dimensions of the Euro-state question have been sacrificed to the impulse to categorize and classify the EU according to the norms of political science, inevitably leading to the conclusion that the EU is a unique case and therefore 'represents an *n* of 1.'

Why is the question of the state-like qualities of the EU so high on the European studies agenda? One reason is that the EU is clearly not a nation-state writ large, a super-state, or even simply a collection of member states, but does possess governmental institutions and policy-making machinery and therefore invites comparison with known state forms. There are many other contributory factors. There are those who see the state-like qualities of the EU as being desirable. For example, one interpretation of the European Social Model (Chapter 6) sees the distinctiveness of Europe inhering in statist models of social protection. On this reading the EU should become more like a welfare state. These ideas resonate with more left wing invocations of a welfarist dimension to the EU and the need to protect workers' rights with state-sponsored forms of social protection. Connected with this is the idea that the European social model is under threat and the EU needs to develop state-like qualities in order to organize European resistance to globalization. In other words, European society needs something like a European state to defend it. In sum then, there exists a strong assumption in EU studies that the EU is a state of some description. Reasons for this generally fall into one of two camps: the analytic, which holds that the EU displays state-like qualities therefore it must be some kind of state; and the normative, which sees a Euro-state as necessary in order for the EU to discharge its duties and protect its citizens.

The difficulty in placing the EU within a typology of state forms has led, over the past decade or so, to the consideration of forms of governance through which the EU works. While government is generally associated with national administration and domestic organization, the idea of governance points to a different range of activities both within and beyond the national level: of firms and NGOs, independent agencies and multi- and international organizations, and state activities at different levels (local, regional, metropolitan, etc.). So whereas government implies centrally coordinated rule over a territory, governance is not just the business of the state but allows for the involvement of a variety of state, non-state, public, private, national and international institutions, including civil society.

There are certainly good reasons to see the EU less in terms of a state (or collection of states) and more in terms of governance, and this shift in emphasis has produced some positive results. According to Le Gales (2002: 86), there are three features of the EU which suggest that governance is the appropriate approach. First, there exists interpenetration of different levels of government. In short, a state-centred approach is too simplistic to account for the complexity of EU governance. Second, a range of actors and organized non-state interests exist coupled with public policy networks displaying varying degrees of organization. The EU clearly works in ways which go beyond conventional versions of state activities. Third, despite democratic shortcomings 'decisions are made and rules imposed on citizens.' The EU may not conform to the idea of a nation-state writ-large but it does have the ability to make policy and govern its territory, albeit in novel ways. There have been a number of attempts to interpret the state-like qualities of the EU through the lens of governance, and one particular approach, multi-level governance, has become the most common and, many would argue, the most appropriate way to view the EU-as-state.

This chapter examines some recent attempts to understand the EU as a state and/or a novel form of governance, and the way these approaches have gained purchase in social theory explanations of the EU-as-state. As we shall see, social theorists have largely followed political scientists in their attempts to develop approaches to the question of what kind of state the EU represents. In terms of approaches which see the EU as a form of state we will look at the idea of the EU as a regulatory state, associated with the work of Majone (1996), and advanced by Walby (1999), amongst many others. As for governance approaches we will look at the multi-level governance thesis, originally developed within EU studies to account for the growing importance of the sub-national regions (Hooghe and Marks, 2001), and endorsed by Held *et al.* (1999) in their thesis on 'global transformations.' Jessop's (2004) idea of metagovernance, which utilizes Weiler's ideas on 'infrantionalism' and points in the direction of the EU as the orchestrator of a European sphere of operation, is also worthy of mention in this context. We will also look at Castells' (2000c) idea of the European Union as a network state, which combines elements of a multi-level governance approach with the idea that the EU constitutes a novel form of state, and places it all with the context of the impact of globalization on postwar Europe.

Rather than favouring either a statist or governance approach (or even a combination of the two), in this chapter it is suggested that a more productive line of enquiry is to understand the ways in which the EU works to secure the means of government in the face of forces which make effective governance increasingly difficult. In doing so we seek to broaden the question of the EU-as-state and not seek only to identify and categorize its governance structures to the neglect of equally important questions pertaining to the ways in which the EU has formatted Europe as a governable entity – through constructing European policy spaces within which European solutions to European problems can be identified (Barry, 1993). It will be argued that the fundamental feature of EU governance is its ability to construct Europe as something to be governed, and to this end it mobilizes a range of actors (state institutions, businesses, interest groups, professionals, citizens, urban networks, and public-private partnerships) to assist in the project of governing. It is the first part of this formulation that is novel. The second part, the mechanics of governance, are not particularly new, different or peculiar to the EU. In many ways, the EU utilizes tried and tested forms of governance and combines these with familiar state-like approaches. What is innovative about EU governance is the means by which the thing to be governed is constituted as such: the EU actively constructs the European realms which it alone is capable of governing. In other words, the key question is not *how* the EU governs or *who* it governs, but *where* it governs.

Social theory, the state, and governance

Social theory has long been concerned with the state. Traditionally, two alternative conceptions of the state have been dominant. One sees the state as a coercive agency, the other as a moral agency, embodying some kind of social consensus (Bottomore, 1987: 146–7). In contemporary readings these approaches to the state are revealed as complementary (and this is reinforced by many interpretations of civil society and its relation to the state). What both conceptions share is the idea that the state is a territorial container for social life, and many approaches see this as a natural, necessary or desirable state of affairs. In the modern world the nation-state has been the dominant form of political container, enjoying control over territory and borders, regulating the boundaries between the domestic and the foreign, and establishing a degree of internal uniformity (if not homogeneity) in terms of economic models, political processes, religious affiliation, linguistic norms, education and training, etc. Thus, the state has become associated strongly with the idea that it embodies collective and sovereign agency, defending the national territory and/or its people against enemies both at home and abroad.

Over the past twenty years or so social theory has developed a nuanced understanding of the place of the nation-state in the world: the global diffusion of the nation-state form throughout the twentieth century being one of the key features of a globalizing world (Axford, 1995; Meyer *et al.*, 1997; Robertson, 1992). Thinking about globalization has also been one of the main catalysts for understanding the state beyond Hobbesian and/or realist assumptions where the main purpose of the state is seen as constant preparedness for war in a world characterized by threats and uncertainties. Rather than the goal of the state being defined exclusively in terms of defence and security, globalization has foregrounded a broader range of state objectives, namely modernization, rational organization, progress, welfare, rights and justice. Formation of nation-states proceeded hand-in-hand with their mutual recognition and the formation of an international system of states. In the later half of the last century the international system became increasingly regulated and reinforced by international organizations. For Giddens (1985: 291), '[w]ithout the UN and a host of other intergovernmental organizations the nation-state would not be the global form of political ordering that it has become.' In the twentieth century the nation-state became not just the global norm as the basic political unit, but also as the vehicle through which peoples' could both express their sovereignty and demonstate their concern for the wellbeing of the world as a whole.

Opinion is divided on the relationship between globalization and the nation-state. On the one hand, there are those who see globalization as a threat to the nation-state (Barber, 2001; Kaldor and Vejvoda, 2002). The decline of the nation-state is also seen as having a major negative consequence for democracy. On this view, the power of the nation-state is in decline, which for some has accelerated the transfer of sovereignty from member states to the EU. The EU is able to do what member states acting alone could not and resist globalization, for example. Such interpretations tend to support the idea that the EU is becoming more state-like as it works to protect the vulnerabilities of its member states. On the other hand, there exists a broad consensus amongst social scientists that globalization has simultaneously strengthened and weakened the nation-state (Fulcher, 2000; Held *et al.*, 1999; Robertson, 2001; Scholte, 2000). Expectations generated by societies regarding their survival and viability are conditioned by 'an increasingly global sense of how societies should be constructed' (Robertson, 1992: 110).

More important perhaps than the debate on the survival of the nation-state, globalization studies have highlighted areas which the state is unable to control easily: transnational organized crime, terrorism, environmental problems, diseases, and movements of refugees. However, the development of more sophisticated approaches to understanding the role (and limits) of the state in the world has not been matched by comparable developments in understanding modes of governance not directly under the control of the national state. On the one hand, this is not too surprising as supra-national governance can be thought of as a relatively recent development. Predictably there has been a strong interest in institutions of global governance in recent years (Held and McGrew, 2002), matched by that in the role of civil society in emerging global governance arrangements (Chandler, 2003; Keane 2003). On the other hand, supra-national or transnational state forms, as represented by the EU, continue to present problems for social theory, the assumption being that governance mu: in some way from the nation-state: an internationalization of the sta levels of governance, for example.

Statist approaches to the EU

It has become common to follow Majone (1996) and characterize the EU as a regulatory state (Walby, 1999; Abraham and Lewis, 2000). In other words, the EU works not through welfarism and public ownership (the Keynesian state), or through deregulation (the neo-liberal panacea), but by encouraging the development of a panoply of independent or quasi-independent regulatory agencies designed to correct market failure (existence of monopolies or environmental pollution). The EU, rather than acting as a super-state, has set about creating a space across which regulatory innovation can be disseminated, and within which the regulatory systems of the member states can become harmonized. One key theme of the White Paper on Governance (European Commission, 2001b) is the role of independent regulatory authorities in the EU, which now number twenty, working in fields such as the environment, drugs and drug addiction, vocational training, health and safety at work, the internal market, racism and xenophobia, food safety, and aviation safety. In this sense, EU activity has not replaced national activity, but 'created new regulatory responsibilities' (Majone, 1996: 59). Majone's work is important because it supports the idea that the EU is something other than a supranational state and offers an alternative account of the way in which the EU governs: the EU's first governance role is to construct the things that it wishes to govern, in this case a range of Europe-wide activities.

Walby (1999) concurs that the EU does not work through traditional state methods, through redistributive mechanisms (taxation) or the institutions of repression (police, army). The EU has not attempted to institute a European welfare state. Rather the EU is a regulatory state, exercising its legal powers to regulate markets and to deliver social justice in specific areas by deploying legal instruments which 'reach over the heads' of national governments. Walby argues that our understanding of the EU's social dimension must be expanded to include regulatory activity as well as traditional mechanisms of redistribution. In other words, the EU state, which she describes as a supra-state, is not a redistributive welfare state, except in the fields of agricultural and cohesion policy, but it does have a number of policies – such as those targeted at backward regions, social exclusion and re-training – which have a social component. In fact, neither agricultural nor cohesion policy can be accurately termed redistributive policies, although this is the way they are frequently portrayed in the literature (Hix, 1999). Cohesion policy in fact is designed to contribute to the competitiveness of the EU. Neo-liberalism 'induces cohesion policy makers to frame policy in terms of competitiveness rather than social goals such as equality or solidarity' (Hooghe, 1998: 463).

The regulatory state thesis has many strengths, particularly in laying emphasis on the mechanisms through which non-state governance is structured, and has prompted some sociological research on the regulatory activity of the EU, for example Abraham and Lewis' (2000) work on the regulation of medicines in Europe. As with the multi-level governance approach (discussed below) there is insufficient attention paid to the relationship between globalization and European integration. Globalization is perceived as an external threat which has restricted the range of traditional redistributive mechanisms open to nation-states. On this reading, the development of the European regulatory state is a defensive response to this threat, and thereby conforms to the accepted understanding that contemporary EU integration is a response to external forces; globalization as a series of threats or challenges which have resulted in greater economic integration, political coherence, and which has enabled the EU to control (regulate) internal developments.

Castells (2000c) terms the European Union a network state, the result of a transfer of sovereignty from the national to supranational level. The resulting Euro-polity takes the form of a complex network of European, national and sub-national institutions mixing together federal, supranational and intergovernmental arrangements for exercising power. To understand Castells' ideas on Europe and the network state it is first necessary to appreciate the extent to which they are shaped by his interpretation of globalization. Networks arise from the need to accommodate various centres of national and regional political authority across Europe and, at the same time, to respond to the forces of globalization. According to Castells (2000a: 502), the original and dominant networks are those of the 'new economy' which is 'organized around global networks of capital, management and information.'

Castells' appreciation of globalization is an economistic one in which global movements of capital and technological knowledge are the key indices. Castells writes, 'the network state ... is the response of political systems to the challenges of globalization. And the European Union may be the clearest manifestation of this emerging form of state' (Castells, 2000c: 364). In Castells' hands the idea of the EU as a network state is an alternative way of formulating the familiar idea that the EU represents a new form of multi-level state comprising institutions of government 'created at the European, national, regional, and local levels' (Castells, 2000c: 339). At the same time, it is the approach which is most obviously aware of the impact of globalization within the European Union, and how European integration, often viewed as a successful defence against globalization, is actually being reorganized in order to accommodate globalization.

Governance approaches to the EU

There has been a marked turn towards governance as the best designation for the way the EU seeks to regulate and manage transnational European space (Rosamond, 2000: 109). Indeed, the impact of the idea of the EU as a multi-levelled polity has contributed in no small way to the more general acceptance of governance as an accurate designation for the way the EU works. In its contemporary usage governance is assumed to operate across different levels. For Scholte

(2001), '[c]ontemporary governance is multilayered. It includes important substate regional, suprastate regional, and transworld operations alongside intertwined with national arrangements.' It is not surprising then that w European studies questions of governance have been dominated by the increasingly influential multi-level governance approach (Marks *et al.*, 1996; Hooghe, 1996; Jeffery, 1997; Hooghe and Marks, 2001). Multi-level governance offers an account of the EU as a series of interlocking and mutually reinforcing levels: regional, national and supranational. Its appeal is that it both strives to capture the capacity of the EU as a complex polity and gives expression to its aspirations for greater democracy, social inclusion, and citizen participation. The multi-level governance thesis represents a positive step in integration studies as it embraces the plurality of levels, centres and agencies operational in the exercise of power. More importantly perhaps, it encourages a wider perspective on European issues and does not emphasize state building or centralized supra-national power as such, but the exercise of rule and authority throughout the Euro-polity. To this end, it has been aided by 'new institutionalism,' an approach to EU integration which advances the idea that non-state institutions and informal structures of governance should be accorded an important role. New institutionalism also places emphasis on the beliefs, cultures and knowledge embedded in institutions. In doing so, it links politics, polity and policy (Bulmer, 1998).

In addition to the emergence of the multi-level governance approach within EU studies there have been moves more generally within social science and sociological approaches to the relationship between globalization and the EU to appropriate a multi-level metaphor. For example, Mann (1998) develops a multi-level perspective on networks of power in the European context, and Nash (2000) and Castells (2000c) utilize the evocative imagery of a multi-level polity. Perhaps the fullest development of the multi-level governance thesis as applied to the relationship between the EU and globalization can be found in Held *et al.* (1999), for whom transnational European space has been impelled by globalization and takes the form of amalgamated levels of governance, displacing but not eliminating the nation-state, which is subject to pressures from supra-national levels of authority creating 'multiple power centres and overlapping spheres of authority' (Held *et al.*, 1999: 441). In relation to the Euro-polity, the transnational level reorders the nation-state level within the overarching integrative framework provided by the EU.

The multi-level governance approach is a sophisticated attempt to understand the complexity of European integration which emphasizes the role of non-state governance and the importance of new institutional networks. In this sense it offers a corrective to approaches which see in the EU evidence of the construction of a super-state or Euro-state. At the same time it advances a rather narrow interpretation of the global dimension in EU affairs, viewing EU integration as a successful response to the threat of (economic) globalization. Globalization is posited as a 'level' beyond the EU which integration prevents it from penetrating. As such, it discounts the possibility that sub-national regions or cities could be animated from beyond the EU (Marks *et al.*, 1996; cf. Albrow, 1998 and Sassen,

2001), or that post-national European citizenship could have a marked global dimension (Streeck, 1996; cf. Soysal, 2000).

The idea that governance comprises a partnership between 'EU institutions, national governments, regional and local authorities and civil society interacting in new ways: consulting one another on a whole range of issues; shaping, implementing and monitoring policy together,' is termed 'network Europe' by former Commission President Romano Prodi (2000b). The debate on the EU-as-state took a new direction as a result of the Commission's White Paper on European Governance in 2001. With its publication, academic work on governance in the EU, which had already developed substantially due to the rising popularity of the idea of multi-level governance coupled with heightened interest in the role of civil society in the architecture of an emerging network polity, found a whole new context for its debates and a new audience for ideas on the polity-like structure of the EU. At the same time, EU policy developments in the field of governance become the topic of widespread and detailed academic debate in a way that transcended the rather narrow focus of much work in EU studies. In other words, the White Paper on governance made EU developments interesting to a broad range of social scientists, and governance in the EU became a 'hot topic' simultaneously in both academic and policy-making circles to an extent not witnessed previously. This had the effect of increasing the interdisciplinarity of EU studies, turning its attention to a range of social issues not previously thought to be of central importance, and providing a forum for contestation over the meaning and direction of European governance, civil society, and harmonized development, amongst other things (Armstrong, 2001; Atkinson, 2001).

The Commission's White Paper understands governance to mean the 'rules, processes and behaviour that affect the way in which powers are exercised at a European level, particularly as regards accountability, clarity, transparency, efficiency and effectiveness' (European Commission, 2000). There are two important facets of this definition. First, the reference to 'rules, processes and behaviour' marks off governance from more statist means of exercising power and points to the EU's interest in new forms of governance such as self-regulation, the open method of coordination, and independent regulatory agencies, in addition to the more familiar governance conduits such as regional and metropolitan administrations, NGOs, public–private partnerships, etc. Second, reference to 'powers exercised at a European level' denotes that the EU is increasingly interested in coordinating the activity of actors and agencies working within a pan-European frame, and also that the EU is interested in promoting and encouraging actors working at the European level. This can be seen most clearly in the case of 'organized civil society' and the way it has become targeted by the Commission as a potential partner in EU governance. Prodi's network society aims to embrace those civil society organizations with a European orientation and a transnational sphere of operation, rather than those operating locally or only in one or more European states: the aim here is the governmentalization of organized civil society. In the Commission's vision of European governance civil society is to be the

means through which emerging forms of state power are to be e>
(Armstrong, 2001: 6–7).

One of the main themes of the White Paper is that the EU can achiev
popular legitimacy through the involvement and participation of its citizens. Civil
society provides the possibility of both the EU working in partnership with a
whole range of non-state actors, giving voice to the concerns of citizens, and
delivering services that meet people's needs (European Commission, 2001b: 14).
Specifically, the Commission seeks to promote participation by involving sub-
national and local governments and civil society organizations in decision-making,
and wishes to enhance its effectiveness by working more closely with relevant
sectors, local and regional governments and civil society in the implementation
of legislation. As Scharpf (2002) points out, the Commission proposals evince a
distrust of member states, whose role in policy-making and implementation the
White Paper seeks to have reduced or bypassed wherever possible.

The Commission would appear to be enlisting the support of civil society and
new forms of partnership in its attempt to alter the balance of power between EU
institutions and member states in its own favour. Additionally, at the same time
as empowering civil society the Commission seeks to regulate it by on the one
hand working to ensure that civil society organizations fulfil the criteria of good
governance (European Commission, 2001b: 14), and on the other by organizing
transnational civil society at the European level. For Armstrong (2001: 6-7),
imposing responsibilities on civil society actors and working towards the
Europeanization of organized civil society are the 'key frames through which the
role of civil society is being constructed within the White Paper discourse.'

The White Paper is particularly interesting in the context of discussions on
the EU-as-state. Although it makes great play of advocating a less 'top-down'
approach to EU governance, and embraces a wide range of policy and non-
legislative instruments, the White Paper has been criticized for giving with one
hand and taking away with the other. After outlining the governance role to be
played by regulatory agencies, civil society organizations, benchmarking, and
voluntary policing of standards, the paper shifts back towards supra-nationalism
by advocating an enhanced role for the Community Method and a stronger guiding
role for the Commission. In short, the White Paper relegates new modes of
governance to a secondary role in the overall EU polity (Wincott, 2001: 3).

Bob Jessop (2004) has recently advanced the idea of multi-level metagovernance in order to apprehend the mix of governance and state-like qualities of the
European Union. Jessop develops this conception out of a critique of governance-
centred approaches, and sees metagovernance as existing in combination with
other forms of governance, for instance states, networks and markets. Importantly,
Jessop wishes to overcome what he sees as an artificial dichotomy between state
and governance-centred approaches. Metagovernance points to a judicious mixing
of markets, networks and hierarchies, and looks towards new forms of coordination
and self-organization. The EU is in a continual process of becoming and hence
cannot easily be characterized according to conventional state schemas. The EU
cannot be characterized by a single pattern of coordination and a fixed pattern of

interdependence. What we have instead is a 'changing equilibrium of compromise.' The EU increasingly engages in 'meta-constitutional dialogue' regarding its future shape and direction, and utilizes 'social dialogue, public–private partnerships, mobilization of non-governmental organizations and social movements' in attempts to further integration and shape policy-making.

To conclude, the success of the multi-level governance thesis can be attributed to the following factors. First, it was accepted widely across the social science spectrum coupled with an endorsement from European policy-makers and politicians. Second, it incorporated civil society, simultaneously giving the model legitimacy and tapping into widespread concern about EU governance lacking a meaningful democratic dimension. Third, its flexibility played a large part. Multi-level approaches can incorporate multi-agency activity and many or few levels, according to preference. Fourth, it was compatible with 'common sense' notions of what the EU is like. Many commentators have found it very useful to appropriate the multi-level governance metaphor as a way of summarizing the essential difference between the EU and more traditional forms of polity.

Constructing EU governance

This chapter seeks to build on these (mainly) political science-inspired approaches in order to develop a social theory alternative. We believe that this alternative will emerge from a shift of focus: rather than looking for evidence of state-building it is important to concentrate on forms of governing within the EU. It is also necessary to engage critically with the current trend to designate as governance forms of government without the state, and question the integrative logic which suggests that EU governance works on a number of 'levels' to further integration and construct an EU state. The EU's governance blend of nation-states, regulatory structures, markets, and non-state partners has one distinctive feature: it requires European domains to be constituted in order that they may be governed.

Urban governance and polycentric development

It would be naïve to think that the EU would ever commit itself to one single form of governance: rather the EU employs a mixture of governance modes. In Axford and Huggins' (1999) neat formulation the EU 'partakes of some elements of state-centred coordination, a whiff of supra-nationalism and a growing amount of non- hierarchical, cross-border networking.' One feature of the White Paper on Governance is that in moving towards a form of governance in which civil society is a central plank, a range of policy tools and coordinating and steering mechanisms have been brought into play. Apart from legislative measures, these include social dialogue, benchmarking, voluntary guidelines, and self-regulation. To this list can be added a range of non-EU initiatives which work to further integration in a number of fields: education, urban management and planning, and social policy amongst them. There exists a range of European actors who work in such a way as to further the goal of European integration but who act

independently of institutions of the EU. This feature of EU govern
researched but is of great relevance to a consideration of both gc
the scope and direction of Europeanization. For examples in the fir
see Lawn and Lingard (2002) and Soysal (2002a); in the field of
Threlfall (2002), and Holmes (2000a). So, EU governance not om,
mixture of state and non-state agencies, and the coordination of non-governmentaı
and non-legislative policy tools, but is being undertaken, to a small degree, by
independent agencies and actors not formally involved (in the sense of being
funded or coordinated) in EU-sponsored projects, although this is not an aspect
of EU governance which will be explored further here.

In order to investigate the nature of EU governance more fully, this section
focuses upon ways in which the EU has developed strategies for the management
of urban regions in Europe. There are many good reasons for studying urban spatial
planning objectives in the context of European governance, not least because it
fits well with the earlier discussions on the European Social Model (Chapter 6),
in which the construction of European education space was seen to be a key
strategy for encouraging European citizenship through a requirement to participate
in lifelong learning. It also dovetails with the discussion on the organization of
European space (Chapter 7), where it was found that the EU's goal of a 'monotopia'
and 'frictionless mobility' was a key component of the drive for competitiveness.

There are other important reasons for choosing urban planning as an example
of EU governance. First, it enables us to further develop the argument that EU
governance is closely linked with the construction of European space. Rather
than state-building the European Commission is most concerned with constructing
European spaces as policy realms over which it has a governance monopoly.
Second, the EU has no urban policy as such (Atkinson, 2001) yet it has developed
strategies for the governance of urban spaces. This rather paradoxical situation
takes us to the heart of the nature of EU governance, which is revealed as a
complex and sometimes contradictory state of affairs. It also suggests that EU
governance cannot be characterized simply in terms of a mix of state, super-state,
and civil society, or as the result of the creation of a networked or multi-levelled
Euro-polity. To understand EU governance we need to be aware of the ability of
the Commission to coordinate a multiplicity of agencies and non-state bodies
and its success in encouraging Europeans to orientate around a common conception of a European issue, and what constitutes an appropriate European response.
In sum, studying urban planning as a mode of governance enables us to see more
clearly how it is possible for the EU to govern in the absence of both state-like
mechanisms and policy competences.

Third, as Neil Brenner (2003: 141–2) points out, urban governance is very
closely linked to the 'rescaling of state space' in the European Union. For Brenner,
the development of EU governance at the local, regional, national and supra-
national level cannot be separated from the way in which urban governance has
encompassed 'not only individual cities and towns but also large scale urban
regions, cross-border metropolitan agglomerations, national city systems, and
supra-national urban hierarchies' (Brenner, 2003: 141). Moreover, the city

occupies a central place in the EU's spatial imaginary, implicated in the idea of 'frictionless mobility' and the transcending of distance in network Europe, and 'framed within EU discourse as a node in an increasingly competition-orientated space economy' (Richardson and Jensen, 2000). Fourth, and related to the preceding point, urban governance is implicated in the EU goal of balanced competitiveness which is central to the EU strategy of becoming the most competitive economy in the world by the end of the decade. The argument here then is that an urban strategy is integral to EU governance, particularly so as the latter has become more and more defined in spatial terms: territorial cohesion and polycentric development have in recent years entered the lexicon of EU governance.

Polycentricity, an idea that has its own social theory provenance in the work of the Chicago School in the early part of the twentieth century (Davoudi, 2003: 979), has, in the hands of EU policy-makers, become associated with the preference for a pattern of economic development which emphasizes the multiplicity of 'centres' in the EU and the need to promote integrated spatial development. Indeed, the EU prefers the idea of polycentricity to the more conventional idea of core-periphery, the latter suggesting unbalanced growth and therefore carrying negative connotations in terms of both competitiveness and cohesion (for an extended discussion of core-periphery relations in the EU see Rumford, 2002 – especially Chapter 7). In contrast, polycentricity stands for balanced growth leading to social and territorial cohesion. The EU's European Spatial Development Perspective (ESDP) – 'the biblical text for European space' (Jensen and Richardson, 2004: 8) – which was finalized in 1999, codified the notion of polycentricity and advocates sustainable development, a polycentric city system, and balanced competitiveness for the EU.

One corollary of polycentric development is the necessity for urban governance: a combination of managing the growth, networking and competitiveness of European cities and organizing the urban agenda in such a way as to further the governance of European space. The Commission has made it clear that the well-being of cities matters to the EU (Atkinson, 2001). The EU is highly urbanized, with around 80 per cent of the population living in urban areas. Further, cities are centres of economic activity and the majority of wealth creation takes place in cities. Urban problems, such as social exclusion, are common to all EU member states and are a focus of remedial policy programmes throughout the EU. Lastly, the EU values cities because they have long played an important role in social and cultural life and the development of 'European civilization.'

As Atkinson (2001) points out, 'there is no legal competence that would currently allow the Commission to pursue the objective of developing an EU urban policy.' While the EU has no urban policy as such, it has developed an 'urban agenda.' Part of the governance role of this urban agenda is to ensure that EU policies which have an impact on urban areas (cohesion, trans-European networks, economic growth and sustainable development) are 'urban sensitive.' The Commission's priorities are to coordinate strategies in different policy domains and encourage cooperation between different levels of government, in short to preside over the Europe-wide coordination of the urban agenda with the aim of enhancing the competitive potential of cities within the framework of the polycentric development of the EU.

Territorial cohesion, defined as 'the balanced distribution of human activities across the Union' (European Communities, 2004: 3) is the designation for the mix of competitiveness and social cohesion aimed for by the Commission. The Commission wishes to develop strategies which would lead to spatially balanced development and avoid an over concentration in the EU's core regions, sometimes referred to as the 'blue banana' – the banana shaped economic heartland of Europe stretching from the south-east of England to the north of Italy. The promotion of polycentrism is central to the aim of territorial cohesion, specifically through the establishment of development centres in non-core regions of the EU. The Commission's position is that polycentric development can be achieved through improving factors of competitiveness, establishing greater cooperation between policy realms, and between governance practices at different 'levels.'

A large number of commentators have dismissed the EU's strategy for territorial cohesion as unrealistic (Atkinson, 2001; Brenner 2003; Davoudi, 2003; Jensen and Richardson, 2004). The main reasons for this being the inherent contradiction between competition and cohesion (capitalistic development produces winners and losers and tends to reinforce the geographical concentration of economic activity), and the fact that the development of lagging regions is predicated on growth rather than redistribution. At the same time, the EU's approach to territorial cohesion does have its supporters who see the goals of increasing competition and reducing regional disparities as compatible, given the right choice of policies (Braunerhjelm *et al.*, 2000). Nevertheless, we can identify five reasons why the EU's drive for territorial cohesion is flawed. One, the need for global competitiveness heightens competition between cities and between regions making balanced development more difficult. Two, the EU is more committed to the economic priorities of the single market and monetary union than balanced development, which while seen as desirable is of secondary importance. Three, the shift from industrial society to knowledge society coveted by the EU will not alter the map of the EU's core regions (Atkinson, 2001). Four, remedial solutions to spatial inequality remain small scale, ameliorative and poorly resourced, and, most importantly, framed by the logic of competition and growth (Allen *et al.*, 1998). Five, ESDP advocates 'healthy competition' but who is to decide how much competition is healthy, and what mechanisms exist to prevent healthy competition becoming unhealthy?

One key feature of European urban governance is that EU strategies are, to a significant degree, framed by the need to manage the problems created by previous governance regimes. On this reading, the abandonment of Keynsianism as a state strategy in the 1980s and 1990s in many EU countries, the rise of entrepreneurial forms of governance, and the consequent growth of regional disparities in Europe (fuelled also by the EU's drive towards the single market) have provided the context for recent attempts to coordinate urban governance. The preference for balanced spatial development, polycentricity, and territorial cohesion has been shaped by the need to compensate for the unbalanced development resulting from previous policy choices. In this sense, European governance represents the governmentalization of governance failure.

Following on from this, and with reference to the criticisms of territorial cohesion advanced above, we can say that the formulation of governance strategies is not simply results-orientated. In the case of the urban agenda the European dimension is more important to the Commission than the efficacy of the proposed solutions. In an environment in which urban regions no longer face the restrictions associated with working exclusively within a national framework for determining economic growth, cities increasingly define themselves in relation to other European and world cities and urban configurations. Globalization is associated with a world of flows: finance, communications, information, persons, diseases, pollution, social movements, and terrorism: 'Cities are, of course, the places that function as initial entry points for these flows' (Le Gales, 2002: 89). While these flows can disrupt the life of cities they also mean that cities pose a potential threat to an orderly European integration, both in terms of importing new ideas, identities and social problems, and in that the city is no longer obliged to work within a national or European frame: global urban connectivity is a growing reality (Sassen, 2000). In such an uncertain situation the EU needs to develop mechanisms of governance through which to harness the potential of European cities, without controlling them too tightly. The EU views the competitive city as a key response to globalization: strategic local spaces positioned competitively within global or supra-national circuits of capital accumulation (Brenner, 2003: 158).

So what, in sum, is distinctive about the form of governance that the EU has adopted in the case of European cities? It is revealed as multifaceted and more complex than suggested by the multi-levelled or supra-national explanations, particularly so as the EU has no urban policy as such. The ESDP, which carries no legal force and exists as a framework for voluntary action, has helped to construct a coordinating narrative through which a wide range of urban initiatives can be rendered complementary. It is responsible for codifying a particular discourse of spatial development which has shaped the urban agenda: the need to combine mobility and polycentricity (Richardson and Jensen, 2000). The ESDP promotes urban networks of cooperation and embraces a strategy for medium and small-sized cities, including cross-border cooperation, designed to enhance the competitiveness of regions: 'cooperation between regions can help overcome counterproductive competition through dissemination of best practices' (European Commission, 2000). As highlighted in the White Paper on Governance, EU governance relies upon the open method of coordination (which emerged with the Maastricht Treaty) through which policy choices remain national but are shaped by common objectives. The shaping of a common agenda is a key element of EU urban governance as is the need to make all EU policies more urban sensitive. In the absence of EU legislation and direct policy-making powers the Commission utilizes a range of methods – exchange of information on best practices, benchmarking, peer review; blaming and shaming; monitoring (Scharpf, 2002). This conforms to the idea that governance is about 'steering, not rowing.'

The EU cannot easily create 'top-down' powers for itself. It can howev
frameworks for interpreting shared problems and a common agenda
disparate actors towards common goals. In fact, the Commission '
orchestration of Europe's urban actors difficult, as each possesses its own powers,
agendas, and a reluctance to be coordinated (Atkinson, 2001). However, this is
not necessarily to the Commission's disadvantage. The difficulty in coordinating
a plethora of agencies, NGOs, enterprises, and state administrations at different
levels creates further opportunities for the Commission to develop a role for itself,
through identifying new governance problems to which its European solutions
can be applied.

The EU's market for gas: national problem, European solution

The single market now embraces the electricity and gas sectors. The form that
liberalization has taken is very much a compromise, and reflects the divergent
views of member states on the issue of the energy market. It is also indicative of a
series of much wider debates on issues such as liberalization versus protectionism,
public service versus competition, and competition versus monopoly rights enjoyed
by power suppliers. Indeed, the EU's energy market is characterized by contradiction between the need to extend competition and the need to ensure security
of supply.

Until recently member states viewed energy supply industries as natural
monopolies to be run strictly along national, protectionist lines. In other words,
their status as public monopolies was justified on the basis that this arrangement
was in the national interest, that is to say, guaranteeing a cheap and regular supply
for domestic industry and household consumers. In short, government of the energy
sectors was largely a domestic matter, policy being determined by member states
and resistant to EU penetration. Despite the gradual liberalization of markets the
energy policy of member states and the EU has still not changed radically. EU
energy policy is caught between competition and cooperation, being fully committed to neither. Security of supply is still the priority, although this is now
couched in EU rather than national terms.

Historically, European governments have been reliant upon imported energy
supplies, and have developed national approaches to managing the problem of
energy dependency. Even the 1973 oil crisis did not inspire member states to
either forge a common European energy supply policy or create a common energy
market. Since this time, some member states have moved in the direction of
ending the state's monopoly over energy supply (notably the UK) but moves
towards a single energy market have been blocked by entrenched national interests.
Despite a gathering momentum towards privatization of state owned assets in
most EU member states over the past two decades, developments in the energy
sector have been much slower.

Until recently the Commission has had limited impact on national energy
policies, despite two of the three treaties upon which the EC was based being
founded upon energy sectors (the ECSC Treaty included coal, and the Euratom

Treaty nuclear energy). Indeed, it has been suggested that member states were more worried about the impact of a common energy policy, than the introduction of a single market for energy (Matlary, 1996: 262). In the mid-1980s it did gain some influence in the area of setting objectives for reducing the overall reliance upon imported energy, but this 'could hardly be thought to constitute a comprehensive Community energy policy' (McGowan, 1996: 145). The situation began to change however as a result of several factors, especially the ever-increasing reliance upon imported energy, the development of plans for the single market, and the need for increased environmental protection. The Commission adopted the role of 'policy entrepreneur,' working to encourage national agencies to identify with a common community perspective, for example, the introduction of an energy tax to encourage greater efficiency and to discourage the use of fossil fuels. Similarly, competition rules place restrictions on the activities of member states and allow the Commission to police their application.

The overarching concern for security of supply manifests itself in the EU's plan to establish cooperative links with major non-EU energy producers. The European Energy Charter is an international legal treaty that aims at stabilizing investment rules for energy exploration, production and transport in the signatory countries. It was adopted in December 1990 as a way of promoting energy co-operation on a Europe-wide basis and facilitating investment in the former Soviet Union. A legally binding Energy Charter Treaty (ECT) was subsequently signed in December 1994 by most western and industrialized countries. The objective of the Energy Charter Treaty is to 'liberalise the trade of energy products and materials between the fifty signatory states' (Touscoz, 1997: 23). But at the same time the ECT is the instrument through which the EU aims to fulfill its ambition to ensure security of supply, particularly from the former Soviet Union. According to Andersen (2000), it was a compromise designed to incorporate national concerns within a broader European perspective: strengthening market solutions while respecting national traditions. The Energy Charter Treaty subordinates competition to cooperation in its desire to ensure security of supply, which works to both undermine national monopolies in the sector and allows for new structures of government to oversee the management of the European strategy.

The Commission's attempt to develop the energy market within a broader policy framework is a good example of EU governance priorities: creating a European space within which a portfolio of energy policies, including environmental protection, the single market and the security of supply, can be deployed in such a way as to introduce European mechanisms of governance to replace those which were resolutely national in scope and operation. The EU is aided in this by the presence of influential pressure groups in the field of environmental protection – whose lobbying activities are subsidized from the EU budget (Hix, 1999: 226) – who have helped create the context in which a coalition of agencies, NGOs and activists favour problems being dealt with at the European level. In short, the Commission has promoted Europe-wide issues for the gas sector which require European solutions which only the EU is equipped to provide.

The policy areas covered in this section – urban regions and gas – could be supplemented with accounts of the changing government structures in respect of other key EU policies: agriculture, the single market, regional and cohesion policy, European civil society, and many others. In all cases, the EU has acted to secure the means of government in response to a new set of challenges. The challenges either take the form of a recognition of situations in which Europe is caught up in profound social and political change, the dynamics of which are beyond the control of the EU, or situations where the European Commission seeks to extend its influence into new areas of competence, thereby circumventing national political structures. The Commission is able to posit the existence of pan-European problems which it alone can mobilize to offset, thereby extending its influence over the integration process and its range of competencies (another good example would be its heralding the problem of the 'democratic deficit' in the early 1990s). In all cases, the challenges are linked to the problem of how best to manage/ accommodate/ameliorate the impact of globalization on the EU.

Conclusion: a new model of European governance

The transformation of the state is central to Europeanization. Governance has been central to this transformation. We can say the shift from state-centric rule to governance has allowed the EU to become more than a collection of nation-states, and upon this foundation the EU has developed new forms of governance in order to become a major actor in the world. The construction of a European space upon which the EU can project its policy preferences and future orientation signals a concern to establish new forms of governance in an environment where traditional (nation-state) forms of government are increasingly found wanting. In this way, the EU is constantly engaged in the negotiation of its government capacities (Nash, 2001: 87).

There are two main aspects of EU governance which have been revealed in this chapter. First, the EU is increasingly concerned with governing a genuinely European sphere, as opposed to increasing its influence over a collection of national domains (which it has also accomplished in various ways). In the case of urban governance and the development of a market for gas the EU has worked to establish Europe as a meaningful domain of governance which it alone has the means and the commitment to govern effectively. In general we can say that EU governance has become increasingly concerned with the government of space: regions, cities, networks, and the 'near abroad' are all examples of new European spatial arrangements around which new European forms of governance have been constructed. This is what makes EU governance distinctive: the mechanisms of governance are not unique, and the partners in governance and those governed are already familiar. The novelty of EU governance is that it has constructed new goals for spatial organization: territorial cohesion and polycentrism obtain their meaning in relation to European, not nation-state, governance. Second, EU governance should be understood as diffuse and variegated and cannot be reduced to policy competences, multi-levelled structures, and state-like powers. The European Union has developed strategies through which it is able to influence outcomes by influencing the preferences of a wide range of actors, many of whom remain beyond its institutional orbit.

In sum, we can say that theorizing about the nature of the EU state has never managed to escape from the shadow of nation-building models. This means that discussion of the EU-as-state has long been locked into a particular set of questions, none of which advance the argument to any great extent: will the EU become more like a nation-state? Can the EU compete with the nation-state (in terms of guaranteeing democracy or winning the loyalty of its citizens)? Approaches which emphasize that the EU is better understood in terms of governance do not automatically fare any better. A major weakness in state and governance approach to the EU is that they assume a state/society distinction. Many governance approaches in fact reinforce this distinction through their reification of civil society. Approaches to the question of the EU-as-state, whether approaching from the governance angle or from the more conventional state centric position, lack a theory of society: accounts which place emphasis on civil society and citizenship are but a poor substitute. What EU studies needs, returning to the theme with which this chapter opened, is not a satisfactory theory of the Euro-state (or even a Euro-polity, see Chapter 9). Indeed, a search for an EU state is misguided. What is required instead is a theory of society.

9 Towards a European polity?

Europe meets the world

It is now common to encounter the idea that the EU represents some form of polity: a Euro-polity, a multi-level polity, a post-national polity, a network polity, to name but a few variations upon this theme. Of late, the assumption that the EU is engaged in polity-building has eclipsed the idea that the European Union represents some kind of super-state (although see Haseler, 2004). Not surprisingly, understanding the nature of this putative Euro-polity is a theme of growing importance within EU studies, particularly so as it dovetails with other developments of note: the preference for governance as a designation for the way the EU coordinates state and non-state actors; the normative value accorded civil society in the construction of an integrated Europe; and the replacement of a deterministic view of integration in favour of a focus on the Europeanization of nation-states, candidate countries and non-members. We can agree with Friese and Wagner (2002: 342) who suggest that the study of the European Union has shifted from the process of integration 'towards exploration of the specific features of the emerging European polity'.

Polity is deemed to be an appropriate designation for an EU characterized by new forms of governance, the search for civil society, the consolidation of citizenship rights, a turn towards constitutionalism, and wide-ranging processes of Europeanization. However, what is not adequately reflected in current efforts to study the EU-as-polity is that framing EU studies more broadly than allowed for by the previous focus on integration has made it more necessary to study the EU within a wider European and global context. The nature of a polity – defined as the institutional structure of a political community through which society constitutes itself – means that it does not presume a unity between territory, society and political organization. As such, it cannot be routinely bounded and demarcated in the same way as the nation-state, nor can it easily maintain a strict inside/outside distinction. Moreover, in the case of the EU polity the core components – governance, civil society, citizenship – each have an applicability or sphere of operation that extends beyond the EU. As we saw in Chapter 7 the organization of European space is not limited to the membership of the EU. Furthermore, the importance of governance, civil society and citizenship to the polity has been highlighted by studies of globalization and globality: they have been imported into EU studies after development in other social science disciplines. This means that debate on the nature of the EU polity requires an understanding of the relation between the EU and the rest of the world. However, this is certainly not the case in many EU studies attempts to understand the EU-as-polity where the global dimensions are largely ignored. EU studies' usage of polity displays a lack of awareness of both of its possible global dimensions and the social theory traditions of studying it in this way.

This is not to say that the shift towards thinking about the EU in terms of a polity is an unwelcome development, although a strong suspicion remains that its popularity stems from being a convenient term with which to fill the gap created by the abandonment of the idea of the EU-as-super-state. Somewhat predictably, the EU quickly becomes a 'non-state polity' (Shaw and Wiener, 1999). Broadly speaking the idea of the EU as a polity can be seen as a positive development for the following reasons. First, it accords a central role for society in the construction of Europe. Polity is the first designation for the EU which incorporates society into EU dynamics. Under the heading of polity the EU is seen as much more than a collection of states or a supra-state complex. Second, it suggests a degree of self-constitution, and allows for the possibility that Europe could be built from the 'bottom-up', although this exists mainly as a figure of EU rhetoric and/or a possible future scenario, rather than a feature of the existing political community. Third, it requires Europe to be studied within a global frame, 'world polity' being the only available model against which to compare the EU polity.

Definitional issues

The choice of polity as a designation for the EU is an interesting development, although not without its problems given the lack of clarity inherent in the term. What exactly is a polity, and how does it differ from a state? There can be few terms in the current political science lexicon which are so poorly defined (or not defined: many political science dictionaries do not contain an entry for the term). One consequence is that there is much freedom when choosing how to use the idea of polity, resulting in a wide range of meanings when applied to the EU. Another consequence is that polity is often used descriptively, in the case of 'the EU is a network polity', for example. In this case state or society could easily be substituted for polity and the meaning would not be altered to any significant degree (it is worth noting that Castells switches between network state and network society). So what does it mean when it is asserted that the EU is some kind of polity? What claims are being made? Polity, in the context of contemporary Europe, indicates that the EU exercises governance but is not a state. Polity also suggests a looser, less hierarchical form of organization, with disparate components. More optimistically perhaps, polity suggests a degree of self-organization within the political community.

We need to ascertain whether polity has a specific meaning in political and social theory, or whether it can serve as a generic descriptive term for all institutional structures involved in the government of a political community. Beyond that, the key question is whether it can be legitimately applied to an emerging form of supra-national governance such as the European Union. Before addressing these issues it is important to establish that polity is a term with a very long history in political science. For Aristotle, polity was a combination of two different principles of rule – oligarchy and democracy – bringing together the authority associated with rule of the few with the political power associated with the rule of the many, in pursuit of the common good. In Aristotle's formulation, polity signals a 'middle way' between types of rule associated with the elites and the masses, and which by curtailing the excesses of each, could form a pragmatic basis for political rule. Aristotle's usage of the term is interesting not least because he locates the essence of polity within society rather than with the institutions of the state.

According to Ritzer (1996: 144), 'Weber defined the polity as a community whose social action is aimed at subordinating to orderly domination by the participants a territory and the conduct of the persons within it, through readiness to resort to physical force, including normally force of arms', although Ritzer here conflates Weber's use of the terms 'political community' and 'polity'. In contemporary political and social science polity is used most often in a broad, ill-defined and descriptive sense, rather than as a technical term for a particular type of organized political community. There now follows a brief survey of a few definitions to give some idea as to its popular meaning. At the most general, it is used as a synonym for political community. It refers to the institutions of political rule, whether located within the state or society: institutions by means of which a society is governed (*Penguin Dictionary of Sociology*). Also, polity can refer to a body of citizens as well as institutions of government: 'form of political organization: a body of people organized under a system of government' (*Chambers 20th Century Dictionary: New Edition*). Some definitions are far less precise. For example, *The New Fowler's Modern English Usage* tells us that polity is 'a society or country as a political entity', which fails to differentiate it from the nation-state (and according to which definition the EU would hardly qualify).

In a more social scientific vein, the *Online Dictionary of the Social Sciences*[1] talks of polity as an 'umbrella term used to refer to the roles and institutions in society that directly shape the way that society is governed'. Interestingly, this entry mentions that there exists a debate about what institutions should be included in a polity, and indicates that state institutions of government, political parties, interest and advocacy groups, and the media may all be included. These dictionary definitions are enlightening in two main ways. First, they indicate that polity can refer to institutional arrangements which are not subordinated to a nation-state, thereby supporting the idea that it may be an appropriate term for describing the EU. Second, they accord an important role to society. It is not simply that society is seen as having a role in governance (as with some interpretations of civil society), but that there is a sense in which polity can be equated to the self-government of a community.

In more recent times an appreciation of the complex nature of the EU-as-state has added to the attractiveness of the idea of the EU-as-polity. In addition, recent definitions of polity have been formulated with the EU polity in mind. For example, Baubock (2003) sees the EU as a nested polity 'composed of member states that are themselves nested polities with autonomous municipalities and regions'. This leads to a definition of polity in the following terms. A polity is 'a politically organized society or community with its own institutions for making collectively binding decisions for a specified group of persons and/or within a bounded territory'. Again, the emphasis here is on the political organization of society, rather than the state *per se*. In a similar vein, for Chryssochoou (1998), polity refers to 'a system of governance capable of producing authoritative political decisions over a given population'.

In the field of contemporary sociological and social theory there have also been a number of attempts to grapple with the idea of polity. Walby (2003) defines polity as:

> an entity which has authority over a specific social group, territory, or set of institutions; some degree of internal coherence and centralized control; some rules and the ability to enforce sanctions against those members who break the rules; the ability to command deference from other polities in specific arenas over which it claims jurisdiction; and which has authority over a broad and significant range of social institutions and domains.
>
> Walby (2003: 534)

It is a definition constructed from the perspective of accounting for the European Union, and is particularly concerned to break with the social science paradigm that assumes the nation-state is the basic unit of collective political organization in the world. Imig and Tarrow (2001: 15) move away from the idea that polity must refer to either state-building or governance towards a conception that emphasizes the role of politics and the public sphere in the construction of a political community. As an alternative designation for contemporary Europe they offer 'composite polity': a system of political relations in which actors at various levels and in different geographical units within a loosely linked system face both horizontal and vertical interlocutors and find corresponding opportunities for alliance building across both axes.

This definition has the merit of not conflating the EU with Europe, and at the same time moves decisively away from state centric or governance models of Europe-as-polity so common in EU studies (Anderson, 2002: 799). Ulrich Beck (1997: 103) defines polity as 'the institutional construction of the political community with which society organizes itself'. This formulation has several advantages. First, it does not equate polity with the state. Second, Beck's emphasis on the 'institutional construction of political community' seems appropriate to the EU case. Third, and most important, it draws attention to the self-constitution and self-organization of society. Another benefit of following Beck's definition is that it questions the modernist social science assumption that polity, state and society obtain their meaning through association with the nation-state and must form an underlying unity contained by national borders. In earlier chapters we have seen how the nation-state can no longer be assumed to contain society, and the ways in which nation, state, and society are not necessarily coincident under conditions of globalization. In short, the principle of unity which was pervasive in modernity is less compelling in the global age.

This survey of definitions and usage of polity has revealed the existence of an enormous variety of meanings attributed to the term. It also reveals that while the idea of polity dovetails with the 'governance turn' in EU studies the term itself has mainly descriptive value, indicating a looser, less territorial institutional arrangement. Put bluntly, it provides a convenient way of not having to refer to the EU as some kind of state. As a result the preference for polity as a designation for the EU is more the result of current fashion rather than a reflection of changes in the way the EU works or a new direction in thinking about EU integration. There exists no theory of the EU-as-polity. There is no consensus on what it comprises, and there is no template with which to construct a model of the EU-as-polity. Nevertheless, there are two reasons why we should persevere with the idea. The 'governance turn' in EU studies and the union's own moves towards constitutionalism mean that it is possible that a coherent agenda for studying the EU as a polity may still emerge from within EU studies. Second, and more importantly, it allows us to compare the EU to the 'world polity' identified by some commentators as a key feature of a globalization. This brings two immediate benefits: it allows us to introduce a major social theory of globalization into the EU studies field (hitherto strangely ignored), namely the 'world polity thesis' of Meyer *et al.*; and gives a sound comparative basis upon which to assess the EU-as-polity, notable by its absence in EU studies.

Polity and the new governance agenda

One theme to emerge from debate on the EU-as-polity in the EU studies literature is the inclusive nature of polity-building: it is less about states and 'top-down' institution-building and more about governance, citizens, and civil society. This corresponds to the self-organization understanding which is a marked feature of some definitions (see Beck, above). In a discussion of citizenship and civil identity in Europe, Chryssochoou (2001b) advances the idea that 'all major actors engaged in European governance see themselves as part of a polity-building exercise that has to evolve from the lower level "upwards"'. On this (somewhat optimistic) view, polity-building is not just about governance frameworks and para-state instruments: it is an affair of the people and rests upon a common identity or project. This signposts a double shift in EU studies: towards a concern with the 'democractic deficit' and questions of popular legitimacy, and the cultural and social dimensions of Europe which have hitherto been of secondary importance. It is certainly the case that over the past decade or so the EU has become much more concerned with how it is perceived by European publics and the extent to which its policies connect with the concerns of its citizens.

The turn towards multi-level polity-building and the incorporation of civil society in the governance of the EU have both resulted from the importance accorded the 'democratic deficit' perceived by many commentators to undermine the popular legitimacy of the union's project. The 'new governance agenda' initiated by the European Commission and centring on the White Paper on Governance (European Commission, 2001b) self-consciously reinvents EU governance in more inclusive terms: key themes being openness, communication, participation, and partnership. The range of concerns brought together under the governance banner have also inspired the EU's move towards a constitution, and the Convention on the Future of Europe that preceded it.

The Convention of the Future of Europe established by the Laeken Council in December 2001 was a deliberate attempt by the EU to approach institutional change not as 'high politics' but in more inclusive, popular terms. Rather than deal with the reforms necessary for widespread enlargement to the east via an intergovernmental conference (IGC) as had been the case in the past, the EU opted for a more public, consultative affair which aimed to take into account a wide range of views; from member states' governments, EU officials, and civil society organizations. The Draft Constitution produced after a year of deliberation was made public in June 2004 but was not approved by the Brussels Council later that year. It now requires ratification by each member state, a process that will take some time, and, as in the case of the UK, be the subject of a referendum. The production of a constitutional treaty in this way should not be taken to mean that there was no EU constitution prior to this. In fact, the EU has long possessed a de facto constitution comprising early EU treaties. What the Draft Constitution does is to formalize these within a single document (Kokott and Ruth, 2003). The convention is often portrayed as being either an attempt to bring Europe closer to its citizens, which is how the EU chose to portray it, or an initiative aimed at making decision-making easier in an enlarged EU. Of course, it was motivated by both considerations, and while the institutional reorganization of the EU has proved difficult for the member states to swallow, the benefits to citizens, while not overwhelming – for example the incorporation of the orphaned Charter of Fundamental Rights – do give some substance to the EU claim to be serious about governance reform.

Re-thinking polity: the global context

Whereas models exist for the encouragement of the idea of EU-as-state or European civil society, no models of transnational or supra-national polity are readily available for scholars of the EU to adopt, re-work or reject. Development of the idea of the EU-as-polity has been further hampered by two factors. First, the nature of the EU is unique, and cannot easily be compared to another international institution: no one has thought it appropriate to describe the UN or NATO as a polity. Second, there is the belief at the core of comparative politics that the organization, structure and capacities of the EU should be compared to those of the nation-state.

However, there exists one model of non-national polity which is seldom if ever drawn upon when the EU-as-polity is under consideration. This is the idea of the world as a polity, which has a strong tradition within one particular strand of sociological theorizing about globalization, namely the 'world polity thesis' associated with John W. Meyer and his colleagues at Stanford University. This body of work, stretching over twenty years or more, has been almost completely ignored by EU studies scholars and theorists of integration, even those who have developed their own approach to the position of Europe *vis-à-vis* a projected world polity (Jorgensen and Rosamond, 2002). This neglect is somewhat strange, particularly as the 'world polity' approach speaks directly to issues at the heart of contemporary EU studies: the means through which a transnational polity can be constructed; the importance of human rights and citizenship; the role of the nation-state under conditions of globalization; and the position of Europe in the world.

There is another intellectual tradition which has a relevance to the idea of global or world polity, and that is the International Relations scholarship associated with the 'English school', particularly their idea of an 'international society' of nation-states. This school of thought has also been largely ignored by students of the European Union (Manners, 2000: 4). Hedley Bull, one of the most notable contributors to the 'English school', developed concepts of 'world society' – common interests and values comprising human community – and 'international society' – common rules and institutions which govern a group of like-minded states. Manners argues that these ideas can be utilized in thinking about the EU. For Manners (2000: 9), 'the concept of an EU society is built on those of world society and international society'. The idea here is that the EU is more than an economic or security organization and as such cannot be captured by the idea of a 'system of states'. The concept of 'European society' suggests a community of member-states and citizens, and 'becomes necessary in order to come to terms with the informal state and non-state societies which have grown up within the EU'. European society draws upon world society and international society norms and values, in particular natural law principles 'based on human rights, rather than the rights which states grant their citizens' (Manners, 2000: 9).

Jorgensen and Rosamond's (2002) work on the relation between the EU and global polity chooses not to draw on this earlier IR literature and makes no reference to the ideas of Meyer *et al.*, indeed they discount the idea that a world polity may already exist. Interestingly, Barry Buzan (2004: 72) points out that Meyer and the other 'world polity theorists' similarly ignore the work of the English School. Jorgensen and Rosamond's concern is with the nature of the EU and how best to study it and they see the EU as a test case for a possible future world polity. For Jorgensen and Rosamond the invocation of a global polity provides two main benefits. First, it offers the opportunity to explore the complexities of post-national governance in a globalized world. Second, it shifts European studies away from a narrow concern with integration, thereby escaping the 'insoluble *sui generis*/n = 1 problem which cannot generate anything other than primitive, descriptive social science' (Jorgensen and Rosamond, 2002: 191). Their approach is premised on the idea that the EU is replacing the nation-state as the key political actor in European politics, even though the EU has not done away with the nation-state as such. This leads to the possibility that the EU may be a new type of actor in a potentially new type of world polity.

The framework within which all these developments is being considered is one which makes an attempt to come to terms with a new world order, and in which the classical realist view of international relations provides little guidance: 'world politics is as much about transnational, trans-societal and post-territorial relations as it is about international or intergovernmental forms of interaction' (Jorgensen and Rosamond, 2002: 205). On this reading, global polity becomes an appropriate vision of governance for a world dominated by economic forms of globalization and over which the nation-state no longer holds sway nor which can return to the anarchy of the 'state of nature' resulting from a failure of realpolitik. In sum, the emphasis in Jorgensen and Rosamond's work is not on the extent to which world or global polity has worked to shape the European nation-state and the EU or the extent to which the EU-as-polity has 'borrowed' from an already existing global polity, but a speculative assessment of the possibility of the EU becoming a model for a future global political order.

There are problems with this conceptualization of the relationship between the EU, Europe, and the possibility of a global polity. One centres on the nation-state centric view of global developments upon which it is founded (global transformation is measured by the extent to which the nation-state is no longer the main actor). Another is the direction of causality: from nation-state to Europe to global polity. A third is the assumption that the biggest change brought about by globalization is to the role of the nation-state in the world, whereas Beck amongst others would argue that it is the changes within the nation-state consequent upon globalization that are of particular import. Jorgensen and Rosamond's approach assumes a one-way relationship from the EU upwards to a future global polity. There is no sense that a world polity already exists and has worked to shape the European nation-state and the EU in important ways. To correct this imbalance we need to examine the extent to which the EU-as-polity has 'borrowed' from an already existing global polity. To do this we need to look at the work of Meyer and his colleagues who, in several detailed empirical studies on various aspects of world culture, have contextualized the nation-state within processes of globalization and the emergence of a world polity, or system of states.

World polity theory starts from the idea that globalization entails the growth and diffusion of world culture. This is not culture in the sense of expressive values or primordial identity but 'cognitive and rational models of identity and action' (Meyer, 2001a: 228). As a result of the spread of this culture there is an increasing isomorphism in the world. In other words, societies are becoming more similar in cultural and political terms. Nation-states around the world, regardless of their level of development, have increasingly adopted common institutions and modes of acquiring and bestowing political legitimacy, through representative democracy and citizenship, for example. Meyer (2001a: 238) states that 'Nation-states employ common definitions of nation-state goals: principally socio-economic development and justice or equality'. Nation-states not only pursue common models of national identity and purpose but themselves gain authority from being interdependent participants in a worldwide system of states. It is a system of states and the common rational culture which unites them that constitutes the world as a polity.

There is no world state. The impulse towards 'institutional isomorphism' is not the outcome of central political organizations organizing the international system of states. There are, however, a number of organized interests – nation-states themselves, business concerns, professional organizations, NGOs – involved in the construction and diffusion of shared norms of actorhood and models of institutional organization. Actors of this kind can achieve a high degree of autonomy but are not necessarily embedded in structures of regulation. The stabilization and common cultural identification of the actors described by Meyer has been further encouraged by the growth and increasing importance of international organizations in the postwar period, the OSCE, the UN, NATO, and GATT foremost amongst them. These have been important developments, not least in the foundation they have given European states upon which to construct pan-European organizations – the Council of Europe and the European Union – which have further consolidated the cultural and institutional commonality of European nation-states.

For Meyer (2001a: 227) the European Union is a stateless, centreless, and networked polity and has much in common with the world polity: it is difficult to draw sharp distinctions between Europe and the world. The more Europe assumes polity-like qualities the more difficult it is to demarcate boundaries between the EU, the rest of Europe, and the world in general. On this view, 'Europe is an especially intense form of an elaborating global system' (Meyer, 2001a: 238). Meyer makes a significant contribution to our understanding of the place of Europe in the world through his ideas on world polity. His work, and that of his colleagues, also throws light on another important area of EU studies, that is the question of European identity and values, and indirectly makes an important contribution to the debate on the nature of the EU-as-state. Europe is not like a nation-state in that, for Meyer (2001a: 239), it is 'massively and deliberately boring … gray men in gray Mercedes' discussing issues designed to be technical and mindbogglingly uninteresting'. However, this is no emotional rant against 'faceless Eurocrats'. That Europe is boring is a consequence of it being patterned and structured to a very high degree by the cultural norms associated with world polity. Not only have European countries (which may still possess the drama and heroes lacking from the European Union) internalized the 'standard actorhood' exhibited by responsible nation-states, Europe is also characterized by 'massive amounts of cultural Otherhood' (Meyer, 2001a: 234). This requires further explanation.

Otherhood refers to a particular cultural posture adopted by those operating in a system of rationalized Actors. Otherhood is a form of 'disinterested professionalism' and possessed by consultants, advisors, scientists, experts, and NGOs, who advocate programmes and solutions couched in terms of the universal good rather than the narrow interest of their constituencies. In Europe, as in the world polity more generally, cultural control is exerted by those who are seen to work for the common good rather than self-interest, framing their calls for development, progress, standardization, and rational organization in terms of the potential benefits to everyone. For Meyer (2001a: 234), 'Europe is all otherhood, not action'. We can see this at work in a number of situations. The EU has campaigned against the use of anti-personnel landmines, assisted in the creation of the International Criminal Court, developed a European climate change programme, and supported moves to reduce debt for the poorest countries in the world. Most notably, in the field of human rights 'the EU has developed a pro-active policy of being at the vanguard of the abolitionist movement against capital punishment and the death penalty' (Manners, 2000: 36). In Meyer's (2001a: 237) terms, 'Europe is filled with Otherhood – rules and associations advising actors and regulating what national and organizational actors do and are responsible for'.

Thus, European culture, to the extent that it can be said to exist, is characterized by rationality, liberalism, and reasonableness. This culture is more intense in Europe than anywhere else in the world, and this intensity is the result of the greater interdependence, the absence of a coordinating state, and the proliferation of Otherness. This all ties in to the nature of EU governance in an interesting way. In Chapter 8 it was mentioned that one characteristic of contemporary EU governance is its interest in correcting failures or rectifying mistakes made by previous governance regimes and institutional orders, what Brenner (2003: 162) refers to as the 'crisis of crisis management'. One problem the nation-state has in measuring up to the exacting standards demanded by the world polity – commitment to progress, rational organization, human rights guarantees – is that 'no nation-state can live up to these expectations, and thus the modern period experiences an enormous expansion in the number and range of perceived social problems' (Meyer, 2001b: 8). In other words, because we have high hopes of social fairness, for example the ability to address social problems through a redistribution of wealth based on progressive taxation or the harmonizing potential of citizenship rights, we become aware of deficiencies in the ability of the state to allocate economic and social resources in an equitable fashion. Meyer advances the view that European governance, drawing upon its vast reservoirs of Otherness, works through 'the creation of perceived crises and problems' (Meyer, 2001a: 232). Examples could include the identification by the European Commission in the 1980s of a 'technology gap' between Europe and the US and Japan, or in the early 1990s that Europe possessed a 'democratic deficit', or the way in which the EU is always pursuing reform of its policies, treaties, and institutional structure. In the world polity, '[f]or every problem solved, two new ones are generated by a worldwide system of associations and professions for which problem-creation is a main (and highly) rewarded business' (Meyer, 2001b: 8). On this view, governance is rooted in the constant discovery of large and small crises and the proffering of new solutions and techniques for their containment and management.

We can see that it is possible to construct a link between the world polity, EU governance and the regulation exerted by global cultural norms. In doing so, Meyer's thesis makes a valuable addition to current thinking on the usefulness of the idea of polity and the relationship between the European Union and globalization. However, there are aspects of the 'world polity thesis' that are more problematic. One problem is that the diffusion of world culture and the principles of Otherness works in a 'top-down' fashion. Models of development are aimed at standardizing the actorhood roles of nation-states, and the rights of individuals are conferred by nation-states adopting global norms. Peoples are entitled to expressive forms of culture precisely because it does not really count in a rationalized, scientized environment. As Boli and Thomas (1999: 5) make plain, 'the structural isomorphism that characterizes actors, interests, and behaviours in the world polity operates increasingly via "top-down" rather than "bottom-up" processes'. As such, there is little room for contestation and conflict in the setting of goals, the democratic orientation of change, and debates over outcomes, winners and losers, and the like. The scripting of actors and others according to rational cultural norms does not lend itself to a multiplicity of outcomes. The second issue follows from this, and relates to the rather singular and narrow view of modernity which underpins the world polity thesis. For Meyer *et al.* there is one modernity which comprises rationalized culture, norms of progress and development, and the scientization of social problems. This is somewhat out of step with important strands in current thinking on the nature of modernity as multiple, overlapping, and contested (Therborn, 2003).

The third issue concerns the status of the nation-state in the world polity. Global culture and its diffusion presumes a central role for the nation-state and its 'standardized actorhood'. It would be difficult to imagine a world polity and the global culture that underpins it existing in a world in which the nation state was not the primary actor. Despite Meyer's attempts to place the EU within the 'world polity' framework one is left with the impression that global culture needs the nation-state and that the EU model, if successfully transplanted to other regions of the world and thereby generalized, could erode the foundations of the world system. States may derive their structure and authority from the world polity, but this larger system of which they are a part requires the nation state in order to function: 'the culture of world society allocates responsible and authoritative actorhood to nation-states' (Meyer *et al.*, 1997: 169). In this respect, 'world polity thesis' shares the realist assumption of a world of nation-states, and it is not clear that the regulating culture associated with Otherhood could have the same influence outside of this context. An important and unresolved problem with Meyer's work is whether the huge quantities of Otherhood generated by the EU exist to serve the ends of European nation-states (and those beyond). The centrality of the nation-state to Meyer's thesis suggests that this is indeed the case: 'international organizations often posture as objective disinterested others who help nation-states pursue their exogenously derived goals' (Meyer *et al.*, 2004: 89). On this reading, placing the EU within the context of a world polity leads back to a Europe of nation-states.

Conclusion: towards a theory of society?

The popularity of polity as a designation for the EU is one consequence of the 'governance turn' which has marked EU studies over the past decade. During this time there has been a decisive shift away from an almost exclusive focus on integration and its corollary, the idea that the EU must be explained in terms of a state. As Chryssochoou (1998) notes, 'it is now possible to contemplate the idea of replacing the rather deterministic concept of "integration" with that of "polity-formation"'. In any case, in the 1990s integration was fast becoming a worn-out concept, undermined on the one hand by the prospect of massive enlargement featuring the former communist countries of eastern and central Europe, and on the other by the idea that EU integration, understood in the conventional sense, had reached a plateau after the Maastricht and Amsterdam Treaties. What has emerged is an EU studies agenda within which polity-building, governance and Europeanization have priority. Through the preference for polity, EU studies now routinely refers to the governance of society (rather than by the state). But while theories of Europeanization and governance abound there exists no theory of society.

For all its positive benefits, the way polity has been employed in EU studies has some serious limitations. For a start, the idea of polity that has become incorporated into EU scholarship – the construction of a political community and its institutions – tends to hold a rather singular view of the community of Europe. The plurality of 'Europes' and the communities to be found there and the ways in which they extend beyond Europe is not reflected in the polity-building literature. Also, polity, according to its current usage, stands for a normative vision of the EU. The idea of EU-as-polity includes that which is deemed currently missing: a civil society, a demos, political legitimacy, self-constitution. In this sense polity is an overly optimistic designation for the EU. Another problem with the EU studies version of polity is that, as with ideas of a supra-state or multi-level governance, the EU polity is thought of narrowly as the polity built by the EU. There is no sense that the European polity connects to the world polity in any meaningful way (although Manners' idea of 'European society' does make this connection). This suggests that polity is used too narrowly in EU studies, as a stand-in for the outmoded idea of EU-as-supra-state, and retains the imprint of a statist logic to thinking about governance and Europeanization.

We have argued that the idea of the EU as a polity requires a rethink of the relationship between the EU and the rest of the world. Put simply, polity begs the question, 'where does Europe stop and the rest of the world begin?' This question is at the heart of the study of Europeanization and is becoming increasingly relevant to an understanding of the EU. To aid the debate it is possible to identify three main dimensions to the relationship of the EU polity and the rest of the world. One, the only model of transnational polity which exists and which can be used as a comparison with the EU is 'world polity', particularly in the terms outlined by John Meyer and his colleagues. On this basis, it makes more sense to compare the EU with the world system than the model of the nation-state. This is a new idea in EU studies (and a possible new direction for comparative politics) and makes an understanding of the relationship between the EU and globalization which goes beyond simple economic causality an urgent task for EU scholars. Two, the idea of polity should be associated with a looser, less hierarchical, more networked entity than a state. This means that the significance of borders and boundaries and the shifting relations between inside and outside are greatly enhanced. Polity cannot be conceived of in the same territorial terms as the state and there is no formal boundary separating Europe from the rest of the world. This alone necessitates a new understanding of how European space is organized (see Chapter 7). Three, the attempt to construct the EU as an integrated, trans-national organization with polity-like qualities and a multi-levelled structure also make Europe more integrated with the rest of the world. This may appear para-doxical, but there exists a link between a self-aware reflexive political community and the need to be open to the world beyond and supportive of universalistic values (Entrikin, 2003: 61). Meyer makes a very strong case for the continuity between Europe and the world, and especially the extent to which rationalistic models of world culture are embedded with the member states of the EU.

'Society' has been short changed by EU studies in the way it has adopted polity as the designation of choice for characterizing EU governance structures. Put another way, the notion of society brought in by discussion of the EU-as-polity is seriously deficient. There are two dimensions to this. One, society has been reduced to civil society and deemed important only as a consequence of its role in EU governance. Two, society is seen as containing all those elements of polity-building which do not yet exist: a European demos; popular identification with the EU project; and a civil society organized at the European level. This accords society a dependent status, positions it as something which has to be constructed by the EU and therefore amenable to domestication and direction, and views it in functional terms as the missing piece of the EU jigsaw the location of which will complete the EU polity. Current thinking of the EU-as-polity therefore holds to many of the same assumptions about the dynamics of EU governance and the unidirectional nature of integration as the more statist approaches which preceded it. What is needed, as we have argued throughout this book, is an approach to Europeanization underpinned by a theory of society.

This will only come about with a sea-change in EU studies. The discussion of polity in this chapter has reinforced the need to study the EU within a global frame: a solipsistic view of the EU cannot hope to understand the EU-as-polity. Fundamentally, there are two ways of looking at the place of the EU in the world. The first, favoured by EU studies, is to look upwards and outwards. From this perspective the EU and the global are 'levels' increasingly removed from the baseline of the European nation-state (sub-national regions can be found by looking 'downwards' from the nation-state vantage point). This perspective is irrevocably wedded to a statist frame of reference. The second view on the place of the EU in the world, and favoured here, is to see the world as the baseline polity and the EU as a sub-unit of a global community to which it is intimately related. In sum, a new global dimension to EU studies, currently underdeveloped and favouring economistic readings (Wincott, 2000), is the necessary concomitant of the idea of the EU as a polity.

10 Rethinking European society
The global civil society context

The idea of the EU-as-polity contains a normative vision of a European civil society, but one which is rooted in nation-states, functional for integration, and amenable to organization and management by the European Union. For most commentators on EU affairs, a European civil society does not exist at the present time (although see Kastoryano, 2003: 80) and is generally perceived as an absence (Chryssochoou, 2001b; Grundmann, 1999; Habermas, 2001a), or at best an aggregation of the national societies of EU member states (Closa, 2001). Some commentators have discerned the emergence of public spheres, mainly limited to activities of European political and economic elites (Lord, 1998; Mann, 1998; Schlesinger, 1999) or constituted by networks of actors or social movements (Eriksen and Fossum, 2001). Others see the search for a European civil society as evidence of the continued dominance of modernist social science categories (Albrow, 1998; Calhoun, 1999) or the tendency to think about society through the lens of the nation-state (Soysal, 2001). In recent times, the expectation that the EU could help construct 'civil society organized at the European level' has gained ground, and not surprisingly the academic debate on European civil society has focused on and been stimulated by the publication of the European Commission's (2001b) White Paper on Governance (Armstrong, 2002; De Schutter, 2002; Smismans, 2003).

European civil society, whether seen in terms of a present lack or a future task for EU governance, has become the dominant way of addressing the question of European society within EU studies. There is a shortage of treatments of contemporary Europe which look at the existence or possibility of a European society, in the sense of a society not organized by the EU or encompassing a wider Europe, and which do not automatically assume that European society will take the form of civil society, although a fledgling literature does exist (Delanty, 1998; Offe, 2002; Outhwaite, 2001; Rumford, 2001, 2003). In short, the question has become formulated in terms of 'when will a European civil society exist?', rather than 'what form will European society take (if it takes one at all)?'. The White Paper on Governance and the direction that studies of European society have taken since its publication make the development of broader considerations of European society less, rather than more likely: the agenda is set firmly around the potential for an EU civil society. This trend is reinforced by other recent developments.

First is the preference for seeing national civil societies in Europe as an important bulwark against the threat of economic globalization (Kaldor and Vejvoda, 2002: x). On this reading civil society should continue to be national as it is functional for the integrity of the nation-state. Second is the failure of EU studies literature on European civil society to connect with a large body of social theory on the nature of European public spheres. Third is the failure to incorporate advances in the conceptualization of global civil society into EU studies. Scholars of the European Union have opted for an autochthonous reading of civil society and in doing so have cut themselves off from some important themes emerging within social science research on global civil society.

Although it now dominates the agenda, the extent to which a European civil society has come into being and the role of the EU in constructing it has entered the EU studies agenda relatively recently, and is still accorded relatively low status in relation to citizenship, governance, the democratic deficit and other related topics. During the same period there has, by contrast, been an explosion of interest in the idea of global civil society (Baker, 2002; Florini and Simmons, 2000; Kaldor, 2003; Keane, 2003; Scholte, 2001). The existence of global or transnational civil society is now being seen as a key issue in understanding the nature and dynamics of globalization, transnational governance, the emerging world polity, the politics of affect and identity, and international relations in its most general sense. So on the one hand there is massive interest in the emerging global civil society, on the other there is significantly less interest in the idea of a European civil society. In other words, while the consensus view finds little evidence for the existence of EU civil society, a much stronger case is being made for viewing global civil society as an actually existing reality, leading to an interesting situation where there appears to be much more global than European civil society.

There is no one dominant interpretation of global civil society, although commonly it refers to a complex of global social movements and advocacy networks which have developed global reach and which are seen as a force for good (measured in terms of enhanced democracy and greater individual freedom, or more commonly human rights) and work to challenge the power of nation-states and/or global capitalism. Some theorists choose to invoke global civil society in relation to the operation of international NGOs (Florini and Simmons, 2000; Kohler, 1998), or the prospects of increasing democracy in global governance (Colas, 2001; Held, 1999). Alternatively, it can be taken to designate an increasing cosmopolitan orientation amongst citizens and an awareness of global risks (Beck, 2000a), or a denationalization of political activity and the increasing salience of global networks (Axford and Huggins, 2001). Scholte (2002: 285) defines global civil society as a realm of civic activity which is global in organizational scope, where transworld issues are addressed, transborder communications are established, and in which actors organize on the basis of supra-territorial solidarity. On the face of it, there is no reason why global civil society should be more prevalent than European civil society, indeed the latter might be more easy to realize given the smaller theatre of operation, the institutional base from which it could draw, and the high level of encouragement offered by the EU itself.

So why is it that global civil society is on the up-and-up, and has sprung into life without the need for a 'world state' to organize it, while European civil society awaits the 'invisible hand' of the EU to mould it and give it substance? Leaving aside the question of whether global civil society 'lacks ontology' (although there is no reason to suppose that EU civil society must be different in this respect) this does appear to be a rather odd state of affairs. One possible reason, already mentioned briefly, is that EU studies has displayed a reluctance to import ideas on global civil society from other social science disciplines and apply them to the European case. Similarly, work on European public spheres tends not to be incorporated into debates on civil society. However, this situation has not just come about because of different disciplines 'not talking to each other'. The core reason for the disparity is that very different ways of viewing civil society have been adopted in each case. In EU studies, European civil society is seen as an aggregate of national societies which can only become meaningful at the European level if organized by the Commission. Theorists of global civil society emphasize the non-national orientation of civil society activity and the ways in which conflicts and contestations can no longer be mapped onto national politics. Global civil society also points to a world in which international politics is no longer premised on a worldwide system of nation-states. EU studies is still working with national models in which civil society is functional for European integration, while a global perspective encourages us to transcend the national scheme of things and think in terms of the new political spaces caused by processes of globalization. This in turn points to a more fundamental difference in the way civil society and global civil society are theorized in contemporary social and political thought. Civil society rests on a certain set of assumptions (civility, national community, autonomy from the state), global civil society on completely different precepts (human rights, the individual, deterritorialization, universality). Indeed, the differences are so great that it is a mistake to view global civil society as an extension or natural continuation of national civil society.

There is much that could be written about the non-existence of European civil society and the possibility of the EU bringing it into being. There is also much that could be said about the merits of the idea of European civil society versus European society, and the usefulness of the term 'civil society' in social and political thought (Rumford, 2002). This chapter takes as its theme the differences between civil society, as traditionally conceived (and the way it continues to be thought of within EU studies), and global civil society as it has emerged in contemporary discourses of globalization. Two main areas of difference are highlighted. First, it is frequently assumed that civil society was originally national and only recently has become transnational. One consequence of this view is that important global processes which could account for the formation of national civil societies are ignored. Second, while civil society was originally conceived as a realm distinct from and/or an improvement upon the natural world, many interpretations of global civil society draw attention to the commonality between society and nature. The implications for thinking about European civil society are quite profound, it is argued. Approaches to European civil society are limited by the preference for seeing it as being formed out of the increasing connectivity of national civil societies. In this sense, theories of European civil society are blind to any global dimension and remain constrained by a national frame of reference. The chapter concludes that conventional approaches to civil society are not useful in thinking about European civil society. A preferable starting point would be to view European civil society as part of global civil society, but there is little or no tradition of scholarship of this kind upon which to build.

The neglected global dimension to civil society

The concept of civil society has long occupied a central place in the social scientific imagination, being closely associated with citizenship, democracy, social cohesion, self-organization, participation, stability, and peaceful political change. Democracy needs civil society: it is the prerequisite for freedom, plurality and social harmony. In Hall's (1998: 54) formulation, 'it is civil society which makes liberalism and democracy truly desirable'. However, there exists little consensus regarding what constitutes civil society or what its functions are. Indeed, it has an extremely wide application and depending upon the political discourse within which it is articulated can be employed to emphasize limitations on the power of the state, the transformatory potential of social movements, or the resilience of community. For Seligman (1998: 81) the fact that 'any concept could be invested with such varied and often contradictory meanings should make us suspect of its usefulness within the social sciences'. Nevertheless, its appeal would appear to be limitless, appearing in political discourses of the left and the right, nationalists and cosmopolitans, and democrats of every stripe. Nor has its promiscuity diminished its applicability. Civil society has been employed to characterize struggles against communism and, at the same time, finds some of its most subtle expression in Marxist theory. It has a strong liberal economic tradition, yet finds a home in the repertoire of socialist thought. For many, civil society presupposes a democratic nation-state, while for others it is firm evidence of post-national democracy.

Keane (1988: 3) defines civil society as 'the realm of social (privately owned, market-directed, voluntarily run or friendship-based) activities which are legally recognized and guaranteed by the state'. Similarly, for Held (1989: 6) civil society 'connotes those areas of social life – the domestic world, the economic sphere, cultural activities and political interaction – which are organized by private or voluntary arrangements between individuals and groups outside the *direct* control of the state'. It should be noted that some versions of civil society exclude economic activity and others include it. Likewise, the distinction between political and civil society is unclear in many accounts (for a full discussion see Foley and Edwards, 1996). Over recent years, the idea of civil society has grown in stature as a result of the centrality accorded to it in the democratic struggles against communism in the countries of the former Soviet bloc in the 1970s and 1980s, its increasing employment to designate a widening of democracy beyond the parliamentary sphere in western Europe in the same period (Keane, 1998), and its potential for re-orienting radical politics in contexts in which socialism has lost its relevance (Kumar, 1993). The positive connotations and optimism surrounding civil society are summarized by Outhwaite (2001) for whom, 'civil society politics in both its Western and Eastern European forms from the 1970s onwards remains one of our most fruitful political experiences and resources'.

At root, the importance (and popularity) of the idea of civil society is that it promises to combine democratic pluralism with state regulation and guidance (Kumar, 1993: 375) through the integration of a cohesive social unit, a participatory democratic regime, and a moral order. It suggests that society can be self-organizing and self-regulating, rather than being commanded by the state, an idea that has its modern origins in the 'societalism' of Adam Fergusson. In order to exist, civil society must become relatively autonomous from other domains which stand to threaten or dominate it. Within social theory it is possible to identify three such domains from which civil society is generally distinguished: the state; community; and nature (Kaviraj, 2001: 288–9). The idea of 'relative autonomy' is crucial, as the domains from which civil society is differentiated are also needed in some degree to sustain it, or to provide it with meaning and identity.

In relation to autonomy from the state, perhaps the domain most frequently associated with civil society in contemporary social theory, freedom, democracy and self-regulation are deemed not to be possible under conditions where the state is overly authoritarian or repressive. As intimated above, the idea of civil society gained wide currency during the 1980s as a result of popular struggles against communist regimes in eastern Europe (Keane, 1988; Kumar, 1993; Pelczynski, 1988; Tismaneanu, 1990). What totalitarian states denied was a public space free of interference and coercion. But while civil society is theorized as a realm autonomous from the state it also requires the state in order to function. The state, as a law-making and law enforcing apparatus – or a 'night-watchman' in classical liberal theory – is necessary if society is to be 'refereed' fairly, the freedoms of civil society enjoyed, and a common political culture instilled among citizens. The freedom to pursue chosen interests, establish pluralist identities, and secure political representation can only come about if all civil society actors abide by a common set of rules (Khilnani, 2001: 26). Thus, the state remains accountable for important protective, regulatory, and educative functions, and is essential to ensure both free association and democratic contestation.

The state and civil society are not antithetical but comprise the 'two moments of democracy' (Keane, 1998: 8). It is not a question of choosing one over the other but of acquiring a judicious measure of both. 'Only a democratic state can create a democratic civil society; only a democratic civil society can sustain a democratic state' (Walzer, 1995: 24). One problematic feature of this state/civil society nexus is that it foregrounds the democratic institutions of the state and their role in the protection of civil society, whilst having very little to say regarding its more repressive functions. Furthermore, the separation of responsibilities between state and civil society with regards to government and democratic regulation may not be as clear cut as liberal supporters of civil society supporters believe: rule can also be exercised via civil society (Cruickshank, 1999; Gramsci, 1971; Rose, 1999).

Sociological thinking about the usefulness of the concept of civil society has tended to focus on the problem of its independence *vis-à-vis* the state (Kumar, 1993), one consequence of which has been to reinforce the idea that civil society should be understood within a national context. But it is not only autonomy from the state which concerns theorists of civil society. The liberal tradition in particular works to distinguish it from the state of nature, a pre-societal human existence. The best known expression of this idea is to be found in the work of Hobbes and Locke. Man desires to leave the state of nature because of its uncertain or threatening qualities and makes a social contract in order to enter civil society, a realm within which social life is enhanced, laws can be upheld, and freedoms more fully enjoyed. For Hobbes civil society is not self-constituting but guaranteed by an all-powerful sovereign, the beneficiary of the social contract. For Locke, civil society is guaranteed by natural law, which was also present in the state of nature but where adherence to its principles could not be guaranteed. For both, the idea of the state of nature remains as a warning to citizens that failure to respect and safeguard the conventions of civil society may result in a return to this undesirable realm. It is only in the hands of Rousseau that civil society achieves the robustness necessary to make a return to the state of nature impossible, and hence permits the more fundamental transformation of society envisaged by Rousseau when invoking the social contract (McLelland, 1996: 257–64). Furthermore, man in civil society is marked off from man in the state of nature by the civility which is now the defining feature of human relations. In civil society people develop both a civilized self-interest and a concern for the equitable treatment of fellow citizens regardless of their interests and sensibilities (Bryant, 1993: 399). Civility underpins the shared 'rules of engagement' without which the state is unable to protect civil society, and a common political culture is thus one important outcome of life in civil society. In sum, we can say that civil society is threatened both by no state (in which case the state of nature would return) and by too much state (which would stifle individual freedoms).

Another strand within civil society theorizing distinguishes it from community, in the sense resonant with Tonnies' ideas of *Gemeinschaft* (community) and *Gesellschaft* (civil society). Here civil society denotes modern forms of association rather than pre-modern communal bonds. Civil society thus implies specialization, differentiation and social complexity. But this is not to say that civil society can function without a principle of solidarity. In fact, civil society relies upon a form of collective identity, or commonality. We have already seen how civil society requires shared norms of democratic participation and a common moral code of civility. Both of these are threatened by political movements which place undue emphasis on individuality, popular identifications or ethnic or religious ascription, for example. In other words, civil society requires a principle of internal coherence as well as the external scaffolding provided by the state. In the modern idiom, the principle vehicle for achieving solidarity has been nationalism. Civil societies have been nationally constituted and coextensive with nation-states.

From the perspective of internal cohesion nationalism has the added advantage of being able to forge a collective identity capable of nourishing and sustaining the other key civil society values; participatory and pluralistic democracy, and civility. A nationally constituted civil society combines individual rights with the public good in such a way as to preclude fragmentation and incoherence. Civil society has become a successful model for imagining society because it promises a sense of cohesion, forges communal bonds, and promotes the belief that political communities can control their destinies and promote the common good (Held, 1999: 90). Similarly, civil society promises to resolve the problem of how trust, reciprocity and cooperation can be guaranteed while at the same time permitting the existence of private life and protecting a public sphere of individual and collective rights.

The preoccupation with the national origins of and location for the flourishing of civil society has been reinforced in the literature on the rise of European civil society by the assumption that in its original form civil society was national, and only recently has it assumed a transnational dimension (Axford and Huggins, 2001). In contrast to this view, we prefer the idea that 'Europe has always been a transnational space' (Kumar, 2003: 34). Conventional approaches to European civil society remain blind to the ways in which civil society has always exhibited a strong global dimension, even in its national setting.

The global dimension of national civil society can be identified in relation to each of the domains (outlined above) by which it distinguishes itself: civility, participatory democracy, and national community. To begin with, in relation to the development of the national principle, the expectations generated by societies regarding their survival and viability are conditioned by 'an increasingly global sense of how societies should be constructed' (Robertson, 1992: 110). In short, in the modern period the nation-state became the global norm for the political unit. The formation of national societies proceeded hand-in-hand with their mutual recognition and the formation of an international system of states. Within this international system of states, dominant or hegemonic states are able to impose rules of behaviour on competitors (Smith, 1999: 238–9). Furthermore, nation-states have become interdependent within an international balance of power such that developments within one state, such as a threat to political elites or the domestic balance of power, has implications for the internal coherence and security of others (Elias, 2000: 235). For example, during the Cold War the orientation of social forces in 'Third World' countries were aligned 'as if in a magnetic field, with the axis of tension between the great powers' (Mennell, 1990: 365). The international division of states between democracies and their communist opponents 'radically altered their domestic politics' (Hirst, 2001: 257). In contemporary Europe, the role of the EU in patterning domestic politics and structuring the institutional and governmental priorities of member states, candidate countries, and third countries is well documented.

Rather than simply serving as a principle for regulating and homogenizing the behaviour of members of a national community, not to mention constituting a major investment in social capital, civility has long been an important regulative principle in inter-state relations and a constraint on the behaviour of nation-states (Robertson, 1992: 121). Whether catalysed by the need for economic development, accession to the membership of international organizations, or the acquisition of the international legitimacy which facilitates domestic political hegemony, the promotion of civility among the population has been a key task associated with the development of the nation-state. Moreover, the promotion of civility and a shared political culture in domestic affairs can help to regulate damaging internal dissension and hence provides the basis for national success in a competitive world of nation-states. Furthermore, greater knowledge of the level of civilization achieved within one's own society relative to that of rivals can give an impetus to national competitiveness (Keane, 1998), and may facilitate inter-state cooperation. Relations between states can also have a major impact upon the development of a culture of democratic civility in the sense that enlightened self-interest and codes of civil behaviour are facilitated by contact between societies, for example through trade, sporting fixtures, and exchange of diplomats.

Relations between states conditions domestic democratic participation to a significant degree. During the Cold War, western powers were content to support dictatorships in order to expand their sphere of influence or preclude the expansion of that of their rivals. Competition between nation-states may lead to attempts to mobilize opposition to an existing regime in a rival state, thereby weakening social cohesion or promoting instability and change. As mentioned above, fractures within the domestic social order can prove debilitating and may be resisted through measures to curb the autonomy of civil society. Freedom of association and contestation between contending policies or political philosophies in the public sphere may be curtailed in order to ensure national unity. As de Tocqueville reminds us, 'unlimited freedom of association for political ends is, of all forms of liberty, the last that a nation can sustain' (quoted in Foley and Edwards, 1996: 45). Social forces comprising civil society may be seen as 'the enemy within' and repression may follow. Conversely, under conditions of international peace (or at least stability amongst proximate states) civil freedoms may flourish. The absence of an external enemy may translate into a state/civil society relationship in which the state interferes to a minimal degree and provides optimal conditions for autonomous self-organization: the classic conditions for the development of national civil society.

As understood here, civil society has always demonstrated a strong transnational or global dimension, an aspect largely ignored in the mainstream literature. Recent scholarship in European civil society largely ignores the possibility that the reciprocal shaping of civil societies has taken place over a very long time, and starts from the assumption that existing (national) civil societies can now be connected in new ways across the continent. This helps explain the way in which civil society is typically seen as having a role in European integration: nation-state societies are the repositories of European democracy and, as such, a democratic European Union must work to integrate them within a greater whole (Perez-Diaz, 2000; Siedentop, 2000). What gets ignored in this approach is the possibility that the mutual interdependence of national civil societies – the globalization of human interdependencies (Mennell, 1990: 368) – may long ago have contributed to the Europeanization of nation-state society.

Global civil society as a natural realm

There are many important ways in which global civil society, in the way it has come to be viewed as both a consequence and facilitator of globalization, has been conceptualized in very different terms from (national) civil society. Before looking in some detail at the most significant difference – the conceptualization of global civil society as continuous with nature rather than resulting from separation from and domination over nature – we will outline several other key areas of difference. This involves, as may be imagined, some generalizations about both positions and does scant justice to either the many variations on the civil society theme or the nuances to be found in the work of many theorists. Nevertheless, the disjuncture between civil society and global civil society is an important one in social theory and has major implications for the way European society is understood.

We can identify the following differences between civil society and global civil society. First, civil society, in both its liberal and more contemporary versions, rests upon a bedrock of pluralism and tolerance, whereas global civil society advocates respect for diversity, what Mignolo (2002) terms 'diversality': diversity as a universal project. Second, civil society is premised upon a unity of citizenship rights, territorial identification, and political community. Global civil society recognizes no such unity and sees individual human rights as coterminous with the biosphere. Third, civil society brings with it expectations of (enhanced) democracy. Global civil society does not focus exclusively upon democracy, which is viewed as largely contingent, and instead promotes human rights, which are deemed to have a greater universality than democracy (Beetham, 1998: 59). Fourth, while economic activity is often excluded from accounts of civil society (civil society theorists are deeply divided on this issue: see Cohen and Arato, 1992; Foley and Edwards, 1996) it is rarely excluded from global civil society. Models of governance which accompany global civil society emphasize a role for regulation of and by economic and business actors. Global civil society is also associated with extending economic rights in a way that civil society is not (being associated with civil, political and sometimes social rights). Fifth, while civil society is associated with the containment or amelioration of class struggle (or its prosecution, in the Marxist variant), global civil society does not prioritize class struggle or struggles against the state – to the chagrin of some neo-Marxist critics (Halperin and Laxer, 2003) – preferring a diversity of struggles against a number of 'centres'.

Perhaps the most striking of all the differences is that global civil society is portrayed as a natural realm, free from the artificiality of nation-building and arbitrary social divisions associated with the modern age, and, most importantly, underpinned by natural law assumptions concerning the intrinsic equality of rights, capacities and responsibilities possessed by human beings. Civil society has long been conceptualized in terms of the emancipation of humans from nature, which is seen as external to society (Delanty, 2000c: 21). In thinking about global civil society social theory has undergone a major transformation: civil society is man-made and contractual (unnatural), while global civil society is not separate from nature but underpinned by natural law conceptions of human rights. This is encapsulated rather neatly by Ulrich Beck (2004: 160) in the context of a discussion of cosmopolitan thought where he states that [n]ature is no longer separated from national or international society: nature is associated with society.

The argument here then is that in thinking about global civil society theorists have revisited natural law explanations, and in doing so are drawing upon pre-modern political understandings about the constitution of society. The central line linking natural law and global civil society is human rights. Emphasizing this particular dimension of global civil society may lead, it could be argued, to a rather one dimensional interpretation. What is being argued here is not that global civil society should be reduced to human rights, but that the foundations upon which human rights have been imagined have encouraged a political culture within which the idea of global civil society has developed. There is a good deal of support for this position from within contemporary social theory. For example, Mary Kaldor sees global civil society as 'equated with the notion of human rights culture' (quoted in Baker, 2002: 939), and global civil society as an adjunct to human rights. From a different perspective, John Meyer (2001a: 229) identifies 'cultural notions of a "natural law" kind about human rights and capacities', as central to any idea of global (and European) society.

Civil society is presented (in the work of Hobbes and Locke, for example) as a solution, that is to say, as protection from a prior, more natural human existence in which life, as famously depicted by Hobbes, was 'nasty, brutish and short'. In this sense, civil society represents escape from and possible control over nature: emancipation can only be achieved if man is liberated from nature. Nature is undesirable not only because it is threatening but because it is equated with waste. For Locke, nature had no intrinsic value, and it was the task of men to improve it with their labour. Not only was the goal of dominating nature through science, technology, and social organization part of civil society thinking, but the need for individuals to master their own human natures, particularly the passions, emotions and desires which were seen as the less positive elements of human nature was also of central importance. Self-mastery, rationality in thought, and civilized behaviour were the necessary prerequisites for true social life, hence the emphasis on civility, the role of education in disciplining the population, and the importance of the family in regulating and stabilizing sexual relations. Gramsci (1971: 298) talks of the 'often painful and bloody process of subjugating natural (i.e. animal and primitive) instincts to new, more complex and rigid norms and habits of order, exactitude and precision which can make possible the increasingly complex forms of collective life which are the necessary consequence of industrial development'.

Global civil society posits a world of natural (human) rights and assumes a natural law framework within which individuals and social groups relate to each other. Natural law, originating with the Stoic thinkers of the classical world, also has a long history in association with Christian belief: that the law of God is superior to that imposed by the state. Natural law, particularly as interpreted by Grotius, contains an injunction to respect another's rights and thereby preserve social peace (Tuck, 1979: 72–3), although it should be mentioned that these rights were in part property rights, as they were for Locke (rights to life, liberty and property). For Kant, respect for humanity is related to living in accordance with universal natural law (Heater, 2002: 35). Individuals are subject to universal natural law and, as a consequence, members of international society. In other words, international society is composed of individuals (not states) who are subject to natural law.

The emergence of international law (positive law rather than natural law) and a framework of international relations based on nation-states has been a fundamental characteristic of the modern world. This is no longer the case. As Beck (2000b: 83) points out, 'the principle that *international law precedes human rights* which held during the (nation-state) first age of modernity is being replaced by the principle of the (world society) second age of modernity, that *human rights precedes international law*'. Holton (1998: 88) uses the example of the International Tribunal (for Nazi war criminals) held in the aftermath of the Second World War to show how the rights and obligations of individuals began to 'take precedence over those of the nation-states of which they are members'. The important shift is that bearers of human rights are recognized to be individuals and not nation-states: international relations based on positive law have given way to human rights founded upon natural law principles, and the result is 'a legally binding world society of individuals' (Beck, 2000b: 84). This mirrors the distinction between individual rights based upon membership of a particular civil society (citizenship), and an ethical concept of the individual imbued with natural rights. Theories of civil society emphasize that rights are bestowed by the state, and therefore can be taken away; theories of global civil society look to the pre-social natural rights discounted by theorists of civil society, recasting them as human and personhood rights in an attempt to give substance to the otherwise abstract notion of the shared human condition. Adding a twist to the natural rights versus civil society debate, Claus Offe (2002) suggests that in the case of the EU, the lack of state-sponsored institutional frameworks for bargaining and compromise, plus the predominance of the market as a social regulator, point in the direction of Europe possessing a 'peaceful state of nature' rather than a European civil society, a rather interesting idea in the context of the foregoing discussion of natural law traditions.

The question of the public sphere

While there is a big question mark over the possibility of a European civil society, the existence of a European public sphere has long been pointed to by many commentators, and can be seen as both a particularly important dimension of Europeanization, and an important prerequisite for the emergence of a transnational civil society. It connects to the foregoing discussion about the natural law underpinnings of global civil society in interesting ways, as we shall see. Discussion of the public sphere is also characterized by the issue of whether national publics can be coordinated or harmonized within an overarching European version

(Grundmann, 1999), particularly as public spheres tend to be seen in terms of national media and/or cultures. Indeed, the assumption that national spheres are unitary has been identified as a problematic starting point for such a debate (van de Steeg, 2002). For our purposes, one of the most salient aspects of the public sphere is the extent to which it is the location for compromise and contestation, and the formulations of consensus and dissent in European society. This places the public sphere in an important role *vis-à-vis* civil society in as much as while the latter is generally (although not exclusively) conceived of as a realm of cohesion, solidarity and unity, the former allows for greater conflict.

In contemporary social theory the idea of the public sphere is dominated by the work of Jürgen Habermas who sees it primarily as a communicative space. The public sphere, according to Calhoun (2000: 258), 'exists uniquely in, through, and for talk'. Moreover, the public sphere is a key element of democracy and cannot be reduced to a function of either the state or civil society. For Habermas, the public sphere is less dependent upon the state (it exists to influence it) and can be thought of as prior to and independent of civil society, although it works to constitute it. Civil society, whether national or global, thus requires a public sphere around which to cohere. Extended to the case of the EU this suggests that 'the public sphere is a crucial setting for the production and shaping of European integration', both because democratic communication and contestation is at the core of any attempt at integration, and a central plank in the construction of solidarity. Indeed, it is precisely because Habermas moves the debate away from a preoccupation with European media, common culture, and a unified demos that his ideas are so relevant to the European case.

One problem with Habermas' version of the public sphere is that it assumes (in a parallel to more liberal formulations) the existence of a pre-political private existence which individuals leave behind when they move into the public sphere. Associated with this is the idea that identity-formation takes places prior to entry into the public sphere, the latter being a realm in which individuals need to transcend their private selves and their narrow self-interest, this transition being constitutive of citizenship. 'Habermas presumes that identities will be formed in private (and/or in other public contexts) prior to entry into the public sphere' (Calhoun, 2000: 534–5). Discussion of a European public sphere has been much influenced by Habermas' work and has given rise to interpretations which emphasize the need to coordinate national public spheres, which being language-specific resist easy aggregation into a unified European public sphere (Closa, 2001). Alternatively, it has been suggested that debate on the democratic deficits and institutional blockages which hinder the construction of a European civil society itself contributes to the formation of a European public sphere (Trenz and Eder, 2004).

There is another approach to the question of the European public sphere which requires consideration. For Yasemin Soysal (1997: 518) the public sphere is not so much separated from the private world of individuals but increasingly saturated by it. In other words, rather than assume the separation of public and private it recasts them as one form of contestation that may take place. Narratives of identity are played out in the public sphere where groups engage in contestations over issues of identity, equality, rights, emancipation, and difference. The terms in which claims are made and which give form to conflict and struggle tends to be the 'universalistic discourse of rights' within which identity is recast as a 'natural good' (Soysal, 1997: 519). In other words, the European public sphere is a realm of (natural) rights in which individuals relate to each other using human rights as a reference point. National community is easily transcended through the utilization of universalistic discourses. Indeed, it becomes increasingly difficult to construct a national public sphere: 'as the universal individual becomes the norm, and identities are defined as rights, the national closure of political communities (and the public spheres in which they are realized) presents a formidable task' (Soysal, 1997: 521).

Soysal's work makes a compelling case for the existence of a European public sphere. Identities form the basis for contestation in the European public sphere and this, more than its communicative function, makes it central to Europeanization. Identities are not constructed in the public sphere, however. On Soysal's model identities can be claimed, realized or exercised in the public sphere, but not formed as such. Whereas for Habermas identities are formed prior to immersion in the public sphere, for Soysal they already exist there but have hitherto gone unclaimed (because individuals and groups are denied equal access to the public sphere). Identities are guaranteed by human rights and in order to express those identities individuals or groups must achieve access to the public sphere. Thus, the goals of social movements, minorities and the marginalized is to participate in a public sphere within which new forms of recognition exist along with a whole range of opportunities for claims-making, all of which follow naturally from possession of human rights. For Soysal, the movement from the private to the public sphere is a rights-endowing process. Natural, rightful identities can be claimed and difference expressed in a public sphere governed by universal principles.

To conclude this short account of the importance of public spheres in the context of the development of European civil society we can make two points. One is that the case for the existence of a European public sphere is much stronger than the corresponding case for a civil society. While human rights work to undermine nationally contained civil societies (which is what it is assumed European civil society must be based on) they are the foundation of the European public sphere (which unlike the case of European civil society is not seen as separate from its corresponding global realm). It is in the interests of all claims-makers, political activists, and those involved in the politics of redistribution to strengthen the European public sphere as its existence is the precondition for the realization of an expanded range of identities, rights and struggles. The second point is that neither approach to the public sphere under consideration here necessarily makes the existence of a future European civil society more likely. Either Europe is imagined as irrevocably national, or there is no compelling link between the public sphere and civil society. Nevertheless, the public sphere exists as a major resource upon which civil society can draw in its attempts at self-constitution, and a strong public sphere makes it less likely that a civil society linked to it could be easily dominated or co-opted by supra-national agencies of EU governance.

Conclusion: rethinking European civil society

The global dimensions of civil society highlighted in this chapter reinforce the idea that it is not possible to continue with the fiction that civil society can be nationally constituted and maintained independently from other such societies. The dominant approach to viewing European civil society, which sees it as either the aggregation of existing national societies or the pet project of a European supra-state, is therefore deeply flawed. The argument developed here is that global civil society, in the way that it has emerged as a key trope in contemporary debates on globalization, exists as an important untapped resource for scholars of EU integration. In short, there are more compelling reasons to see European civil society as part of global civil society rather than an outcome of supra-national governance in the EU.

In EU studies, the absence of European civil society is lamented but relations between a nascent European civil society and global civil society are rarely explored. Similarly, the development of a European public sphere is too often treated in isolation from the question of civil society, to the detriment of EU studies (although social theory approaches to the European public sphere are better at relating this to questions of civil society than EU studies approaches to civil society are at placing it alongside consideration of the public sphere). The more conflictual and antagonistic elements of civil society are downplayed in the EU's vision of a 'civil society organized at European level' which is imagined as both consensual and functional for European integration. More importantly perhaps, EU studies must face up to the rather inconvenient truth that it is unable to explain why there appears to be much more global civil society than European civil society. Explaining the reasons for this disparity has been the main thrust of the chapter, and can be summarized in the following terms. Thinking about European civil society is still locked into a liberal-conventional view of civil society as a realm of civility and autonomy from the state within which a cohesive political community can thrive. It has yet to embrace the possibility that civil society is global rather than national, and that ways in which global civil society have been conceived could also be applied to the emerging European civil society. This would in turn require scholars of the EU to see it less in terms of a collection of nation-states and more in terms of cosmopolitan linkages. The artificial divide between civil society and the public sphere (and downplaying of the importance of the latter) has also worked to conceal the full extent of the civil society that may be emerging in Europe.

Beck (2000b) criticizes the tendency to see transnational society in terms of the increasing connectivity between nation-state societies. This is unsatisfactory because,

> globalization not only alters the interconnectedness of nation-states and national societies but the internal quality of the social. Whatever constitutes

'society' and 'politics' becomes in itself questionable, because the principles of territoriality, collectivity and frontier are becoming questioned.

(Beck, 2000b: 87–8)

We can go further and say that the general understanding of what constitutes a society is subject to a new regime of global expectations. Previously, the internationally institutionalized norm was the nation-state society. This is no longer the case and all manner of interested parties – governments, corporations, NGOs and citizens – are searching for the meaning of society in a world where social coherence, democratic participation and political legitimacy are being redefined. The activities of diverse actors – transnational communities of interest (religious, ethnic), multinational corporations, INGOs, organized crime and terrorist networks – can circumvent national and even supra-national structures and create new constituencies, communities, and new social relationships which have no necessary allegiance to previous norms of association. That the outcome of such processes could ever be a 'civil society organized at European level', as wished for by the Commission, is doubtful. However, the idea of European civil society is more realistic when it is viewed as constituted through global civil society, of which it forms a part. Parenthetically, it can be mentioned that the whole idea of civil society, once worn out and implicated in an outmoded discourse of modernity, has been given fresh impetus when recast as global civil society and imbued with pre-modern natural law qualities.

There is a final irony for those who still prefer to see European civil society in terms of a liberal-national project. The development of a European civil society as part of the Euro-polity could lead, as an unintended outcome, to less rather than more identification with Europe. To a significant degree civil society values, particularly those etched in contemporary discourse, are universal values more than European values. In constituting Europe as a civil society architects of the EU polity would also be providing its citizens with reasons to think of themselves as citizens of the world. The solidarity and community which are seen as an indispensable part of civil society can also lead to the concretization of certain forms of universalism, thereby threatening the cohesion of the civil society which gave rise to them. As Entrikin (2003: 62) points out, 'the universalism embedded in democratic principles would seem to entail the elimination of borders or at least to the creation of highly permeable boundaries'. What this means is that civil societies, even as traditionally conceived, once consolidated become more open to the world, and 'conducive to practices supportive of the universalistic ideals of a common humanity' (Entrikin, 2003: 61).

In earlier chapters we have seen how the European Union should not be conceived as separate from the world, even if this is often how scholars of European integration prefer to see it. The key to understanding Europeanization is to situate the transformation of Europe within a global framework, not only to get a better sense of Europe's role in the world, but in order to see how Europe is continuous with the world. This is true not only of the organization of European space, the polycentric nature of European governance, or the global dimensions of the EU polity, but equally so in the case of European civil society. Indeed, the consti... of European civil society is virtually inconceivable in the terms normally emplo... within EU studies to theorize such a development. If a European civil society comes into being it will be because Europe is seamlessly integrated with the rest of the world, not set apart from it.

ısmopolitan Europe

Studies of contemporary Europe have coalesced around the formation and trajectory of the European Union, its role in the formation of trans-European linkages and institutional structures, and the disseminations of policy preferences. This is a Europe seen in terms of polity-building and governance structures, and which has an over-riding concern with the fate of the nation-state: its rescue, incorporation, and supercession. This focus has led, over a period of time, to the view that the most important transformations in Europe are ones initiated by the EU; creation of an economic bloc, enlargement, creation of the single market, introduction of EU citizenship, the single currency, etc. With a little more reductive thinking it is quite easy to render Europe and the EU synonymous.

This approach avoids confronting the possibility that the most significant feature of contemporary Europe is widespread and rapid social transformation. Over the past two decades or so, the social transformation of Europe has been particularly dramatic, centring on the demise of state-socialism and the widespread social disorientation caused by the end of the Cold War, on the one hand, and the upheavals associated with the transition from industrial to post-industrial society, from Fordism to post-Fordism, and from modernity to postmodernity, on the other. To this mix can be added the fundamental transformations associated with globalization which both provides a context within which the other changes can be understood and creates yet another dynamic of transformation, this time to the very nature of modernity, state, the society, and the individual. This transformative context is of course not restricted to the European theatre, as the idea of globalization would imply. From this perspective it makes great sense to study Europe, not in terms of integration, but in terms of the social transformations which have a much wider and more profound impact; indeed they form the context for the shaping of European polity-building. To date, European Union studies, and cognate disciplines in the fields of social and political science, have not attempted to account for these broader social transformations and have not concerned themselves with the formulation of a theory of society.

To understand Europeanization therefore we need a theory of society. Developing such a theory recasts the study of contemporary Europe and places the role of the EU in European affairs and Europe in the world in a new and different light. Put simply, the global nature of social transformation makes Europe less separate from the rest of the world. In this context it is interesting to reflect upon the way in which globalization has been incorporated into discourses of EU integration over the past decade or so. Although globalization represents a major social transformation this aspect has been seriously downplayed and EU studies has chosen to interpret it in terms familiar to that discipline; as an external threat to the nation-state, as a catalyst for economic integration, a new set of challenges to Europe which the EU alone is capable of solving, and more recently, as an opportunity for the EU to project itself on a world stage.

EU studies' understanding of society remains seriously underdeveloped. Society is seen not in terms of social transformations but in terms of a project to be realized by the EU, following from economic and political integration. The idea that society has a reality outside of the context of an EU project or the residual societies contained within nation-states is absent, and the extent to which global civil society permeates and shapes European political life is not acknowledged. EU studies' appreciation of social transformation extends only to a limited range of outcomes to processes not in fact seen as primarily social: institutionalization, or in a more recent variant, new forms of governance. A policy-led or statist approach to the EU cannot yield a theory of society, and the existence of European citizens, a 'civil society organized at the European level', and greater national inter-connectedness is scant evidence that a European society is about to emerge from EU integration.

Although the 'governance turn' has been a positive one for EU studies in many respects it has had two important consequences for the way society has been conceived. First, society has been reduced to the idea of civil society which in turn is seen as a partner in governance, thereby rendering it instrumental and dependent. On this reading civil society beyond the nation-state cannot develop under its own steam. Second, social transformation has been interpreted as an opportunity for the introduction of new modes of coordinated governance: Europe as a space to be governed. This is a small advance on the earlier preference for seeing social transformation in terms of institutionalization: EU scholars are still desperately seeking a state. To understand the centrality of society to contemporary European transformation it is necessary to step outside the terms in which the debate is currently being conducted. We need to move away from an understanding of society which depends upon the architecture of the (nation-) state and is reducible to a combination civil society, governance, and citizenship and rights.

The argument, simply put, is that the transformations of the current period, conveniently summarized under the heading of globalization, have made much conventional social scientific theorizing about Europe redundant. Specifically, the questioning of the statist and territorial foundations of political life means that to understand Europe in the present period we need to start with theory of society, rather than a theory of the state, integration or governance. The corollary of this is that a social theory approach to social transformation is a more adequate starting point for understanding Europe.

Dimensions of social transformation

...e and extent of the social transformations which have shaped Europe in ...emporary period requires elaboration in order that the complexity and .... nce of the question of society can be fully appreciated. The role of the state is one area in which this transformation has been felt particularly strongly. The nation-state has been relativized by globalization to an extent where the state is no longer the singular reference point for the individual *vis-à-vis* the world. Whereas the state was once a primary source of identity, belonging, recognition, rights, order, and welfare it can no longer claim a monopoly in any of these areas. The state is but one institutional arrangement which attempts to organize, shape and give meaning to social life. In large part, this is because the nation-state is no longer exclusively defined by its role as welfare provider, having acquired increasingly a wider regulatory role. Whereas the welfare state was once a model of society to be emulated (a marker of European social justice), Europeans are now searching for a new normative social model. This is a major deficiency of the development of the EU and for the moment the national welfare state still remains the main source of social solidarity for people. The EU has failed to construct a compelling model of society which would be distinctive to itself. It has jettisoned the welfare state yet tries to cling to the legitimacy of that model through the evocation of a European Social Model comprising a blend of markets and social justice. However, this social model based on the need for a dynamic and knowledge-based economy has failed to connect to the lived experience of most Europeans, and although the most recent expression of the social model – the learning society – offers a future orientation and social promise coupled with a degree of reflexive awareness, it remains subordinated to the economic logic of enhanced competitiveness.

A European Social Model which remains instrumental and functional for integration is unlikely to offer a normative direction to Europeanization or serve as a template for the 'good society' which is necessary in order to make sense of the plethora of rights, freedoms and benefits which the EU offers its residents. The problem with the way the European Social Model has been conceived, we would argue, is that it remains wedded to a future shaped by the European Union, and to a vision of Europe which is largely indifferent to the rest of the world. What is needed is a more cosmopolitan interpretation of the European Social Model. While such a model is far from fully formed there are encouraging signs that one may emerge in the future. The Strauss-Khan group's deliberation on a sustainable future for Europe saw the European Social Model in these terms and recognized the need for it to defend 'the dignity of all human beings, not just of Europeans' (Strauss-Kahn, 2004).

Associated with the loss of a dominant social model and welfarist orientation of the 'good society', and indeed what underlies this, is the displacement of modernity as the organizing principle for social experience. Modernity is associated with the primacy of the nation-state, the institutionalized cleavage resulting from class struggles, a belief in rationality and progress, and faith in a technologically driven future. In the current period, especially in Europe, modernity has come to be imagined as plural and multiple, progress less certain, faith in scientism problematic, and the striving for modernization has been overshadowed by a concern with 'risk society'. The pluralization of modernity can be equated to the decentring of Europe in the world.

This is connected with the fragmentation of political imaginaries. The predominance of nationalism and class as organizing principles for peoples and their political ambitions has given way to a multiplicity of narratives of belief, which have given rise to multiple identifications and conflicts over belonging and loyalty. A vision of a singular social model or aspirational community has to accommodate the reality that ethnicity, religion, neo-liberalism, social movements, environmental awareness, and human rights all generate new expectations of living in the world, new social formations, new narratives of connectivity, and new imaginings of family, community, and individuality. All of this is given a further twist by the fact that democracy is no longer the overarching organizational principle for the autonomous political community. There are several dimensions to this. First, rights discourses are not dependent upon democratic imaginaries to sustain them. For many groups and movements the claiming of rights is a more important goal than democratic community, which is seen as contingent not preconditional. Second, there has been a rise in anti-democratic discourses and these have taken their place alongside more liberal and communitarian political traditions. Examples would include exclusive forms of nationalism and ethnicity; movements under the heading of 'uncivil society' (campaigns against immigrant and refugee groups, for example); religious fundamentalism in all its forms; and the incorporation of more extreme forms of politics into the political 'mainstream', as represented by the figures of Haider and Le Pen. Third, there has been a marked trend towards 'democracy lite' in many European countries. For example, low voter participation in elections, the 'elective dictatorship' of Prime Minister Blair, and identification of multiple 'democratic deficits'. Moreover, it can no longer be assumed that Western nation-states can be trusted to uphold justice and civil liberties, as controversies surrounding Belmarsh prison, Guantanamo Bay, and Abu Ghraib have shown.

Related to these transformations is the loss of social imaginaries which were previously influential, and indeed formative of many European political traditions. It could be argued that the problem of identifying a European Social Model around which Europeans can coalesce and which could give content and meaning to the project of European integration is that the erosion of many of the core beliefs associated with modernity has left Europeans without a notion of emancipation. The importance of emancipatory politics, romantic narratives of autonomy, and utopian social aspirations to European culture cannot be underestimated. The postmodern challenge to the necessity and inherent value of progress, and the displacement of nation and class from the political imaginary, has fatally weakened the claims of emancipatory politics and its hold over the imagination of Europeans. Radical socialism, feminism, and workerism have lost ground in the face of the diffuse possibilities offered by the politics of identity, and this in turn has transformed thinking about a social model from a goal to be realized by self-

social transformation to a much narrower debate on the capacities and
bilities of the individual.

y, the interconnectedness of Europe within a globalizing world and the
recognition of the possibilities inherent in this connectivity have led to the
realization that neither the nation-state nor the European Union has the answers
to problems which are global in nature (terrorism, disease, pollution). In this
sense, global civil society may hold many attractions, particularly if it is recognized
that Europe cannot be dissociated from its location in world society or the global
polity. Globalization has acted upon Europe in many ways, including changing
the role of the nation-state and untying the bonds that previously held political
community in thrall to national security. Globalization has changed our
appreciation of the importance of spaces and borders to the organization of society.
Society has no boundaries in the way that was assumed within the logic of
modernist social science and borders can no longer be taken to distinguish inside
from outside. At its very root, globalization leads to a blurring of borders and the
interpenetration of interior/exterior, self and other. Europe has been defined by
borders, from nations and states to the EU and the new borderlands of the global
era. The border defines self and other. With the growing importance of the EU
and conditions created by globalization, borders will not disappear; they will
continue to be important but will take a huge variety of forms. If anything
characterizes the border in Europe today it is that they are directly implicated in
complicated issues of democratization. Borders are everywhere – in cores and in
peripheries – and need to be democratized. Europe can itself be seen as a borderland,
defined only in relation to differences, which are culturally (cognitively and
symbolically), politically and geographically constructed. There is no longer a
'great frontier', an imperial *limes*, whether an expanding western or a closed eastern
frontier. The border no longer separates an inside from an outside. In societies
organized along the lines of global networks, borders exist in a more complicated
relation to inside and outside.

There is now a cosmopolitan aspect to society in Europe which was not
previously evident. It is argued that a cosmopolitan perspective can help us theorize
society in the present context. In particular, it provides new ways of thinking
about history, community, the individual, the world, and the relationships between
them, in ways which connect strongly to thinking about the search for a European
Model of Society. A cosmopolitan perspective holds many attractions, not least
of them being that a major problem in the way Europe is studied, perhaps *the*
problem, is that the political and social science associated with the study of the
nation-state still permeates EU studies. The nation-state has long been the horizon
of possibility when studying social transformation. As Ulrich Beck and his
colleagues have pointed out, 'continuous change became eternalized into the
idea of an autonomous self-reproducing society, into the structures and categories
of the nation-state' (Beck *et al.*, 2003: 11). This is changing, in part as a result of
the recognition that comparing the EU with the nation-state does not necessarily
make for good social science, and also due to the recognition that the relationship
between globalization and the EU needs a fresh, postetatic context.

We argue that cosmopolitanism can help to apprehend Europe in ways which do not refer back to a national imaginary. In brief, there are three main advantages of adopting a cosmopolitan stance towards Europe. One, cosmopolitanism offers the possibility of placing Europe in relation to the world (and to globalization). It is a mistake to create an artificial separation between Europe and the world. In our consideration of civil society, European space, and Euro-polity for example, we have found that Europe is less distinct from the world than is commonly thought. One consequence of this realization is that it is unhelpful to look for specific, unique forms of European identity, culture, and belonging. To be European is at the same time to be part of the world and is in part a recognition of the fact there is no essential underlying essence to peoplehood. Two, a cosmopolitanism perspective does not see social change as inherently threatening. For EU studies, and more generally with conventional social science, continual social change is perceived as destabilization, the antidote to which is the social order associated with cohesive national community. Three, cosmopolitanism allows for new forms of connectivity. Europe becomes a space within which individuals can experience history, society and identity in new ways, and in doing so start to create society afresh by generating new social relations and norms of social justice.

However, before we look at the cosmopolitan dimensions of Europe we must look at other ways in which it is possible to imagine a future Europe.

European futures

The vision of Europe that has been dominant throughout the modern period and which has been the basis of the European Union until now needs readjustment. If the project of European integration – which is but the latest and the most successful of all those modernist projects aimed at the political unification of the western powers – was one driven by the economic and political interests of the major powers, we have come to a significant caesura in that movement, which in many ways has achieved its aim. For the moment the focus is shifting to the peripheries of Europe, where from the idea of Europe itself derived. Viewed in the wider global context, a very much enlarged and politically embellished Europe is no longer the eastern frontier of the United States of America and the battleground of an east–west conflict. To a significant extent this east–west conflict has taken on a different character with the USA and China the new global powers. Europe's place in this reconfiguration of centres and peripheries is uncertain although it is unlikely that the EU will become a major political-military player, but what is sure is that Europe and Asia are defining their relation with each other. In 2003–4 we have seen a new chapter in Europe's relation to the United States. It is particularly significant that this has occurred at a time when Europe is redefining its relations with Asia, especially with those countries that have historically occupied the dividing lines between the Occident and lands of the Eurasian belt. Inevitably, the Mediterranean will take the place of the Atlantic in shaping the identity of Europe in the twenty-first century. In short, Europe is moving eastwards and as it does so earlier and more ancient visions of Europe emerge to ind us of the origins of the idea of Europe in the cultures and civilization of the Mediterranean and Asia Minor. The European Union and Europe more generally is at a decisive point in terms of its fundamental identity and orientation in the world. There are four options facing it. The first is a return to an 'Old Europe' of nation-states; the second is a post-national federalist 'New Europe'; the third is a universalistic occidentalist Europe allied to the United States; and the fourth is a cosmopolitan Europe based on an inter-EuroAsian civilization.

There is considerable support today for a return to a Europe of nation-states but within the wider context of the European Union. While the Eurosceptics will continue to demand a return to the comforting illusion of a Europe of sovereign nation-states, the reality today is that sovereignty has been progressively transferred to Brussels. However, there is still room for nation-states to continue to play a major role in terms of social integration and political identification. In this scenario Old Europe will not be rendered irrelevant by the continued momentum of Europeanization.

The second option is the post-national vision of a New Europe that has jettisoned the nation-state for a federalist future in which democracy would be embedded in regional, national and, above all, in a supra-federalist state. As is best expressed in Habermas's writings, Europe must give to itself a constitution in recognition of the fact that a European people must be created, if it does not already exist. In this view, it is possible to speak of a European demos which is bound together by a constitutional patriotism and post-national forms of loyalty. The existence of a European ethnos does not preclude the possibility of a post-national demos, which is manifest in a whole range of expressions of European civil society in recent years.

However, this model comes at a price; while post-national trends are in evidence, a post-national political entity is ultimately confined to a limited number of societies and ones that are at a similar level of development in terms of social, cultural and political structures and values. It does not lend itself easily to the current situation of a large-scale polity composed of very diverse societies. Moreover, as in Habermas's theory, it presupposes secular, liberal and post-cultural forms of identification and may be ill-equipped to deal with major conflicts over belonging and identity. For those attracted to it, the tendency has been to trade more democracy for a smaller and more closed Fortress. The viability of this model – which assumes a European people can be called into existence by a constitution – has been called into question by the current enlargement of the European Union and growing post-liberal anxieties.

Where the vision of a post-national Europe is fuelled by anti-Americanism, the third is a universalistic occidental Europe allied to the United States. This is a view of Europe that sees the European Union as a global player and one that is closely linked to NATO. The assumption here is that something called 'the west' matters and must be defended by Europe, which shares with the United States a common cultural community based upon the values of western civilization. As is apparent from the support many European governments – with the exception of France and Germany – gave to the United States invasion of Iraq last year this has considerable support, especially among the political right. The UK's alleged 'special relation' with the US is of course too a major factor in the reality of this model of Europe. Indeed, when it comes to the test this Atlanticist Europe is still very powerful and it is notable that the draft treaty appeals to the values of western civilization rather than to values that might be termed specifically European. But there is no denying the vision of a universalistic occidentalist Europe has its limits, as the results of the 2004 Spanish election reveal in sealing the fate of the occidentalist government; moreover, the impact of anti-war protests in several European countries cannot be underestimated in leading to a more assertive Europe. It is also unlikely that Europe can be a global player simply because it lacks the military clout.

There is also a fourth option, which might be called a cosmopolitan Europe. Rather than being universalistic and Atlanticist, it is a more limited cosmopolitanism based on an inter-Euro–Asian civilizational constellation. The articulation of this model is a major challenge for Europe and might be the appropriate *imaginaire* for our time. Given the limits of the post-national model and the dangers of the Occidentalist position, Europe can sustain the drive towards greater integration without the comforting illusion of Old Europe. A cosmopolitan Europe is one that is more open to diversity, especially to its more than 15 million Muslims and many other minorities, and content with a limited unity in diversity, where the nation can rediscover itself without atavistic nationalism, and where the federalist tendency does not erode national autonomy.

The really important challenge for this conception of Europe is to open itself to the wider east that is now also a part of itself. A cosmopolitan Europe is one that does not have a clear distinction between east and west or between Self and Other. Without retreating into pointless anti-Americanism or searching in vain for an elusive European people that could be enshrined in a European constitution and a new we-feeling, or aspiring to be a global player, the cosmopolitan challenge is to rediscover the diversity of Europe. In the context of the eventual membership of Turkey and other near Eastern countries and the ongoing renegotiation of borders, Europe will become more post-western and also more cosmopolitan with cultural questions concerning belonging more and more important. One of the arguments made in this book is that there is no underlying European identity that makes this impossible, that is there is no foundational European identity that prevents Europe from adopting a more inclusive kind of identity.

This cosmopolitan Europe will have to redefine not only its identity but will have to articulate a deeper civilizational *imaginaire*, that is the way people imagine their society in terms of its values and meaning. This is more than an intellectual understanding and also more than a consciously articulated identity; it refers to the very condition of social existence, political possibility and cultural creativity. It might be suggested that essential to this *imaginaire* will be a rediscovery of the unity of the inter-European–Asian civilizational constellation. Perhaps, then, this is a model for the future, an openness to the east in a rethinking of the civilizational basis of Europe in cultures and civilizations of the Mediterreanean and Near East.

Cosmopolitan Europe

The connection between cosmopolitanism and Europe has not been made by scholars of EU integration for much the same reasons as ideas of global civil society have not informed thinking about EU civil society to any great extent. There is much more interest in cosmopolitan Europe within social theory approaches to Europe. So on the one hand the EU has been described as the first international organization with cosmopolitan credentials (Archibugi, 1998), while the EU itself never invokes cosmopolitanism in its deliberations on citizenship, civil society or European identity, and cosmopolitanism is not part of the self-identity of the European Union. In other words, at the same time as the EU is being interpreted as a cosmopolitan polity-in-the-making by social scientists, mainly on the strength of its capacity for transnationalized decision-making, EU institutions and their policy-makers eschew the idea of cosmopolitanism in their official discourses, although the idea that European values are universal values (some but not all of which can be construed as having a cosmopolitan component) has had an impact on EU thinking over a long period.

In the past few years, cosmopolitanism has once more emerged as a key theme within social theory, although this is not to say that there exists a great deal of consensus on what constitutes cosmopolitanism, who can be described as cosmopolitan, or where cosmopolitanism might be found. In fact, a number of contending ways of conceiving cosmopolitanism have been promoted, some drawing upon much older political traditions, others of more recent vintage. One approach, the 'cosmopolitan democracy' thesis of Archibugi, Held and their colleagues (Archibugi and Held, 1995; Archibugi *et al.*, 1998), has a direct line to studies of contemporary Europe. Their cosmopolitanism is a normative model of international order, a post-national vision of global democractic governance. A slightly different version of this position is represented by Habermas (see Habermas, 2003c). Alternatively, cosmopolitanism can denote a transformative process, as with Beck's (2002: 17) ideas of cosmopolitanization, or globalization from within national societies (see also Beck and Grande, 2004).

Of course, cosmopolitanism is not a new idea, possessing a lineage which can be traced back to the ancient world, and being firmly embedded in various traditions of Western political thought (Rengger, 2003). It was largely eclipsed in the modern period by the ideologies associated with national belonging, and beset by negative associations with the pre-modern, the rootless and the marginal. Some of these associations remain to the present day and work to limit the popularity of cosmopolitan perspectives. There is a different sense in which cosmopolitanism is not new: cosmopolitanism has been a constant feature of everyday social and political life for a very long time. In additional to conscious avowals of cosmopolitan identity amongst elites there exists a sort of 'banal cosmopolitanism' which has remained hidden or has simply not been recognized due to its ordinariness. This cosmopolitanism occurs alongside, and not necessarily in conflict with, nationalism and other identities (Cheah, 1998), and can be found in networks formed by interest groups, in the codes of practice adhered to by groups of

professionals, in the communities of scholars who encircle the globe wit
conferences and publication activities, and in the commonalities genera
workers' organizations, peace campaigners, and the women's movemen
example.

Whereas traditional ideas associated with cosmopolitanism tend to revolve
around world citizenship (Heater, 2002), more recent constructions emphasize a
multiplicity of identities and belongings, and membership in a plurality of
communities. This has formed the basis for a new political content for cosmopolitanism (as an alternative to exclusive forms of nationalism, for example), and
for an idea of world citizenship which is grounded in tangible benefits and
pragmatic policy regimes (environmental responsibility, personhood rights, human
development) rather than abstract notions of universal brotherhood. It is fair to
say that there is no one dominant interpretation of cosmopolitanism today
(Vertovec and Cohen, 2002). It can stand for *inter alia*: world citizenship, as
embodied in the UN's Universal Declaration of Human Rights; the advocacy of
a more democratic world order of national states; an engagement and respect for
the Other and acknowledgement of difference; the recognition of the multiplicity
of identifications which characterizes contemporary social life; or a rejection of
narrow and exclusionary forms of nationalism, or all of these.

While cosmopolitanism has risen rapidly up the social science agenda it has
made very few inroads in relation to European Union studies. By and large, EU
scholars have remained untouched by the emerging cosmopolitan agenda. This
deserves further investigation, particularly when one considers that other political
and social scientists have accorded the EU a privileged place in relation to
cosmopolitanism, and for Archibugi (1998: 219): 'the first international model
which begins to resemble to cosmopolitan model is the European Union'. What
is distinctive about cosmopolitanism, and to what extent can it help us make
sense of developments in contemporary Europe, and the place of Europe in the
world? The re-emergence of cosmopolitanism has occurred against a background
in which globalization has obliged the nation-state to renegotiate its place in the
world order. In addition, there exists a growing appreciation of the importance of
transnational social movements, post-national citizenship, multiple political
identifications, and global civil society, all of which have encouraged social
theorists and political commentators to explore new ways of thinking about
political attachments and new ways of thinking about the place of individuals,
communities, organizations, and nation-states in the emerging world polity.

Cosmopolitanism posits a new relationship between the individual and society,
and one in which the nation-state has a far less pivotal role as a pole of attraction
(if not in terms of implementing or resisting global regimes of human rights). In
current EU studies these linkages are short-circuited by the impulse to locate the
universality of European citizenship in its national origins. If globalization is
understood in terms of the growing interconnectedness of the world coupled with
a recognition of the palpable 'oneness' of the world, to paraphrase Roland
Robertson, then a cosmopolitan outlook contributes to an increasing global
consciousness. The more we think through cosmopolitan categories – the univer-

salism of human rights, the world as a risk society, the indivisibility of humankind – the more we make the idea of global society meaningful. Cosmopolitanism also points to new forms of political community, not simply in the sense that it offers new possibilities for transnational or global attachments, but in the ways it recognizes the multiplicity of communities into which people are inserted, and the means through which inclusion/exclusion operates in a world of communities of choice and multiple attachments. Communities and loyalties are therefore not an either/or choice but inherently pluralistic. This has some purchase on the European context in which proponents of both nationalism and supra-nationalism have yet to find a means of inscribing multiple identities within political discourse in a way that does not result in divisions and conflicts. Cosmopolitanism takes multiple belonging as the norm and does not seek to deny the plurality of selves to which this can give rise. Cosmopolitanism aspires to be at home with difference and diversity, societal tensions which national citizenship and multicultural identity have engaged with but failed to resolve.

Cosmopolitanism can offer a fresh perspective on the question of what it is to be European, a question which has become increasingly important in thinking about the EU. Rather than a European identity rooted in common cultural heritage and shared ancestry, cosmopolitanism encourages a reflexive stance towards individual and collective identity and, importantly, a positive embrace of the values of the Other. Cosmopolitanism includes an engagement with difference which, in addition to the liberal principles of tolerance and respect, goes much further in encouraging an identification with the Other. Cosmopolitanism is alert to the importance of contestation and difference in a pluralistic society and understands the positive value of agonistic democracy. Moreover, cosmopolitanism encourages the recognition that we contain some of these conflicts and tensions in our own biographies: we each contain a clash of cultures (Beck, 2000a). In our encounters we are able to both recognize people as strangers and accept them as internal Others. Cosmopolitanism thus enables the expression of sympathies and emotions associated with close-knit communities while simultaneously promoting the cool distancing associated with encounters with strangers or action-at-a-distance.

On this reading, being European is about adopting a particular stance towards the world. This involves embracing difference, embodying otherness, and existing in a state of becoming rather than being. In this sense, we have never been European, but, with a cosmopolitan mindset, we might now aspire to it. The possibility of a cosmopolitan European society leaves open the possibility that once constituted as cosmopolitan Europeans would have less rather than more reasons to become attached to Europe, preferring instead to lend support to a cosmopolitan world order. Many commentators have considered the likelihood or otherwise of a European demos coming into existence (for example, Delanty, 1998; Soysal, 2002a), but what would happen to European solidarity if it should turn out that the European demos is made up of cosmopolitans? This dilemma may go some way to explaining why cosmopolitanism is absent from European Commission and European Council debates on integration, enlargement, the

democratic deficit, citizenship, and civil society. The EU is much happier to th
of European citizens as nationals/Europeans rather than cosmopolitans.

While the EU has not been too successful in turning national citizens in..
Europeans, it may turn out to be rather good at producing cosmopolitans. It is not
impossible that in the future Europeans, particularly those who exhibit a high
degree of reflexivity towards their own national identities and who find European
identity to be artificial and empty of content, could identify with cosmopolitanism.
Cosmopolitanism can offer a content and meaning to identity which the EU,
with its emphasis on citizens as workers, consumers, students, or even lifelong
learners, cannot match.

Notes

2 History, modernity and the multiple conceptions of Europe

1   Some of the following is based on papers given by Gerard Delanty at Koc University, Istanbul, 2 May 2003; University of Konstanz, 21 May 2003; European Sociological Association Murcia, Spain, 24 September 2003; Israel Academy of Sciences and Humanities, Jersualem, 4 November 2003; and also draws from ideas originally published in Gerard Delanty (2003) 'The making of a post-western Europe: a civilizational analysis', *Thesis Eleven*, 72: 8–24.

2   Cited in the Regular Reports from the Commission on Progress towards Accession, 8 November 2000. See: http://www.europa.eu.int/enlargement/report_report_11_00/index.htm.

3 Is there a European identity?

1   Some of the following is based on a paper given by Gerard Delanty for the ARENA Conference, University of Oslo, 3 October 2003. An earlier version was published as Gerard Delanty (2003) 'Is there a European identity?', *Global Dialogue*, 6(3–4): 76–86.

2   Some of the following is based on a paper presented by Gerard Delanty in September 2002 at the Conference on the Future of Europe at the University of Maastricht, Netherlands and 16–17 January 2003 at the Conference 'Whither Europe: Borders, Boundaries, Frontiers in a Changing World', Gothenburg University. An earlier version was published as Gerard Delanty (2003) 'Europe and the idea of "unity in diversity"', in Rutger Lindahl (ed.) *Whither Europe: Borders, Boundaries, Frontiers in a Changing World*, Gothenburg: CERGU.

3   *Bulletin of the European Communities*, 1973, No. 12, Section 5, Clause 2501, pp. 118–22.

4   The Charta was proposed by Václav Havel in 1994 and was taken up by Europa-Union Deutschland and was drafted in 1995. See http://www.europa-web.de/europa/02wwswww/203chart/chart_gb.htm.

4 What does it mean to be a 'European'?

1   This chapter is based on a paper originally given by Gerard Delanty at the Conference 'Cosmopolitanism and Europe', Royal Holloway University of London, 22 April 2004 and another paper part of which appeared as Delanty (2003) 'Loyalty and the European Union', in Michael Waller, Andrew Linklater and Patrick Thonberry (eds) *Loyalty and the Postnational State*, London: Routledge.

5 The new cultural logic of Europeanization

1   Some of the following discussion on citizenship derives from Gerard Delanty (2004) 'From nationality to citizenship: cultural identity and cosmopolitan challenges in Ireland', in Andrew Finlay (ed.) *Nationalism and Multiculturalism: Irish Identity, Citizenship and the Peace Process*, London, Berlin and Hamburg: LIT Verlag.

7 Organizing European space

1   The European Neighbourhood Policy covers: Belarus, Ukraine, Moldova, Georgia, Armenia, Azerbaijan, Morocco, Algeria, Tunisia, Libya, Egypt, Israel, Jordan, Lebanon, Syria, Palestinian Authority.

9 Towards a European polity?

1   http://socialsciencedictionary.nelson.com.

References

Abraham, J. and Lewis, G. (2000) *Regulating Medicines in Europe: Competition, Expertise and Public Health*, London: Routledge.

Adorno, T.W. (1986) 'What does coming to terms with the past mean?', in G. Hartman (ed.) *Bitburg in Moral and Political Perspective*, Bloomington, IN: Indiana University Press.

Albrow, M. (1998) 'Europe in the global age', Amalfi Prize Lecture, 30 May, Amalfi, Italy.

Alexander, J., Eyerman, R., Giesen, B., Smelser, N. and Sztompka, P. (2004) *Cultural Trauma and Collective Identity*, Cambridge: Cambridge University Press.

Allen, J., Massey, D. and Cochrane, A. (1998) *Rethinking the Region*, London: Routledge.

Amin, A. (2001) 'Spatialities of globalization', *Environment and Planning A*, 34: 385–99.

Amin, A. (2004) 'Regions unbound: towards a new politics of place', *Geografiska Annaler*, 86B(1): 33–44.

Anderson, B. (1983) *Imagined Communities*, London: Verso.

Anderson, J. (2002) 'Europeanization and the transformation of the democratic polity, 1945–2000', *Journal of Common Market Studies*, 40(5): 793–822.

Anderson, M. (1996) *Frontiers: Territory and State Formation in the Modern World*, Oxford: Polity Press.

Anderson, M. and Bort, E. (eds) (1998) *The Frontiers of Europe*, London: Pinter.

Andersen, S.S. (2000) 'EU energy policy: interest interaction and supranational authority', Arena Working Papers WP 00/5. Available online http://www.arena.uio.no/publications/wp00_5.htm.

Appadurai, R. (1996) *Modernity at Large: Cultural Dimension of Globalization*, Minneapolis, MN: University of Minnesota Press.

Archibugi, D. (1998) 'Principles of cosmopolitan democracy', in D. Archibugi, D. Held and M. Kohler (eds) *Re-imagining Political Community: Studies in Cosmopolitan Democracy*, Cambridge: Polity Press.

Archibugi, D. and Held, D. (1995) 'Editors' introduction', in D. Archibugi and D. Held (eds) *Cosmopolitan Democracy: An Agenda for a New World Order*, Cambridge: Polity Press.

Archibugi, D., Held, D. and Köhler, M. (eds) (1998) *Re-imagining Political Community: Studies in Cosmopolitan Democracy*, Cambridge: Polity Press.

Armstrong, K.A. (2001) 'The White Paper and the rediscovery of civil society', *EUSA Review*, 14(4): 3–8.

Armstrong, K.A. (2002) 'Rediscovering civil society: the European Union and the White Paper on Governance', *European Law Journal*, 8(1): 102–32.

Arnason, J. (1991) 'Modernity as a project and as a field of tension', in A. Honneth and H. Joas (eds) *Communicative Action*, Cambridge: Polity Press.

Arnason, J. (1993) *The Future that Failed: Origins and Destinies of the Soviet Model*, London: Routledge.

Arnason, J. (2000) 'Approaching Byzantium: identity, predicament and afterlife', *Thesis Eleven*, 62: 39–69.

Arnason, J. (2003a) *Civilizations in Dispute: Historical Questions and Theoretical Traditions*, Leiden: Brill.

Arnason, J. (2003b) 'Entangled communisms: imperial revolutions in Russia and China', *European Journal of Social Theory*, 6(3): 307–25.

Asad, T. (2002) 'Muslims and European identity: can Europe represent Islam?', in A. Pagden (ed.) *The Idea of Europe: From Antiquity to the European Union*, Cambridge: Cambridge University Press.

Ash, T. Garton (2003) 'Anti-Europeanism in America', *New York Review of Books*, 13 February.

Ashplant, T., Dawson, G. and Roper, M. (eds) (2001) *The Politics of War, Memory and Commemoration*, London: Routledge.

Atkinson, R. (2001) 'The emerging "urban agenda" and the European spatial development perspective: towards an EU urban policy?', *European Planning Studies*, 9(3): 385–406.

Axford, B. (1995) *The Global System: Economics, Politics, and Culture*, Cambridge: Polity Press.

Axford, B. (2001) 'Enacting globalization: transnational networks and the deterritorialization of social relationships in the global system', *Protosociology*, 15: 119–47.

Axford, B. and Huggins, R. (1999) 'Towards a post-national polity: the emergence of the Network Society in Europe', in D. Smith and S. Wright (eds) *Whose Europe?: The Turn Towards Democracy*, Oxford: Blackwell.

Axford, B. and Huggins, R. (2001) 'Globalization and the prospects for cosmopolitan world society', in B. Axford, K. Browning and R. Huggins (eds) *Democracy and Democratization*, Routledge: London.

Bach, M. (ed.) (2000) *Die Europäisierung nationaler Gesellschaften*, Wiesbaden: Westdeutscher Verlag.

Baker, G. (2002) 'Problems in the theorization of global civil society', *Political Studies*, 50: 928–43.

Balibar, E. (1991) 'Es gibt keinen Staat in Europa: racism and politics in Europe today', *New Left Review*, 186: 5–19.

Balibar, E. (2004) *We the People of Europe: Reflections on Transnational Citizenship*, Princeton, NJ: Princeton University Press.

Banus, E. (2002) 'Cultural policy in the EU and the European identity', in M. Farell, S. Fella and M. Newman (eds) *European Integration in the 21st Century: Unity in Diversity?* London: Sage.

Barber, B. (2001) 'Challenges to democracy in an age of globalization', in R. Axtmann (ed.) *Balancing Democracy*, London: Continuum.

Barlett, R. (1993) *The Making of Europe: Conquest, Colonization and Cultural Change, 950–1350*, London: Allen Lane.

Barnett, C. (2001) 'Culture, policy, and subsidiarity in the European Union: from symbolic identity to the governmentalization of culture', *Political Geography*, 20: 405–26.

Barry, A. (1993) 'The European Community and European government: harmonization, mobility and space', *Economy and Society*, 22(3): 314–26.

Barry, A. (2001) *Political Machines: Governing a Technological Society*, London: Athlone Press.

Barth, F. (ed.) (1969) *Ethnic Groups and Boundaries: The Social Organization of Cultural Difference*, London: Allen and Unwin.

Bassim, M. (1991) 'Russia between Europe and Asia: the ideological construction of geographical space', *Slavic Review*, 50: 1–17.

Batt, J. (2003) 'The EU's new borderlands', London: CER Working Paper.

Baubock, R. (2003) 'Multilevel citizenship and territorial borders in the EU polity', IWE Working Paper No. 37. Available online http://www.iwe-oeaw.ac.at/workingpapers/WP37.pdf.

Bauman, Z. (1973) *Culture as Praxis*, London: Routledge and Kegan Paul.

Bauman, Z. (2001) *Liquid Modernity*, Cambridge: Polity Press.

Bauman, Z. (2003) *Liquid Love*, Cambridge: Polity Press.

Bauman, Z. (2004) *Identity*, Cambridge: Polity Press.

Beck, U. (1997) *The Reinvention of Politics: Rethinking Modernity in the Global Social Order*, Cambridge: Polity Press.

Beck, U. (1999) *World Risk Society*, Cambridge: Polity Press.

Beck, U. (2000a) *What is Globalization?* Cambridge: Polity Press.

Beck, U. (2000b) 'The cosmopolitian perspective: sociology of the second age of modernity', *British Journal of Sociology*, 51(1): 79–105.

Beck, U. (2002) 'The cosmopolitan society and its enemies', *Theory, Culture and Society*, 19(1–2): 17–44.

Beck, U. (2003) 'Understanding the real Europe', *Dissent*, Summer. Available online http://www.dissentmagazine.orgImenutest/articles/su03/beck.htm.

Beck, U. (2004) 'The cosmopolitan turn', in N. Gane (ed.) *The Future of Social Theory*, London: Continuum.

Beck, U. and Grande, E. (2004) *Das kosmopolitische Europa*, Frankfurt: Suhrkamp.

Beck, U., Bonns, W. and Lau, C. (2003) 'The theory of reflexive modernization', *Theory, Culture and Society*, 20(2): 1–33.

Beetham, D. (1991) *The Legitimation of Power*, Basingstoke: Macmillan.

Beetham, D. (1998) 'Human rights as a model for cosmopolitan democracy', in D. Archibugi, D. Held and M. Kohler (eds) *Re-imagining Political Community: Studies in Cosmopolitan Democracy*, Polity Press: Cambridge.

Bellier, I. and Wilson, T. (eds) (2000) *An Anthropology of the European Union: Building, Imagining and Experiencing the New Europe*, Oxford: Berg.

Benhabib, S. (2002) *The Claims of Culture: Equality and Diversity in the Global Era*, Princeton, NJ: Princeton University Press.

Bennett, T. (2001) *Differing Diversities: Cultural Policy and Cultural Diversity*, Strasbourg: Council of Europe Publications.

Berezin, M. (2003) 'Introduction: territory, emotion and identity: spatial recalibration in a new Europe', in M. Berezin and M. Schain (eds) *Europe Without Borders: Remapping Territory, Citizenship and Identity in a Transnational Age*, Baltimore, MD: Johns Hopkins University Press.

Berezin, M. and Schain, M. (2003a) 'Preface', in M. Berezin and M. Schain (eds) *Europe Without Borders: Remapping Territory, Citizenship and Identity in a Transnational Age*, Baltimore, MD: Johns Hopkins University Press.

Berezin, M. and Schain, M. (eds) (2003b) *Europe without Borders: Remapping Territory, Citizenship and Identity in a Transnational Age*, Princeton, NJ: Princeton University Press.

Berger, T. and Luckmann, T. (1966) *The Social Construction of Reality*, Harmondsworth: Penguin.

Billington, J. (2004) *Russia in Search of Itself*, Baltimore, MD: Johns Hopkins University Press.

Bloom, H. (1990) *Personal Identity, National Identity and International Relations*, Cambridge: Cambridge University Press.

Bodei, R. (1995) 'Historical memory and European identity', *Philosophy and Social Criticism*, 21(4): 1–13.

Bohman, J. (2005) 'Constitution-making and democratic innovation: the European Union and transnational governance', in E. Eriksen (ed.) *Making the Euro-Polity: Reflexive Integration in Europe*, London: Routledge.

Boje, T., van Steenbergen, B. and Walby, S. (eds) (1999) *European Societies: Fusion or Fission?* London: Routledge.

Boli, J. and Thomas, G. (eds) (1999) *Constructing World Culture: International Non-governmental Organizations Since 1875*, Stanford, CA: Stanford University Press.

Boltanski, L. and Thévenot, L. (1991) *De La justification: Les Économies de la grandeur*, Paris: Gallimard.

Boltanski, L. and Thévenot, L. (1999) 'Critical and pragmatic sociology', *European Journal of Social Theory*, 2(3): 359–77.

Bonnell, V. and Hunt, L. (eds) (1999) *Beyond the Cultural Turn*, Berkeley, CA: University of California Press.

Bonnett, A. (2004) *The Idea of the West*, Basingstoke: Palgrave.

Borneman, J. and Fowler, N. (1997) 'Europeanization', *Annual Review of Anthropology*, 26: 487–514.

Bornschier, V. (1997) 'European processes and the state of the European Union', Paper presented at the 1997 European Sociological Association Conference, University of Essex. Available online http://www.suz.unizh.ch/bornschier/european_processes.pdf.

Börzel, T. and Risse, T. (2003) 'Conceptualizing the domestic impact of Europe', in K. Featherstone and C. Radaelli (eds) *The Politics of Europeanisation*, Oxford: Oxford University Press.

Bottomore, T. (1987) *Sociology: A Guide to Problems and Literature*, 3rd edn, London: Allen and Unwin.

Bourdieu, P. (1984) *Distinction: A Social Critique of the Judgement of Taste*, Cambridge: Polity Press.

Bozdogan, S. and Kasaba, R. (eds) (1997) *Rethinking Modernity and National Identity in Turkey*, Seattle, WA: University of Washington Press.

Brague, R. (2002) *Eccentric Culture: A Theory of Western Civilization*, South Bend, IN: St Augustine's Press.

Braudel, F. (1972/3) *The Mediterranean and the Mediterranean World in the Age of Philip II*, London: Fontana.

Braunerhjelm, P., Faini, R., Norman, V., Ruane, F. and Seabright, P. (2000) *Integration and the Regions of Europe: How the Right Policies Can Prevent Polarization*, London: Centre for Economic Policy Research.

Breakwell, G. (2004) 'Identity change in the context of the growing influence of the European Union institutions', in R.K. Herrmann, T. Risse and M.B. Brewer (eds) *Transnational Identities: Becoming European in the EU*, New York: Rowman and Littlefield.

Breakwell, G. and Lyons, E. (eds) (1996) *Changing European Identities: Social Psychological Analyses of Change*, Oxford: Butterworth-Heinemann.

Breckenridge, C., Pollock, S., Bhabha, H.K. and Chakrabarty, D. (eds) (2002) *Cosmopolitanism*, Durham, NC: Duke University Press.

Brenner, N. (1999) 'Beyond state-centrism? Space, territoriality, and geographical scale in globalization studies', *Theory and Society*, 28: 39–78.

Brenner, N. (2003) 'Rescaling state space in western Europe: urban governance and the rise of glocalizing competition state regimes (GCSRs)', in M. Berezin and M. Schain (eds) *Europe Without Borders: Remapping Territory, Citizenship, and Identity in a Transnational Age*, Baltimore, MD: Johns Hopkins University Press.

Brotton, J. (2002) *The Renaissance Bazaar: From the Silk Road to Michelangelo*, Oxford: Oxford University Press.

Brubaker, R. and Cooper, F. (2000) 'Beyond "identity"', *Theory and Society*, 29: 1–47.

Bryant, C.G.A. (1993) 'Social self-organization, civility and sociology: a comment on Kumar's "civil society"', *British Journal of Sociology*, 44: 397–401.

Bulmer, S.J. (1998) 'New institutionalism and the governance of the single European market', *Journal of European Public Policy*, 5(3): 365–86.

Buss, A. (2004) *The Russian Orthodox Tradition and Modernity*, Leiden: Brill.

Buzan, B. (2004) *From International to World Society? English School Theory and the Social Structures of Globalisation*, Cambridge: Cambridge University Press.

Cacciari, M. (1997) *L'Arcipelago*, Milan: Adelphi.

Calhoun, C. (ed.) (1994) *Social Theory and the Politics of Social Identity*, Oxford: Blackwell.

Calhoun, C. (1999) 'Nationalism, political community and the representation of society: or, why feeling at home is not a substitute for public space', *European Journal of Social Theory*, 2(2): 217–31.

Calhoun, C. (2000) 'Social theory and the public sphere', in B. Turner (ed.) *The Blackwell Companion to Social Theory*, 2nd edn, Oxford: Blackwell.

Calhoun, C. (2003) 'The democratic integration of Europe: interests, identity, and the public sphere', in M. Berezin and M. Schain (eds) *Europe without Borders: Remapping Territory, Citizenship, and Identity in a Transnational Age*, Baltimore, MD: Johns Hopkins University Press.

Capozza, D. and Brown, R. (eds) (2000) *Social Identity Processes*, London: Sage.

Castano, E. (2004) 'European identity: a socio-psychological perspective', in R.K. Herrmann, T. Risse and M.B. Brewer (eds) *Transnational Identities: Becoming European in the EU*, New York: Rowman and Littlefield.

Castells, M. (1996) *The Rise of the Network State. Volume 1: The Information Age*, Oxford: Blackwell.

Castells, M. (1998) 'The unification of Europe', in M Castells (ed.) *End of the Millennium, Volume 3: The Information Age*, Oxford: Blackwell.

Castells, M. (2000a) *The Rise of the Network Society. The Information Age: Economy, Society and Culture, Volume 1*, 2nd edn, Oxford: Blackwell.

Castells, M. (2000b) 'Materials for an exploratory theory of the network society', *British Journal of Sociology*, 51(1): 5–24.

Castells, M. (2000c) *End of Millennium, The Information Age: Economy, Society and Culture, Volume 3*, 2nd edn, Oxford: Blackwell.

Castoriadis, C. (1987) *The Imaginary Institution of Society*, Cambridge: Polity Press.

Castoriadis, C. (1993) *World in Fragments: Writings on Politics, Society, Psychoanalysis, and the Imagination*, Stanford, CA: Stanford University Press.

Cederman, L.-E. (ed.) (2001) *Constructing Europe's Identity: The External Dimension*, London: Lynne Rienner.

Cerutti, F. (1992) 'Can there be a supranational identity?', *Philosophy and Social Criticism*, 18(2): 147–62.

Cerutti, F. (2003) 'A political identity of the Europeans', *Thesis Eleven*, 72: 26–45.

Cesarani, D. and Fulbrook, M. (eds) (1996) *Citizenship, Nationality and Migration in Europe*, London: Routledge.

Chakarbarty, D. (2000) *Deprovencializing Europe: Postcolonial Thought and Historical Difference*, Princeton, NJ: Princeton University Press.

Chandler, D. (2003) 'International justice', in D. Archibugi (ed.) *Debating Cosmopolitics*, London: Verso.

Chaney, D. (1994) *The Cultural Turn: Scene-Setting Essays on Contemporary Cultural History*, London: Routledge.

Cheah, P. (1998) 'Introduction part II: the cosmopolitical – today', in P. Cheah and B. Robbins (eds) (1998) *Cosmopolitics: Thinking and Feeling Beyond the Nation*, Minneapolis, MN: Minnesota University Press.

Cheah, P. and Robbins, B. (eds) (1998) *Cosmopolitics: Thinking and Feeling Beyond the Nation*, Minneapolis, MN: Minnesota University Press.

Checkel, J. (1999) 'Social construction and integration', *Journal of European Public Policy*, 6(4): 545–60.

Christiansen, F. and Hedetoft, U. (eds) (2004) *The Politics of Multiple Belonging*, Aldershot: Ashgate.

Christiansen, T., Jorgensen, K.N. and Wiener, A. (eds) (2001) *The Social Construction of Europe*, London: Sage.

Christin, T. and Trechsel, A. (2000) 'Joining the EU: explaining public opinion in Switzerland', *European Union Politics*, 3(4): 415–43.

Chryssochoou, D. (1998) 'Democracy and integration theory in the 1990s: a study in European polity-formation', Jean Monnet Working Papers in Comparative and International Politics. Available online http://aei.pitt.edu/archive/00000409/01/jmwp14.htm.

Chryssochoou, D. (2001a) *Theorizing European Integration*, London: Sage.

Chryssochoou, D. (2001b) 'Towards a civic conception of the European polity', ESRC 'One Europe or Several?' Programme Working Paper 33/01. Available online http://www.one-europe.ac.uk

Citrin, J. (2001) 'The end of American identity?', in S. Renshon (ed.) *One America? Political Leadership, National Identity and the Dilemmas of Diversity*, Washington, DC: Georgetown University Press.

Citrin, J. and Sides, J. (2004) 'More than just nationals: how identity choice matters in the new Europe', in R.K. Herrmann, T. Risse and M.B. Brewer (eds) *Transnational Identities: Becoming European in the EU*, New York: Rowman and Littlefield.

Closa, C. (2001) 'Requirements of a European public sphere: civil society, self and the institutionalisation of citizenship', in K. Eder and B. Giesen (eds) *European Citizenship Between National Legacies and Postnational Projects*, Oxford: Oxford University Press.

Coakley, J. (1982) 'Political territories and cultural frontiers: conflicts of principle in the formation of states in Europe', *West European Politics*, 5(4): 34–49.

Cohen, A. (1985) *The Symbolic Construction of Community*, London: Routledge.

Cohen, J. and Arato, A. (1992) *Civil Society and Political Theory*, Cambridge, MA: MIT Press.

Colas, A. (2001) 'The promises of international civil society: global governance, cosmopolitan democracy and the end of sovereignty?' Avaiable online http://www.theglobalsite.ac.uk.

Commission of the European Communities (1992) *Treaty on European Union*, Luxembourg: OOPEC.

Commission of the European Communities (1995) White Paper on Education and Training: Teaching and Learning – Towards the Learning Society. Brussels, COM(95) 590 final, 29 November.

Cowan, J.K., Dembour, M.-B. and Wilson, R. (eds) (2001) *Culture and Rights: Anthropological Perspectives*, Cambridge: Cambridge University Press.

Cronin, A. (2002) 'Consumer rights/cultural rights: a new politics of European belonging', *European Journal of Cultural Studies*, 5(3): 507–25.

Crouch, C. (1999) *Social Change in Western Europe*, Oxford: Oxford University Press.

Cruikshank, B. (1999) *The Will To Empower: Democratic Citizens and Other Subjects*, Ithaca, NY: Cornell University Press.

Cunningham, M. (1999) 'Saying sorry: the politics of the apology', *The Political Quarterly*, 70(3): 285–93.

Davies, N. (1996) *Europe: A History*, Oxford: Oxford University Press.

Davoudi, S. (2003) 'Polycentricity in European spatial planning: from an analytical tool to a normative agenda', *European Planning Studies*, 11(8): 979–99.

Delanty, G. (1995a) *Inventing Europe: Idea, Identity, Reality*, Basingstoke: Macmillan.

Delanty, G. (1995b) 'The limits and possibility of a European identity: a critique of cultural essentialism', *Philosophy and Social Criticism*, 21(4): 15–36.

Delanty, G. (1996a) 'The frontier and identities of exclusion in European history', *History of European Ideas*, 22(2): 93–103.

Delanty, G. (1996b) 'The resonance of Mitteleuropa: a Habsburg myth or anti-politics?', *Theory, Culture and Society*, 14(4): 93–108.

Delanty, G. (1997a) 'Habermas and occidental rationalism: the politics of identity, social learning and the cultural limits of moral universalism', *Sociological Theory*, 15(3): 30–59.

Delanty, G. (1997b) *Social Science: Beyond Realism and Constructivism*, Buckingham: Open University Press.

Delanty, G. (1998) 'Social theory and European transformation: is there a European society?' *Sociological Research Online*, 3(1).

Delanty, G. (1999) *Social Theory in a Changing World: Conceptions of Modernity*, Cambridge: Polity Press.

Delanty, G. (2000a) *Modernity and Postmodernity: Knowledge, Power, the Self*, London: Sage.

Delanty, G. (2000b) *Citizenship in the Global Age: Culture, Society and Politics*, Buckingham: Open University Press.

Delanty, G. (2000c) 'The foundations of social theory: origins and trajectories', in B. Turner (ed.) *The Blackwell Companion to Social Theory*, 2nd edn, Oxford: Blackwell.

Delanty, G. and Jones, P. (2002) 'Architecture and Social Theory', *European Journal of Social Theory*, 5(4): 453–66.

Delanty, G. and O'Mahony, P. (2002) *Nationalism and Social Theory*, London: Sage.

Delanty, G. and Strydom, P. (eds) (2003) *Philosophies of Social Science: Classic and Contemporary Readings*, Buckingham: Open University Press.

Derrida, J. (1994) *The Other Heading: Reflections on Today's Europe*, Bloomington, IN: Indiana University Press.

De Schutter, O. (2002) 'Europe in search of its civil society', *European Law Journal*, 8(2): 198–217.

Diamantopoulou, A. (2000a) 'The European social model and enlargement', Speech at a seminar on harmonization of Turkey's social policy and legislation with EU standards, 23 June, Istanbul. Speech/00/235.

Diamantopoulou, A. (2000b) 'The European social model: past its sell-by date?' Speech at the Institute for European Affairs, 20 July, Dublin.

Diamantopoulou, A. (2003) 'Future perspectives for the European Social Model', Speech at PES seminar on the European Social Model, 17 September, Bologna.

DiMaggio, P. (1997) 'Culture as cognition', *Annual Review of Sociology*, 23: 263–87

Dingsdale (2000) *Mapping Modernities: Geographies of Central and Eastern Europe, 1920–2000*, London: Routledge.

Durkheim, É. (1960) *The Division of Labour in Society*, Glencoe, IL: The Free Press.

Durkheim, É. (1995) *The Elementary Structures of the Religious Life*, New York: Free Press.

Eder, K. (2000a) 'Zur Transformation nationalstaatlicher Öffentlichkeit in Europa', *Berliner Journal für Soziologie*, 10(2): 167–84.

Eder, K. (2000b) *Kulturelle Identität zwischen Tradition und Utopia*, Frankfurt: Campus.

Eder, K. (2001) 'Integration through culture? The paradox of the search for a European identity', in K. Eder and B. Giesen (eds) *European Citizenship between National Legacies and Postnational Projects*, Oxford: Oxford University Press.

Eder, K. and Giesen, B. (eds) (2001) *European Citizenship: National Legacies and Trans-national Projects*, Oxford: Oxford University Press.

Eder, K., Giesen, B., Schmidtke, O. and Tambini, T. (2002) *Collective Identities in Action: A Sociological Approach to Ethnicity*, Aldershot: Ashgate.

Edwards, M. (2004) *Civil Society*, Cambridge: Polity Press.

Eisenstadt, S.N. (2000a) 'The civilizational dimension in sociological analysis', *Thesis Eleven*, 62: 1–21.

Eisenstadt, S.N. (2000b) 'Multiple modernities', *Daedalus*, 129(1): 1–29.

Eisenstadt, S.N. (2003) *Comparative Civilizations and Multiple Modernities*, Volumes 1 and 2, Leiden: Brill.

Eisenstadt, S.N. and Giesen, B. (1995) 'The construction of collective identity', *Archives Européennes de Sociologie*, 26(1): 72–102.

Elias, N. (2000) *The Civilizing Process* (revised edition), Blackwell: Oxford.

Emerson, M. (2003) 'Institutionalizing the wider Europe', CEPS Policy Brief No. 42. Available online http://www.ceps.be.

Emirbayer, M. (1997) 'Manifesto for a relational sociology', *American Journal of Sociology*, 103: 281–317.

Entrikin, N. (2003) 'Political community, identity, and cosmopolitan place', in M. Berezin and M. Schain (eds.) *Europe without Borders: Remapping Territory, Citizenship, and Identity in a Transnational Age*, Baltimore, MD: Johns Hopkins University Press.

Eriksen, T.H. (2001) 'Between universalism and relativism: a critique of the UNESCO concept of culture', in J.K. Cowan, M.-B. Dembour and R. Wilson (eds) *Culture and Rights: Anthropological Perspectives*, Cambridge: Cambridge University Press.

Eriksen, E.O. and Fossum, J.E. (2001) 'Democracy through strong publics in the European Union?', ARENA Working Paper WP01/16. Available online http://www.arena.uio.no/publications/wp01_16.htm.

European Commission (1995) White Paper on education and training: 'Teaching and Learning – Towards the Learning Society', COM(95) 590.

European Commission (2000) White Paper on European Governance: 'Enhancing democracy in the European Union', Work Programme. Commission Staff Working Document SEC(2000) 154/7 final, 11 October.

European Commission (2001a) 'Unity, solidarity, diversity for Europe, its people and its territory'. Second Report on Economic and Social Cohesion. Available online http://www.inforegio.cec.eu.int/wbdoc/docoffic/official/report2/contentpdf_en.htm.

European Commission (2001b) White Paper on Governance, COM(2001) 428 final.

European Commission (2002) Communication from the Commission to the Council and the European Parliament: 'Towards integrated management of the external borders of the member states of the European Union', COM(2002) 233 final, Brussels: Commission of the European Communities.

European Commission (2003) Communication from the Commission to the Council and the European Parliament: 'Wider Europe – neighbourhood: a new framework for relations with our eastern and southern neighbours', COM(2003) 104 final, Brussels: Commission of the European Communities.

European Commission (2004a) 'Beyond enlargement: Commission shifts European neighbourhood policy into higher gear', press release IP/04/308 Brussels, 12 May.

European Commission (2004b) 'The European neighbourhood policy', speech/04/141 by Günter Verheugen given to Prime Ministerial Conference of the Vilnius and Visegrad Democracies: 'Towards a Wider Europe: the new agenda', 19 March, Bratislava.

European Commission (2004c) 'Building our common future: financial and political outlook for the enlarged union 2007–2013', press release IP/04/189, 10 February.

European Communities (2004) Interim territorial cohesion Report. DG Regional Policy. Luxembourg: Office for Official Publications of the European Communities.

European Council (2001) Presidency conclusions, Laeken Council 14 and 15 December.

European Council (2002) Barcelona European Council, presidency conclusions, 15–16 March.

European Council (2003) 'A secure Europe in a better world: European security strategy', 12 December, Brussels.

Evans, M. and Lunn, K. (eds) (1997) *War and Memory in the Twentieth Century*, Oxford: Berg.

Eyerman, R, and Jamison, A. (1991) *Social Movements: A Cognitive Approach*, Cambridge: Polity Press.

Fairclough, N. (2000) *New Labour, New Language*, London: Routledge.

Featherstone, K. (2003) 'Introduction: In the name of Europe', in K. Featherstone and C. Radaelli (eds) *The Politics of Europeanization*, Oxford: Oxford University Press.

Featherstone, K. and Kazamias, G. (eds) (2001) *Europeanization and the Southern Periphery*, London: Frank Cass.

Field, J. (1997) 'The European Union and the Learning Society: contested sovereignty in an age of globalisation'. Available online http://www.leeds.ac.uk/educol/documents/000000432.htm.

Florini A.M. and Simmons, P.J. (2000) 'What the world needs now?', in A.M. Florini (ed.) *The Third Force: The Rise Of Transnational Civil Society*, Washington, DC: Carnegie Endowement for International Peace.

Foley, M. and Edwards, B. (1996) 'The paradox of civil society', *Journal of Democracy*, 7(3): 38–52.

Fontana, J. (1995) *The Distorted Past: A Reinterpretation of European History*, Oxford: Blackwell.

Foucher, M. (1998) 'The geopolitics of European frontiers', in M. Anderson and E. Bort (eds) *The Frontiers of Europe*, London: Pinter.

Frankenfeld, P. (1992) 'Technological citizenship: a normative framework for r
Science and Technology and Human Values, 17(4): 459–84.

Friedmann, J. (1994) *Cultural Identity and Global Process*, London: Sage.

Friedmann, J. (2000) 'Reading Castells: Zeitdiagnose and social theory', *E*
and Planning D: Society and Space, 18(1): 111–20.

Friese, H. (ed.) (2002) *Identities*, Providence, RI: Berghahn.

Friese, H. and Wagner, P. (2002) 'The Nascent political philosophy of the European polity', *The Journal of Political Philosophy*, 10(3): 342–64.

Fuchs, D. and Klingeman, H.-D. (2002) 'Eastward enlargement of the European Union and the identity of Europe', *West European Politics*, 25(2): 19–54.

Fulbrook, M. (1999) *German National Identity after the Holocaust*, Cambridge: Polity Press.

Fulcher, J. (2000) 'Globalisation, the nation-state and global society', *The Sociological Review*, 48(4): 522–43.

Gadamer, H.-G. (1992) 'The diversity of Europe: inheritance and future', in D. Misgeld and G. Nicholson (eds) *Applied Hermeneutics*, New York: SUNY.

Gane, N. (ed.) (2004) *The Future of Social Theory*, New York: Continuum.

Gaonkar, D.P. (ed.) (2001) *Alternative Modernities*, Durham, NC: Duke University Press.

Garcia, S. (ed.) (1993) *European Identity and the Search for Legitimacy*, London: Pinter.

Gellner, E. (1983) *Nations and Nationalism*, Oxford: Blackwell.

Geremek, B. (1996) *The Common Roots of Europe*, Cambridge: Polity Press.

Gergen, K. (2001) *Social Constructionism in Context*, London: Sage.

Geyer, R. (2000) *Exploring European Social Policy*, Cambridge: Polity Press.

Giddens, A. (1985) *The Nation-state and Violence: Volume Two of a Contemporary Critique of Historical Critique of Historical Materialism*, Cambridge: Polity Press.

Giddens, A. (1990) *Consequences of Modernity*, Cambridge: Polity Press.

Giddens, A. (1991) *Modernity and Self-Identity*, Cambridge: Polity Press.

Giesen, B. (1998) *Kollektive Identität*, Frankfurt: Surhkamp.

Giesen, B. (2003) 'The collective identity of Europe: constitutional practice of community of memory', in W. Spohn and A. Triandafyllidou (eds) *Europeanization, National Identities and Migration*, London: Routledge.

Giesen, B. (2004a) 'The trauma of perpetrators: the holocaust as the traumatic reference of German national identity', in J. Alexander, R. Eyerman, B. Giesen, N.J. Smelser, and P. Sztompka (eds) *Cultural Trauma and Collective Identity*, Cambridge: Cambridge University Press.

Giesen, B. (2004b) *Triumph and Trauma*, Boulder, CO: Paradigm Press.

Giesen, B. and Junge, K. (2003) 'Historical memory', in G. Delanty and E. Isin (eds) *Handbook of Historical Memory*, London: Sage.

Gillis, J. (ed.) (1994) *Commemorations: The Politics of National Identity*, Princeton, NJ: Princeton University Press.

Gilroy, P. (1993) *The Black Atlantic: Modernity and Double Consciousness*, Cambridge, MA: Harvard University Press.

Gleason, P. (1983) 'Identifying identity: a semantic history', *The Journal of American History*, 69(4): 910–31.

Göle, N. (1996) *The Forbidden Modern: Civilization and Veiling*, Ann Arbor, MI: University of Michigan Press.

Goody, J. (2004) *Islam in Europe*, Cambridge: Polity Press.

Gowan, P. (1995) 'Neo-liberal theory and practice for eastern Europe', *New Left Review* 213(Sept/Oct): 3–60.

Gowan, P. (2002) 'The EU and eastern Europe: diversity without unity?', in M. Farell, S. Fella and M. Newman (eds) *European integration in the 21st Century: Unity in Diversity?* London: Sage.

Grabbe, H. (2004) ' How the EU should help its neighbours', CER policy brief. Available online http://www.cer.org.uk/pdf/policybrief_eu_neighbours.pdf.

Gramsci, A. (1971) *Selections from Prison Notebooks*, London: Lawrence and Wishart.

Gray, P. and Oliver, K. (2001) 'The memory of catastrophe. Views on commemoration of historical disaster', *History Today*, 51(2): 9–15.

Grundmann, R. (1999) 'The European public sphere and the deficit of democracy', in D. Smith and S. Wright (eds) *Whose Europe: The Turn Towards Democracy*, Oxford: Blackwell.

Gutmann, A. (2003) *Identity in Democracy*, Princeton, NJ: Princeton University Press.

Habermas, J. (1976) *Legitimation Crisis*, London: Heinemann.

Habermas, J. (1987) *The Theory of Communicative Action*, volume 2, Cambridge: Polity Press.

Habermas, J. (1988) 'The public use of history', *New German Critique*, 44: 40–50.

Habermas, J. (1989) *The Structural Transformation of the Public Sphere*, Cambridge: Polity Press.

Habermas, J. (1992) 'Citizenship and national identity: some reflections on the future of Europe', *Praxis International*, 12(1): 1–19.

Habermas, J. (1994) 'Struggles for recognition in the democratic constitutional state', in A. Gutmann (ed.) *Multiculturalism: Examining the Politics of Recognition*, Princeton, NJ: Princeton University Press.

Habermas, J. (1996) *Between Facts and Norms: Contributions to a Discourse Theory of Law and Democracy*, Cambridge: Polity Press.

Habermas, J. (1998) *The Inclusion of the Other: Studies in Political Theory*, Cambridge, MA: MIT Press.

Habermas, J. (2001a) 'Why Europe needs a constitution', *New Left Review*, 11(Sept/Oct): 5–26.

Habermas, J. (2001b) *The Postnational Constellation*, Cambridge: Polity Press.

Habermas, J. (2003a) 'Interpreting the fall of a monument', *Constellations*, 10(3): 364–70.

Habermas, J. (2003b) 'Realism after the linguistic-pragmatic turn', in G. Delanty and P. Strydom (eds) *Philosophies of Social Science: Classic and Contemporary Readings*, Buckingham: Open University Press.

Habermas, J. (2003c) 'Toward a cosmopolitan Europe', *Journal of Democracy*, 14(4): 86–100.

Habermas, J. and Derrida, J. (2003) 'February 15, or what binds Europeans together: a plea for a common foreign policy, beginning in the core of Europe', *Constellations*, 10(3): 291–7.

Hacking, I. (1998) *Rewriting the Soul: Multiple Personality and the Sciences of Memory*, Princeton, NJ: Princeton University Press.

Hacking, I. (1999) *The Social Construction of What?* Cambridge, MA: Harvard University Press.

Hakli, J. and Kaplan, D. (2002) 'Learning from Europe: borderlands in social and geographical context', in D. Kaplan and J. Hakli (eds) *Boundaries and Place: European Borderlands in Geographical Context*, Lanham, MD: Rowman and Littlefield.

Halbachs, M. (1980) *The Collective Memory*, New York: Harper & Row.

Hall, D. and Danta, D. (eds) (2000) *Europe Goes West: EU Enlargement, Diversity and Uncertainty*, London: The Stationary Office.

Hall, J. (1998) 'Genealogies of civility', in R.W. Hefner (ed.) *Democratic Civility: The History and Cross-Cultural Possibility of a Modern Political Ideal*, New Brunswick, NJ: Transaction.

Hall, J.S. (1999) *Cultures of Inquiry: From Epistemology to Discourse in the Methodological Practices of Sociohistorical Research*, Cambridge: Cambridge University Press.

Hall, S. and Du Gay, P. (eds) (1996) *Questions of Cultural Identity*, London: Sage.

Haller, M. (2000) ' "European integration and sociology", the difficult balance between the theoretical, empirical and critical approach', *European Societies*, 2(4): 533–48.

Halperin, S. and Laxer, G. (2003) 'Effective resistance to corporate globalization', in G. Laxer and S. Halperin (eds) *Global Civil Society and its Limits*, Basingstoke: Palgrave.

Hansen, P. (2002) 'European integration, European identity and the colonial connection', *European Journal of Social Theory*, 5(4): 483–98.

Hansen, R. and Weil, P. (2001) *Towards a European Nationality: Citizenship, Immigration, and Nationality Law in the EU*, Basingstoke: Palgrave.

Hardt, M. and Negri, A. (2000) *Empire*, Cambridge, MA: Harvard University Press.

Harrington, A. (2004) 'Ernst Troeltsch's concept of Europe', *European Journal of Social Theory*, 7(4): 479–98.

Haseler, S. (2004) *Super-State: The New Europe and its Challenge to America*, London: I. B. Tauris.

Hassner, P. (2002) 'Fixed borders or moving borderlands? A new type of border for a new type of entity', in J. Zielonka (ed.) *Europe Unbound: Enlarging and Reshaping the Boundaries of the European Union*, London: Routledge.

Hay, C., Watson, M. and Wincott, D. (1999) 'Globalization, European integration and the persistence of European social models', Working Paper 3/99 POLSIS, University of Birmingham. Available online http://www.one-europe.ac.uk/pdf/w3.pdf.

Hay, D. (1957) *Europe: History of an Idea*, Edinburgh: Edinburgh University Press.

Heater, D. (2002) *World Citizenship: Cosmopolitan Thinking and its Opponents*, London: Continuum.

Held, D. (1989) *Political Theory and the Modern State*, Cambridge: Polity Press.

Held, D. (1998) 'Democracy and globalization', in D. Archibugi, D. Held and M. Kohler (eds) *Re-imagining Political Community: Studies in Cosmopolitan Democracy*, Cambridge: Polity Press.

Held, D. (1999) 'The transformation of political community: rethinking democracy in the context of globalization', in I. Shapiro and C. Hacker-Cordon (eds) *Democracy's Edges*, Cambridge: Cambridge University Press.

Held, D. (2002) 'Culture and political community: national, global and cosmopolitan', in S. Vertovec and R. Cohen (eds) *Conceiving Cosmopolitanism*, Oxford: Oxford University Press.

Held, D. and McGrew, A. (2002) (eds) *Governing Globalization: Power Authority and Global Governance*, Cambridge: Polity Press.

Held, D., McGrew, A., Goldblatt, D. and Perraton, J. (1999) *Global Transformations: Politics, Economics and Culture*, Cambridge: Polity Press.

Heller, A. (1999) *Theory of Modernity*, Oxford: Blackwell.

Hemerijck, A. (2002) 'The self-transformation of the European social model(s)', in G. Esping-Anderson (ed.) *Why we Need a New Welfare State*, Oxford: Oxford University Press.

Herb, G. and Kaplin, D. (eds) (1999) *Nested Identities: Nationalism, Territory and Space*, New York: Rowman and Littlefield.

Herrmann, R.K., Risse, T. and Brewer, M.B. (eds) (2004) *Transnational Identities: Becoming European in the EU*, New York: Rowman and Littlefield.

Hesse, B. (ed.) (2000) *Un/Settled Multiculturalism: Disaporas, Entanglements, Transruptions*, London: Zed Books.

Hindess, B. (1998) 'Divide and rule: the international character of modern citizenship', *European Journal of Social Theory*, 1(1): 57–70.

Hirst, P. (2001) 'Democracy in the twenty-first century', in R. Axtmann (ed.) *Balancing Democracy*, London: Continuum.

Hirst, P. and Thompson, G. (1996) *Globalization in Question: The International Economy and the Possibilities of Governance*, Cambridge: Polity Press.

Hix, S. (1999) *The Political System of the European Union*, Basingstoke: Palgrave.

Hobsbawm, E. (1997) 'The curious history of Europe', in E. Hobsbawm (ed.) *On History*, London: Abacus.

Hobsbawm, E. and Ranger, T. (eds) (1983) *The Invention of Tradition*, Cambridge: Cambridge University Press.

Hobson, J. (2004) *The Eastern Origins of European Civilization*, Cambridge: Cambridge University Press

Hodge, S. and Howe, J. (1999) 'Can the European social model survive?', *European Urban and Regional Studies*, 6(2): 178–84.

Holmes, D. (2000a) 'Surrogate discourses of power: the European Union and the problem of society', in I. Bellier and T.M. Wilson (eds) *An Anthropology of the European Union*, Oxford: Berg.

Holmes, D. (2000b) *Integral Europe: Fast-Capitalism, Multiculturalism, Neofascism*, Princeton, NJ: Princeton University Press.

Holton, R. (1998) *Globalization and the Nation-State*, Basingstoke: Palgrave.

Honneth, A. (1987) *The Struggle for Recognition*, Cambridge: Polity Press.

Hooghe, L. (1996) 'Reconciling EU-wide policy and national diversity', in L. Hooghe (ed.) *Cohesion Policy and European Integration: Building Multi-level Governance*, Oxford: Oxford University Press.

Hooghe, L. (1998) 'EU cohesion policy and competing models of European capitalism', *Journal of Common Market Studies*, 36(4): 457–77.

Hooghe, L. and Marks, G. (2001) *Multi-level Governance and European Integration*, Lanham, MD: Rowman and Littlefield.

Huntington, S.P. (2004a) *Who Are We? The Challenges to America's National Identity*, New York: Simon & Shuster.

Huntington, S.P. (2004b) 'Dead souls: the denationalization of the American elite', *The National Interest*, Spring: 5–18.

Husserl, E. (1965) *The Crisis of the European Sciences*, New York: Harper & Row.

Hutton, W. (1997) *The State to Come*, London: Vintage.

Hutton, W. (2002) *The World We're in*, London: Little, Brown.

Huyssen, A. (2003) *Present Pasts: Urban Palimpsests and the Politics of Memory*, Stanford, CA: Stanford University Press.

Ifversen, J. (2002) 'Europe and European culture: a conceptual analysis', *European Societies*, 4(1): 1–25.

Imig, D. and Tarrow, S. (2001) *Contentious Europeans: Protest and Politics in an Emerging Polity*, Lanham, MD: Rowman and Littlefield.

Isin, E. and Turner, B. (eds) (2002) *Handbook of Citizenship Studies*, London, Sage.

Isin, E. and Wood, P. (1999) *Citizenship and Identity*, London, Sage.

Jachtenfuchs, M. and Kohler-Koch, B. (2004) 'Governance and institutional development', in A. Wiener and T. Diez (eds) *European Integration Theory*, Oxford: Oxford University Press.

Jacobson, D. (1996) *Rights Across Borders: Immigration and the Decline of Citizenship*, Baltimore, MD: Johns Hopkins University Press.

Jardine, L. and Brotton, J. (eds) (2000) *Global Interests: Renaissance Art between East and West*, London: Reaktion Books.

Jarvis, P. (2000) 'Globalisation, the learning society and comparative education', *Comparative Education*, 36(3): 343–55.

Jeffery, C. (1997) 'Conclusions: sub-national authorities and "European domestic policy"', in C. Jeffery (ed.) *The Regional Dimension of the European Union: Towards a Third Level in Europe?* London: Frank Cass.

Jenkins, B. and Sofos, S. (eds) (1996) *Nation and Identity in Contemporary Europe*, London: Routledge.

Jenkins, R. (1996) *Social Identity*, London: Routledge.

Jensen, O.B. and Richardson, T. (2003) 'Being on the map: the new iconographies of power over European space', *International Planning Studies* 8(1): 9–34.

Jensen, O.B. and Richardson, T. (2004) *Making European Space: Mobility, Power and Territorial Identity*, London: Routledge.

Jepperson, R. (2000) 'Institutional logics: on the constitutive dimensions of the modern nation-state polities', Working Paper 2000/36, Robert Schuman Centre for Advanced Studies, European University Institute, Florence.

Jessop, B. (2004) 'The European Union and recent transformations in statehood'. Available online http://www.comp.lancs.ac.uk/sociology/papers/jessop-eu-transformations-statehood.pdf.

Jönsson, C., Tägel, S. and Törnqvist, G. (2000) *Organizing European Space*, London: Sage.

Jorgensen, K. and Rosamond, B. (2002) 'Europe: regional laboratory for a global polity?', in M. Ougaard and R. Higgot (eds) *Towards a Global Polity*, London: Routledge.

Jowell, R., Curtice, J., Park, A., Brook, L. and Thomson, K. (eds) (2000) *British Social Attitudes. The 17th Report*, London: Sage.

Kagan, R. (2003) *Paradise and Power: America and Europe in the New World Order*, New York: Knopf.

Kaldor, M. (2003) *Global Civil Society: An Answer to War*, Cambridge: Polity Press.

Kaldor, M. and Vejvoda, I. (eds) (2002) *Democratization in Central and Eastern Europe*, London: Continuum.

Kamali, M. (2005) *Multiple Modernities, Civil Society, and Islam: The Case of Iran and Turkey*, Liverpool: Liverpool University Press.

Kastoryano, R. (2002) *Negotiating Identities: States and Immigrants in France and Germany*, Princeton, NJ: Princeton University Press.

Kastoryano, R. (2003) 'Transnational networks and political participation: the place of immigrants in the European Union', in M. Berezin and M. Schain (eds) *Europe without Borders: Remapping Territory, Citizenship, and Identity in a Transnational Age*, Baltimore, MD: Johns Hopkins University Press.

Kaviraj, S. (2001) 'In search of civil society', in S. Kaviraj and S. Khilnani (eds) *Civil Society: History and Possibilities*, Cambridge: Cambridge University Press.

Kaya, I. (2004) *Social Theory and Later Modernities: The Turkish Experience*, Liverpool: Liverpool University Press.

Keane, J. (1988) *Democracy and Civil Society*, London: Verso.

Keane, J. (1998) *Civil Society: Old Images, New Visions*, London: Verso.

Keane, J. (2003) *Global Civil Society*, Cambridge: Polity Press.

Khilnani, S. (2001) 'The development of civil society', in S. Kaviraj and S. Khilnani (eds) *Civil Society: History and Possibilities*, Cambridge University Press: Cambridge.

Kibria, N. (2002) *Becoming Asian American: Second-Generation Chinese and Korean American Identities*, Baltimore, MD: John Hopkins University Press.

Kierzkowski, H. (ed.) (2002) *Europe and Globalization*, Basingstoke: Palgrave.

King, A. (2000) 'Football fandom and post-national identity in the New Europe', *British Journal of Sociology*, 51(3): 419–42.

King, A. (2003) *The European Ritual: Football in the New Europe*, Aldershot: Ashgate.

Kleinman, M. (2002) *A European Welfare State: European Union Social Policy in Context*, Basingstoke: Palgrave.

Kofman, E. (2003) 'Political geography and globalization as we enter the twenty-first century', in E. Kofman and G. Youngs (eds) *Globalization: Theory and Practice*, London: Continuum.

Kohler, M. (1998) 'From the national to the cosmopolitan public sphere', in D. Archibugi, D. Held and M. Kohler (eds) *Re-imagining Political Community: Studies in Cosmopolitan Democracy*, Cambridge: Polity Press.

Kohli, M. (2000) 'The battlegrounds of European Identity', *European Societies*, 2(2): 113–37.

Kokott, J. and Ruth, A. (2003) 'The European convention and its draft treaty establishing a constitution for Europe: appropriate answers to the Laeken questions?', *Common Market Law Review*, 40: 1315–45.

Koopmans, R. and Statham, P. (2000) *Challenging Immigration and Ethnic Relations Politics: Comparative European Perspectives*, Oxford: Oxford University Press.

Kriesi, H., Koopmans, R., Duyvendak, J. and Giugni M. (1995) *New Social Movements in Western Europe: A Comparative Analysis*, London: UCL Press.

Kristeva, J. (1993) *Nations without Nationalism*, New York: Columbia University Press.

Kristeva, J. (2000) *Crisis of the European Subject*, New York: Other Press.

Kumar, K. (1993) 'Civil society: an inquiry into the usefulness of an historical term', *British Journal of Sociology*, 44: 375–96.

Kumar, K. (2003) 'Britain, England and Europe: cultures in contraflow', *European Journal of Social Theory*, 6(1): 5–23.

Kymlicka, W. (1995) *Multicultural Citizenship: A Liberal Theory of Minority Rights*, Oxford: Clarendon Press.

Kymlicka, W. and Norman, W. (eds) (2000) *Citizenship in Diverse Societies*, Oxford: Oxford University Press.

Laclau, E. (ed.) (1994) *The Making of Political Identities*, London: Verso.

Ladrech, R. (2002) 'Europeanization and political parties: towards a framework for analysis', *Party Politics*, 8(4): 389–403.

Laffan, B. (2004) 'The European Union and its institutions as "identity builders"', in R.K. Herrmann, T. Risse and M.B. Brewer (eds) *Transnational Identities: Becoming European in the EU*, New York: Rowman and Littlefield.

Laitin, D. (2002) 'Culture and national identity: "the east" and European integration', *West European Politics*, 25(2): 55–80.

Lamy, P. and Laidi, Z. (2001) 'Governance or making globalization meaningful'. Available online http://www.laidi.com/papiers/governance.pdf.

Lasch, C. (1995) *The Revolt of the Elites and the Betrayal of Democracy*, New York: Norton.

Lawn, M. (2003) 'The "usefulness" of learning: the struggle over governance, meaning and the European education space', *Discourse: Studies in the Cultural Politics of Education* 24(3): 325–36.

Lawn, M. and Lingard, B. (2002) 'Constructing a European policy space in educational governance: the role of transnational policy actors', *European Educational Research Journal*, 1(2): 342–59.

Lehning, P. and Weale, A. (eds) (1997) *Citizenship, Democracy and Justice in the New Europe*, London: Routledge.

Le Gales, P. (2002) *European Cities: Social Conflicts and Governance*, Oxford: Oxford University Press.

Le Goff, J. (1992) *History and Memory*, New York: Columbia University Press.

Levy, D. and Sznaider, N. (2002) 'Memory unbound: the holocaust and the formation of cosmopolitan memory', *European Journal of Social Theory*, 5(1): 87–106.

Linklater, A. (2002) 'Cosmopolitan harm conventions', in S. Vertovec and R. Cohen (eds) *Conceiving Cosmopolitanism*, Oxford: Oxford University Press.

Lister, R. (1997) *Citizenship: Feminist Perspectives*, Basingstoke: Palgrave.

Lister, R. (1998) 'Citizenship and difference: towards a differentiated universalism', *European Journal of Social Theory*, 1(1): 71–90.

Lockwood, D. (1964) 'Social Integration and System Integration', in G.K. Zollschan and W. Hirsch (eds) *Explorations in Social Change*, Boston, MA: Houghton Mifflin.

Lord, C. (1998) *Democracy in the European Union*, Sheffield: Sheffield Academic Press.

Lowenthal, D. (1985) *The Past is a Foreign Country*, Cambridge: Cambridge University Press.

Luhmann, N. (1979) *Trust and Power*, New York: John Wiley.

Luhmann, N. (1982) *The Differentiation of Society*, New York: Columbia University Press.

Luhmann, N. (1990) *Political Theory and the Welfare State*, Berlin: De Gruyter.

Luhmann, N. (1995) *Social Systems*, Stanford, CA: Stanford University Press.

Luhmann, N. (1998) *Observations on Modernity*, Stanford, CA: Stanford University Press.

Lurry, C. (1993) *Cultural Rights*, London: Routledge.

Macdonald, S. (ed.) (1993) *Inside European Identities: Ethnology in Western Europe*, Oxford: Berg.

McCormick, J. (1999) *Understanding the European Union: A Concise Introduction*, Basingstoke: Palgrave.

McDonald, M. (1996) ' "Unity in diversity": some tensions in the construction of Europe', *Social Anthropology*, 4(1): 47–60.

McGowan, F. (1996) 'Energy policy', in H. Kassim and A. Menon (eds) *The European Union and National Industrial Policy*, London: Routledge.

McLelland, D. (1996) *A History of Western Political Thought*, London: Routledge.

Majone, G. (1996) *Regulating Europe*, London: Routledge.

Malmborg, M. and Stråth, B. (eds) (2002) *The Meaning of Europe*, Oxford and New York: Berg.

Mann, M. (1986) *The Sources of Social Power: Volume 1: A History of Power From the Beginning to A.D. 1760*, Cambridge: Cambridge University Press.

Mann, M. (1987) 'Ruling Class Strategies and Citizenship', *Sociology*, 21(3): 339–54.

Mann, M. (1998) 'Is there a society called Euro?', in R. Axtman (ed.) *Globalization and Europe: Theoretical and Empirical Investigations*, London: Pinter.

Manners, I. (2000) 'Normative power Europe: a contradiction in terms?' Available online http://www.copri.dk/publications/wp/wp%20(2000/38–(2000.doc.

Margalit, A. (2002) *The Ethics of Memory*, Cambridge, MA: Harvard University Press.

References

s, G., Scharpf, F., Schmitter, P. and Streek, W. (1996) *Governance in the European nion*, London: Sage.

Marshall, T.H. (1992) *Citizenship and Social Class*, London: Pluto Press.

Marshall, W. (2000) 'Let's expand the winner's circle', *Blueprint Magazine*, 1 June. Available online http://www.ppionline.org/ndol/print.cfm?contentid=927.

Martin, A. (2001) 'EMU and the European model of society: an interim project report', ARENA seminar paper, 21 June, Oslo University. Available online http://www.arena.uio.no/events/papers/AndrewMartin.pdf.

Martin, A. and Ross, G. (eds) (2004) *Euros and Europeans: Monetary Integrations and the European Model of Society*, Cambridge: Cambridge University Press.

Massey, D. (1993) 'Power-geometry and a progressive sense of space', in J. Bird, B. Curtis, T. Putnam, G. Robertson, and L. Tickner (eds) *Mapping the Futures: Local Cultures, Global Change*, London: Routledge.

Massey, D. (2004) 'Geographies of responsibilities', *Geografiska Annaler*, 86B(1): 5–18.

Matlary, J.H. (1996) 'Energy policy: from a national to a European framework?', in H. Wallace and W. Wallace (eds) *Policy-making in the European Union*, Oxford: Oxford University Press.

May, T. (1999) 'Reflexivity and sociological practice', *Sociological Research Online*, 4: 3. Available online http://www.socresonline.org.uk/socresonline/4/3/may.html.

Meehan, E. (1993) *Citizenship and the European Community*, London: Sage.

Meinhof, U.H. (ed.) (2002) *Living (with) Borders: Identity Discourses on East–West Borders in Europe*. Aldershot: Ashgate.

Mellor, P. (2004) *Religion, Realism and Social Theory*, London: Sage.

Melucci, A. (1995) 'The process of collective identity', in H. Johnson and B. Klandermans (eds) *Social Movements and Culture*, London: UCL Press.

Melucci, A. (1996) *Challenging Codes: Collective Action in the Information*, Cambridge: Cambridge University Press.

Mennell, S. (1990) 'The globalization of human society as a very long-term social process: Elias's theory', in M. Featherstone (ed.) *Global Culture: Nationalism, Globalization and Modernity*, London: Sage.

Meyer, J.W. (2000) 'Globalization: sources and effects on national states and societies', *International Sociology*, 15(2): 233–48.

Meyer, J.W. (2001a) 'The European Union and the globalization of culture', in S.S. Andersen (ed.) *Institutional Approaches to the European Union: Arena Report No. 3/2001*, Oslo: ARENA.

Meyer, J.W. (2001b) 'Globalization, national culture, and the future of the world polity', Wei Lun Lecture, 28 November, Chinese University of Hong Kong.

Meyer, J.W., Boli, J., Thomas, G.M. and Ramirez, F.O. (1997) 'World society and the nation-state', *The American Journal of Sociology*, 103(1): 144–81.

Meyer, J.W., Boli, J., Thomas, G.M. and Ramirez, F.O. (2004) 'World society and the nation-state', in F.J. Lechner and J. Boli (eds) *The Globalization Reader*, 2nd edn, Oxford: Blackwell.

Mignolo, W. (2002) 'The many faces of cosmo-polis: border thinking and critical cosmopolitanism', in R. Robertson and K. White (eds) *Globalization: Critical Concepts in Sociology, Volume 3: Global Membership and Participation*, London: Routledge.

Mikkeli, H. (1998) *Europe as an Idea and as an Identity*, Basingstoke: Palgrave.

Miles, L. (2004) 'Theoretical considerations', in N. Nugent (ed.) *European Union Enlargement*, Basingstoke: Palgrave.

Milward, A. (1993) *The European Rescue of the Nation-State*, London: Routledge.

Milward, A. (2002) 'Historical teleologies', in M. Farrell, S. Fella and M. Newman (eds) *European Integration in the 21st Century*, London: Sage.

Misztal, B. (2004) 'The sacralization of memory', *European Journal of Sociology*, 7(1): 67–84.

Morin, E. (1987) *Penser l'Europe*, Paris: Gallimard.

Morin, E. (2002) 'European civilization: properties and challenges', in M. Mozaffari (ed.) *Globalization and Civilizations*, London: Routledge.

Moscovici, S. (2000) *Social Representations*, Cambridge: Polity Press.

Mosse, G. (1990) *Fallen Soldiers: Reshaping the Memory of the World Wars*, Oxford: Oxford University Press.

Mouzelis, N. (1999) 'Modernity: a non-European conceptualization', *British Journal of Sociology*, 50(1): 141–59.

Mozaffari, M. (ed.) (2002) *Globalization and Civilizations*, London: Routledge.

Mulhall, S. and Swift, A. (1996) *Liberalism and Communitarianism*, 2nd edn, Oxford: Blackwell.

Müller, J.-W. (2003) (ed.) *Memory and Power in Post-War Europe: Studies of the Presence of the Past*, Cambridge: Cambridge University Press.

Müller-Graff, P.-C. (1998) 'Whose responsibilities are frontiers?', in M. Anderson and E. Bort (eds) *The Frontiers of Europe*, London: Pinter.

Nash, K. (2000) *Contemporary Political Sociology: Globalization, Politics and Power*, Oxford: Blackwell.

Nash, K. (2001) 'The "cultural turn" in social theory: towards a theory of cultural politics', *Sociology* 35(1): 77–92.

Nava, M. (2002) 'Cosmopolitan modernity: everyday Imaginaries and the register of difference', *Theory, Culture and Society*, 19(1): 81–99.

Navaro-Yashin, Y. (2002) *Faces of the State: Secularism and Public Life in Turkey*, Princeton, NJ: Princeton University Press.

Nederveen Pieterse, J. (1999) 'Europe, travelling light: Europeanization and globalization', *The European Legacy*, 4(3): 3–17.

Nederveen Pieterse, J. (2004) *Globalization and Culture*, New York: Rowman and Littlefield.

Nelson, B., Roberts, D. and Veit, W. (1992) *The Idea of Europe: Problems of National and Transnational Identity*, Oxford: Berg.

Neuman, I. (1996) *Russia and the Idea of Europe*, London: Routledge.

Niethammer, L. (2000) *Kollektive Identität: Heimliche Quellen einer unheimlichen Konjunktur*, Hamburg: Rowohlt.

Nora, P. (1996) *Realms of Memory: Rethinking the French Past*, New York: Columbia University Press.

Novoa, A. (2001) 'The restructuring of the European education space: changing relationships among states, citizens, and educational communities', in J. Fink, G. Lewis and J. Clarke (eds) *Rethinking European Welfare: Transformations of Europe and Social Policy*, London: Sage/Open University Press.

Nugent, N. (ed.) (2004) *European Union Enlargment*, Basingstoke: Palgrave.

Offe, C. (2002) 'Is there, or can there be, a "European society"', in I. Katenhusen and W. Lamping (eds) *Demokratien in Europa: Der Einfluss der europäischen Integration auf Institutionenwandel und der neue Konturen des demokratischen Verfassungsstaates*, Opladen: Leske and Budrich.

Olsen, J. (2002) 'The many faces of Europeanization', *Journal of Common Market Studies*, 40(5): 921–52.

Ong, A. (1999) *Flexible Citizenship: The Cultural Logics of Transnationality*, Durham, NJ: Duke University Press.

Önis, Z. and Keyman, F. (2003) 'Turkey at the polls: a new path emerges', *Journal of Democracy*, 14(2): 95–107.

Oommen, T.K. (2005) 'Socio-political transition in the Indian republic and European Union', *European Journal of Social Theory*, 7(4): 519–37.

Orchard, V. (2002) 'Culture as opposed to what? Cultural belonging in the context of national and European identity', *European Journal of Social Theory*, 5(4): 419–33.

Osterhammel, J. (1998) *Die Entzauberung Asiens*, Munich: Beck.

Outhwaite, W. (2001) 'Civil society in Europe', paper presented at the conference on 'The Shape of the New Europe', May, Warwick University.

Özbundun, E. and Keyman, F. (2002) 'Cultural globalization in Turkey: actors, discourses, strategies', in P. Berger and S. Huntington (eds) *Many Globalizations*, Oxford: Oxford University Press.

Pagden, A. (ed.) (2002) *The Idea of Europe: From Antiquity to the European Union*, Cambridge: Cambridge University Press.

Pahl, R.E. (1991) 'The search for social cohesion: from Durkheim to the European Commission', *Archives Européennes de Sociologie*, XXII: 345–60.

Pantella, M. (1999) 'Unity in diversity: cultural policy and EU legitimacy', in T. Bantoff and M. Smith (eds) *Legitimacy and the European Union*, London: Routledge.

Parekh, B. (2000) *Rethinking Multiculturalism: Cultural Diversity and Political Theory*, Basingstoke: Palgrave.

Passerini, L. (1998) *Europe in Love, Love in Europe: Aspects of Cultural History in 1930s Britain*, London: I. B. Tauris.

Patocka, J. (2001) *Plato and Europe*, Stanford, CA: Stanford University Press.

Pelczynski, Z.A. (1988) 'Solidarity and "the rebirth of civil society"', in J. Keane (ed.) *Civil Society and the State*, London: Verso.

Perez-Diaz, V. (1998) 'The public sphere and a European civil society', in J. Alexander (ed.) *Real Civil Societies: Dilemmas of Institutionalization*, London: Sage.

Perez-Diaz, V. (2000) 'The role of civil nations in the making of Europe', *Social Research*, 67(4): 957–88.

Pierson, P. (1998) 'Social policy and European integration', in A. Moravcsik (ed.) *Centralization or Fragmentation? Europe Facing the Challenge of Deepening, Diversity and Democracy*, New York: Council on Foreign Relations Press.

Potter, J. (1996) *Representing Reality: Discourse, Rhetoric and Social Construction*, London: Sage.

Povinelli, E. (2002) *The Cunning of Recognition: Indigenous Alterities and the Making of Australian Multiculturalism*, Durham, NC: Duke University Press.

Preyer, G. and Bos, M. (2001) 'Introduction: borderlines in time of globalization', *Protosociology*, 15: 4–14.

Prodi, R. (2000a) *Europe As I See it*, Cambridge: Polity Press.

Prodi, R. (2000b) 'Towards a European civil society', speech at the second European social week, 6 April, Bad Honnef.

Prodi, R. (2001) 'Globalisation'. Available online http://europa.eu.int/comm/commissioners/prodi/globalisation_en.htm.

Prodi, R. (2004) 'The role of the EU in a changing world', speech to the CASS European Institute, 12 April, Beijing.

Preston, P. W. (1997) *Political/Cultural Identity: Citizens and Nations in a Global Era*, London: Sage.

Rasch, W. (2000) *Niklas Luhmann's Modernity: The Paradoxes of Differentiation*, Stanford, CA: Stanford University Press.

Rawls, J. (1987) 'The idea of an overlapping consensus', *Oxford Journal of Legal Studies*, 7: 1–25.

Rawls, J. (1999) *The Law of Peoples*, Cambridge, MA: Harvard University Press.

Renan, E. (1990) 'What is a nation?', in H. Bhabha (ed.) *Nation and Narration*, London: Routledge.

Rengger, N. (2003) 'Cosmopolitanism', in R. Axtmann (ed.) *Understanding Democratic Politics: An Introduction*, London: Sage.

Rex, J. (1996) 'National identity in the democratic multinational state', *Sociological Research Online*, 1(2).

Richardson, T. and Jensen, O. (2000) 'Discourses of mobility and polycentric development', *European Planning Studies*, 8(4): 503–20.

Ricoeur, P. (1995) 'Reflections on a New Ethos for Europe', *Philosophy and Social Criticism*, 21(5/6): 3–13.

Ricoeur, P. (2004) *Memory, History, Forgetting*, Chicago: University of Chicago Press.

Rieger, E. (1996) 'The common agricultural policy: external and internal dimensions', in H. Wallace and W. Wallace (eds) *Policy-making in the European Union*, Oxford: Oxford University Press.

Rifkin, J. (2004) *The European Dream: How Europe's Vision of the Future is Quietly Eclipsing the American Dream*, New York: Tarcher/Penguin.

Ritzer, G. (1996) *Sociological Theory: Fourth Edition*, New York: McGraw Hill.

Risse, T. (2004a) 'Social constructivism and European integration', in A. Wiener and T. Diez (eds) *European Integration Theory*, Oxford: Oxford University Press.

Risse, T. (2004b) 'European institutions and identity change', in R.K. Herrmann, T. Risse and M.B. Brewer (eds) *Transnational Identities: Becoming European in the EU*, New York: Rowman and Littlefield.

Robins, K. (1996) 'Interrupting identities: Turkey/Europe', in S. Hall and P. du Gay (eds) *Cultural Identity*, London: Sage.

Robertson, R. (1991) 'Social theory, cultural relativity and the problem of globality', in A.D. King (ed.) *Culture, Globalization and the World-System*, Basingstoke: Palgrave.

Roberston, R. (1992) *Globalization: Social Theory and Global Culture*, London: Sage.

Robertson, R. (2001) 'Globalization theory 2000+: major problematics', in G. Ritzer and B. Smart (eds) *Handbook of Social Theory*, London: Sage.

Roche, M. (2001) 'Citizenship, popular culture and Europe', in N. Stevenson (ed.) *Culture and Citizenship*, London: Sage.

Rosamond, B. (1999) 'Discourses of globalization and the social construction of European identities', *Journal of European Public Policy*, 6(4): 652–68.

Rosamond, B. (2000) *Theories of European Integration*, Basingstoke: Palgrave.

Rosamond, B. (2002) 'Globalisation and the European Union', paper presented to conference on 'Transcending the National', July, University of New South Wales Sydney.

Rose, G. (1998) 'The victim's resentments', in B. Cheyette and L. Marcus (eds) *Modernity, Culture and 'the Jew'*, Oxford: Blackwell.

Rose, N. (1999) *Powers of Freedom: Reframing Political Thought*, Cambridge: Cambridge University Press.

Rose, N. (2000) 'Community, citizenship, and the third way', *American Behavioural Scientist* 43(9): 1395–1411.

Ruggie, G. (1993) 'Territoriality and beyond: problematizing modernity in international relations theory', *International Organization*, 47(1): 168–70.

Rumford, C. (2000a) *European Cohesion? Contradictions in EU Integration*, Basingstoke: Palgrave.

Rumford, C. (2000b) 'European cohesion? Globalization, autonomization, and the dynamics of EU integration', *Innovation: the European Journal of Social Science Research*, 13(2): 183–97.

Rumford, C. (2001) 'Social spaces beyond civil society: European integration, globalization and the sociology of European society', *Innovation: the European Journal of Social Science Research*, 14(3): 205–18.

Rumford, C. (2002) *The European Union: A Political Sociology*, Oxford: Blackwell.

Rumford, C. (2003) 'European civil society or transnational social space? Conceptions of society in discourses of EU citizenship, governance, and democracy: An emerging agenda', *European Journal of Social Theory*, 6(1): 25–44.

Samuel, R. (ed.) (1994) *Theatres of Memory. Volume 1: Past and Present in Contemporary Culture*, London: Verso.

Sassatelli, M. (2002) 'Imagined Europe: the shaping of a European cultural identity through EU cultural policy', *European Journal of Social Theory*, 5(4): 435–51.

Sassen, S. (2000) 'The global city: strategic site/new frontier', in E. Isin (ed.) *Democracy, Citizenship and the Global City*, London: Routledge.

Sassen, S. (2001) 'Spatialities and temporalities of the global: elements for a theorization', in A. Appadurai (ed.) *Globalization*, Durham, NC: Duke University Press.

Scharpf, F. (2002) 'The European social model: coping with the challenges of diversity', *Journal of Common Market Studies*, 40(4): 645–70.

Schlesinger, P. (1992) 'Europeaness: a new cultural battlefield', *Innovation*, 5(2): 11–23.

Schlesinger, P. (1999) 'Changing spaces of political communication: the case of the European Union', *Political Communication*, 16(3): 263–79.

Schlesinger, P. (2001) 'From cultural protection to political culture? Media policy and the EU', in L.-E. Cederman (ed.) *Constructing Europe's Identity: The External Dimension*, London: Lynne Rienner.

Schlesinger, P. (2005) 'The Babel of Europe? An essay on networks and communicative spaces', in D. Castiglione and C. Longman (eds) *The Public Discourses of Law and Politics in Multicultural Societies*, Oxford: Hart Publishing.

Scholte, J.A. (2000) *Globalization: A Critical Introduction*, Basingstoke: Palgrave Macmillan.

Scholte, J.A. (2001) 'Civil society and democracy in global governance', CSGR Working Paper No. 65/01, Department of Politics and International Studies, University of Warwick.

Scholte, J.A. (2002) 'Global civil society', in R. Robertson and K. White (eds) *Globalization: Critical Concepts in Sociology, Volume 3: Global Membership and Participation*, London: Routledge.

Scüzs, J. (1988) 'Three historical regions of Europe', in J. Keane (ed.) *Civil Society and the State*, London: Verso.

Seligman, A.B. (1998) 'Between public and private: towards a sociology of civil society', in R.W. Hefner (ed.) *Democratic Civility: The History and Cross-cultural Possibility of a Modern Political Ideal*, New Brunswick, NJ: Transaction.

Shaw, J. and Wiener, A. (1999) 'The paradox of the European polity'. Available online http://www.jeanmonnetprograme.org/papers/99/991002.html.

Shore, C. (2000) *Building Europe: The Cultural Politics of European Integration*, London: Routledge.

Shore, C. (2004) 'Whither European citizenship: eros and civilization revisited', *European Journal of Social Theory*, 7(1): 27–44.

Siedentop, L. (2000) *Democracy in Europe*, Harmondsworth: Penguin.

Silber, I. (2003) 'Pragmatic sociology as cultural sociology', *European Journal of Social Theory*, 6(4): 427–49.

Singer, P. (2003) *One World: The Ethics of Globalization*, New Haven, CT: Yale University Press.

Smelser, N. and Alexander, J. (eds) (1999) *Diversity and its Discontents: Cultural Conflict and Common Ground in Contemporary American Society*, Princeton, NJ: Princeton University Press.

Smismans, S. (2003) 'European civil society: shaped by discourses and institutional interests', *European Law Journal*, 9(4): 473–495.

Smith, A. (1992) 'National identity and the idea of Europe', *International Affairs*, 68(1): 129–35.

Smith, D. (1999) 'Making Europe – processes of Europe-formation since 1945', in D. Smith and S. Wright (eds) *Whose Europe: The Turn Towards Democracy*, Oxford: Blackwell.

Smith, R.M. (2003) *Stories of Peoplehood: The Politics and Morals of Political Membership*, Cambridge: Cambridge University Press.

Spillane, L. (1997) *Nation and Commemoration: Creating National Identities in the United States and Australia*, Cambridge: Cambridge University Press.

Somers, M. (1994) 'The narrative constitution of identity: a relational and network approach', *Theory and Society*, 23(5): 605–49.

Soysal, Y. (1994) *The Limits of Citizenship*, Chicago, IL: University of Chicago Press.

Soysal, Y. (1997) 'Changing parameters of citizenship and claims-making: organized Islam in European public spheres', *Theory and Society*, 26(4): 509–27.

Soysal, Y. (2000) 'Citizenship and identity: living in diasporas in post-war Europe?', *Ethnic and Racial Studies*, 23(1): 1–15.

Soysal, Y. (2001) 'Changing boundaries of participation in European public spheres: reflections on citizenship and civil society', in K. Eder and B. Giesen (eds) *European Citizenship Between National Legacies and Postnational Projects*, Oxford: Oxford University Press.

Soysal, Y. (2002a) 'Locating Europe', *European Societies*, 4(3): 265–84.

Soysal, Y. (2002b) 'Teaching Europe: conscience in Europe – discussion led by Yasemin Soysal', The Wyndham Place Charlemagne Trust. Available online http://www.wpct.co.uk.

Statham, P. and Gray, E. (2005) 'The public sphere and debates over Europe in Britain: internalised and conflict-driven?', *Innovation: The European Journal of Social Science Research*, 18(): 63–83.

Stevenson, N. (ed.) (2000) *Culture and Citizenship*, London: Sage.

Stevenson, N. (2003) *Cultural Citizenship: Cosmopolitan Questions*, Buckingham: Open University Press.

Stråth, B. (ed.) (2000) *Europe and the Other and Europe as the Other*, Brussels: Peter Lang.

Stråth, B. (2002) 'A European identity: to the historical limits of the concept', *European Journal of Social Theory*, 5(4): 387–401.

Strauss-Kahn, D. (2004) 'Building a political Europe: 50 proposals for tomorrow's Europe', report by Chairperson of the Round Table: A sustainable project for tomorrow's Europe' formed on the initiative of the President of the European Commission. Available online http://europa.eu.int/comm/dgs/policy_advisers/experts_groups/gsk_docs/rapport_europe_strauss_kahn_en.pdf.

Streeck, W. (1996) 'Neo-voluntarism: a new European social policy regime?', in G. Marks, F. Scharpf, P. Schmitter and W. Streek (eds) *Governance in the European Union*, London: Sage.

Streeck, W. (1999) 'Competitive solidarity: rethinking the "European social model"', MPIfG Working Paper 99/8. Available online http://www.mpi-fg-koeln.mpg.de/pu/workpap/wp99–8.html.

Strydom, P. (2002) *Risk, Environment and Society*, Buckingham: Open University Press.

Swaan, A. de (2001) *Words of the World*, Cambridge: Polity Press.

Swidler, A. (1986) 'Culture in action: symbols and strategies', *American Sociological Review*, 51: 273–86.

Taguieff, P.-A. (1993/1994) 'From race to culture: the new right's view of European identity', *Telos*, 98/9: 99–125.

Taguieff, P.-A. (1994) *Sur la Nouvelle Droit*, Paris: Descartes & Co.

Tajifel, H. (1982) *Social Identity and Intergroup Relations*, Cambridge: Cambridge University Press.

Tarrow, S. (1995) 'The Europeanization of conflict: reflections from a social movement perspective', *West European Politics*, 18(2): 223–51.

Taylor, C. (1994) 'The politics of recognition', in A. Gutmann (ed.) *Multiculturalism: Examining the Politics of Recognition*, Princeton NJ: Princeton University Press.

Taylor, C. (2004) *Modern Social Imaginaries*, Durham, NC: Duke University Press.

Taylor, P. (1999) *Modernities: A Geopolitical Interpretation*, Cambridge: Polity Press.

Taylor, R. (ed.) (2001) *Unity in Diversity*, Brussels: European Quality Publications.

Therborn, G. (1995a) 'Routes to/through modernity', in M. Featherstone, S. Lash and R. Robertson (eds) *Global Modernities*, London: Sage.

Therborn, G. (1995b) *Beyond European Modernity: The Trajectory of European Societies, 1945–2000*, London: Sage.

Therborn, G. (1997) 'Europe in the twenty-first century', in P. Gowan and P. Anderson (eds) *The Question of Europe*, London: Verso.

Therborn, G. (2003) 'Entangled modernities', *European Journal of Social Theory*, 6(3): 293–305.

Thévenot, L. and Lamont, L. (eds) (2000) *Rethinking Comparative Cultural Sociology: Politics and Repertoires of Evaluation in France and the United States*, Cambridge: Cambridge University Press.

Threlfall, M. (2002) 'Social integration in the European Union: towards a single social area?', in M. Farell, S. Fella and M. Newman (eds) *European Integration in the 21st Century: Unity in Diversity?*, London: Sage.

Tiersky, R. (ed.) (2001) *Euro-Skepticism*, New York: Rowan and Littlefield.

Tismaneanu, V. (ed.) (1990) *In Search of Civil Society: Independent Peace Movements in the Soviet Bloc*, London: Routledge.

Torpey, J. (2000) *The Invention of the Passport: Surveillance, Citizenship and the State*, Cambridge: Cambridge University Press.

Touscoz, J. (1997) 'The role of the European Union in the framework of the Energy Charter Treaty', *European Foreign Affairs Review*, 2(1): 23–32.

Touraine, A. (1977) *The Self-Production of Society*, Chicago: University of Chicago Press.

Touraine, A. (1994) 'European countries in a post-national era', in C. Rootes and H. Davis (eds) *A New Europe? Social Change and Political Transformation*, London: UVL Press.

Touraine, A. (1997) *What is Democracy?*, Boulder, CO: Westview.

Touraine, A. (2000) *Can We Live Together? Equal and Different*, Cambridge: Polity Press.

Trenz, H.-J. and Eder, K. (2004) 'The democratizing dynamics of a European public sphere', *European Journal of Social Theory*, 7(1): 5–25.

Tuck, R. (1979) *Natural Right Theories: Their Origin and Development*, Cambridge: Cambridge University Press.

Tully, C. (1995) *Strange Multiplicity: Constitutionalism in an Age of Diversity*, Cambridge: Cambridge University Press.

Turner, B.S. (1990) 'Outline of a Theory of Citizenship', *Sociology*, 24(2): 189–217.

Turner, B.S. (ed.) (1993) *Citizenship and Social Theory*, London: Sage.

Turner, C. (2004) 'Jürgen Habermas: European or German', *European Journal of Political Theory*, 3(3) 293–314.

Turner, C. (2005) 'Nation and commemoration', in G. Delanty and K. Kumar (eds) *Handbook of Nations and Nationalism*, London: Sage.

Turner, F. (1921) *The Frontier in American History*, New York: Holt.

Unger, R. (1987) *Politics: A Work in Constructivist Social Theory*, Cambridge: Cambridge University Press.

Urry, J. (2000a) *Sociology Beyond Societies: Mobilities for the Twenty-First Century*, London: Routledge.

Urry, J. (2000b) 'Sociology of time and space', in B. Turner (ed) *The Blackwell Companion to Social Theory*, 2nd edn, Oxford: Blackwell.

Urry, J. (2001) 'The sociology of space and time', in J. Blau (ed) *The Blackwell Companion to Sociology*, Oxford: Blackwell.

Valéry, P. ([1957]1962) 'The European', *History and Politics*, New York: Bolligen.

van de Steeg, M. (2002) 'Rethinking the conditions for a public sphere in the European Union', *European Journal of Social Theory*, 5(4): 497–517.

van Ham, P. (2001) 'Europe's postmodern identity: a critical appraisal', *International Politics*, 38: 229–52.

Varenne, H. (1993) 'The question of Euro-nationalism', in T. Wilson and M.E. Smith (eds) *Cultural Change and the New Europe: Perspectives on the European Community*, Boulder, CO: Westview Press.

Velody, I. and Williams, R. (eds) (1998) *The Politics of Constructionism*, London: Sage.

Venn, C. (2000) *Occidentalism: Modernity and Subjectivity*, London: Sage

Vertovec, S. and Cohen, R. (eds) (2002) *Conceiving Cosmopolitanism*, Oxford: Oxford University Press.

Vertovec, S. and Rogers, A. (eds) (1998) *Muslim European Youth: Reproducing Ethnicity, Religion, Culture*, Aldershot: Ashgate.

Vibert, F. (2001) *Europe Simple Europe Strong: The Future of European Governance*, Cambridge: Polity Press.

Viehoff, R. and Segers, R. (eds) (1999) *Identität, Kultur, Europa*, Frankfurt: Suhrkamp.

Vink, M. (2003) 'What is Europeanisation? And other questions on a new research agenda', *European Political Science*, 3(1): 63–74.

Wagner, P. (1994) *The Sociology of Modernity: Liberty and Discipline*, London: Routledge.

Wagner, P. (2001) *Theorizing Modernity*, London: Sage.

Wagner, P. (2005) 'The political form of Europe: Europe as a political form', *Thesis Eleven*, 80: 47–73.

Walby, S. (1999) 'The new regulatory state: the social powers of the European Union', *British Journal of Sociology*, 50(1): 118–40.

Walby, S. (2003) 'The myth of the nation-state: theorizing society and polity in a global era', *Sociology*, 37(3): 531–46.

Wallace, H. (1999) 'Whose Europe is it anyway?' *European Journal of Political Research*, 35(3): 287–306.

Wallace, W. (2002) 'Where does Europe end? Dilemmas of inclusion and exclusion', in J. Zielonka (ed.) *Europe Unbound: Enlarging and Reshaping the Boundaries of the European Union*, London: Routledge.

Wallace, W. (2003) 'Where should EU enlargement stop?', in Lindahl, R. (ed.) *Whither Europe: Borders, Boundaries, Frontiers in a Changing World*, Gothenburg: CERGU.

Walzer, M. (1990) 'What does it mean to be "American"?', *Social Research*, 57(3): 591–614.

Walzer, M. (1995) 'The concept of civil society', in M. Walzer (ed.) *Towards a Global Civil Society*, Providence, RI: Berghahan Books.

Warleigh, A. (2002) 'Towards network democracy? The potential of flexible integration', in M. Farrell, S. Fella and M. Newman (eds) *European Integration in the 21st Century*, London: Sage.

Webb, W.P. (1952) *The Great Frontier*, Boston, MA: Houghton Mifflin.

Weiler, J. (1999) *The Constitution of Europe*, Cambridge: Cambridge University Press.

Weiler, J. (2003) *Un' europa cristianna*, Milan: Biblioteca Rizzoli. Forthcoming (2005) *A Christian Europe*.

Wendt, A. (1999) *Social Theory of International Relations*, Cambridge: Cambridge University Press.

Westwood, S. and Phizacklea, A. (2000) *Transnationalism and the Politics of Belonging*, London: Routledge.

Whittaker, C. (2000) 'Roman Frontiers and European Perceptions', *Journal of Historical Sociology*, 13(4): 462–82.

Wickham, J. (2002) 'The end of the European social model: before it began?'. Available online http://www.ictu.ie/html/publications/ictu/Essay2.pdf.

Wiener, A. (1998) *European Citizenship Practice: Building Institutions of a Non-State*, Boulder, CO: Westview Press.

Wiener, A. and Diez, T. (eds) (2004) *European Integration Theory*, Oxford: Oxford University Press.

Wincott, D. (2000) 'Globalization and European integration', in C. Hay and D. Marsh (eds) *Demystifying Globalization*, Basingstoke: Palgrave.

Wincott, D. (2001) 'The White Paper, the Commission and the "future of Europe"', *EUSA Review*, 14(4): 3–8.

Wincott, D. (2003) 'The idea of the European social model: limits and paradoxes of Europeanization', in K. Featerstone and C. Radaelli (eds) *The Politics of Europeanization*, Oxford: Oxford University Press.

Wintle, H. (ed.) (1996) *Culture and Identity in Europe*, Aldershot: Avebury.

Wintle, M. (2000) 'The question of European identity and the impact of the changes of 1989/90', in J. Shahin and M. Wintle (eds) *The Idea of a United Europe*, London: Palgrave.

Wittrock, B. (2000) 'Modernity: one, none, or many? European origins and modernity as a global condition', *Daedalus*, 129(1): 31–60.

Wodak, R., de Cillia, R., Resigl, M. and Liebert, K. (1999) *The Discursive Construction of National Identity*, Edinburgh: Edinburgh University Press.

World Commission on Culture and Development (1995) *Our Creative Diversity*, Paris: UNESCO.

Young, I.M. (1990) *Justice and the Politics of Difference*, New Haven, CT: Princeton University Press.

Young, I.M. (2000) *Inclusion and Democracy*, Oxford: Oxford University Press.

Young, J. (1993) *The Texture of Memory: Holocaust Memorials and Meaning*, New Haven, CT: Yale University Press.

Young, J. (1998) 'The arts of Jewish memory in a postmodern age', in B. Cheyette and L. Marcus (eds) *Modernity, Culture and 'the Jew'*, Oxford: Blackwell.

Zerubavel, E. (1997) *Social Mindscapes: An Invitation to Cognitive Sociology*, Cambridge, MA: Harvard University Press.

Zielonka, J. (2002) 'Introduction: boundary making by the European Union', in J. Zielonka (ed.) *Europe Unbound: Enlarging and Reshaping the Boundaries of the European Union*, London: Routledge.

Zimmerman, A. (1995) 'Toward a more democratic ethics of technological governance', *Science, Technology and Human Values*, 20(1): 86–107.

Index